A SICILIAN MAN

ALSO BY CAROLINE MOOREHEAD

Fortune's Hostages

Sidney Bernstein: A Biography

Freya Stark: A Biography

Over the Rim of the World: The Letters of Freya Stark (ed.)

Troublesome People

Betrayed: Children in Today's World (ed.)

Bertrand Russell: A Life

The Lost Treasures of Troy

Dunant's Dream: War, Switzerland and the History of the Red Cross

Iris Origo: Marchesa of Val d'Orcia

Martha Gellhorn: A Life

Human Cargo: A Journey among Refugees

The Letters of Martha Gellhorn (ed.)

Dancing to the Precipice: Lucie de la Tour du Pin and the French Revolution

A Train in Winter: A Story of Resistance, Friendship and Survival

Village of Secrets: Defying the Nazis in Vichy France

A Bold and Dangerous Family: The Rossellis and the Fight Against Mussolini

A House in the Mountains: The Women who Liberated Italy from Fascism

Edda Mussolini: The Most Dangerous Woman in Europe

A SICILIAN MAN

Leonardo Sciascia, the
Rise of the Mafia and the
Struggle for Italy's Soul

CAROLINE MOOREHEAD

Chatto & Windus
LONDON

1 3 5 7 9 10 8 6 4 2

Chatto & Windus, an imprint of Vintage,
is part of the Penguin Random House group of companies

Vintage, Penguin Random House UK, One Embassy Gardens,
8 Viaduct Gardens, London SW11 7BW

penguin.co.uk/vintage
global.penguinrandomhouse.com

First published by Chatto & Windus in 2026

Copyright © Caroline Moorehead, 2026

The moral right of the author has been asserted

Every effort has been made to contact all copyright holders.
The publisher will be pleased to amend in future editions any errors
or omissions brought to their attention.

Penguin Random House values and supports copyright. Copyright fuels creativity, encourages diverse voices, promotes freedom of expression and supports a vibrant culture. Thank you for purchasing an authorised edition of this book and for respecting intellectual property laws by not reproducing, scanning or distributing any part of it by any means without permission. You are supporting authors and enabling Penguin Random House to continue to publish books for everyone. No part of this book may be used or reproduced in any manner for the purpose of training artificial intelligence technologies or systems. In accordance with Article 4(3) of the DSM Directive 2019/790, Penguin Random House expressly reserves this work from the text and data mining exception.

Typeset in 11/14 pt Sabon LT Std by Six Red Marbles UK, Thetford, Norfolk
Printed and bound in Great Britain by Clays Ltd, Elcograf S.p.A.

The authorised representative in the EEA is Penguin Random House Ireland,
Morrison Chambers, 32 Nassau Street, Dublin D02 YH68

A CIP catalogue record for this book is available from the British Library

HB ISBN 9781784745035
TPB ISBN 9781784745042

Penguin Random House is committed to a sustainable future
for our business, our readers and our planet. This book is made
from Forest Stewardship Council® certified paper.

For Peter

'I hate Sicily, I detest her to the same degree that I love her . . . I was born here and am condemned to love her, but there are times when I am overcome with the longing to at least die elsewhere'.

Leonardo Sciascia, *Sicily as Metaphor*

'The intellectual courage to be truthful and political reality are two irreconcilable practices in Italy.'

Pier Paolo Pasolini, *Lettere Luterane*

Contents

Foreword		xiii
Chapter 1	Dancing to another tune	1
Chapter 2	Iron and fire	18
Chapter 3	A society doubly unjust	34
Chapter 4	Terrified of the present and uncertain of the future	50
Chapter 5	Sword thrusts	75
Chapter 6	The reluctant *mafiologo*	94
Chapter 7	Irredeemable Sicily	105
Chapter 8	The *terribiltà* of power	116
Chapter 9	Tweaking the tiger's tail	135
Chapter 10	'Clean, always clean'	152
Chapter 11	A death sentence	165
Chapter 12	A thin and porous line	180
Chapter 13	Pensioning off the dead	196
Chapter 14	Hungry and thirsty for justice	208
Chapter 15	God's policeman	227
Afterword		246
Acknowledgements		255
List of illustrations		257
Select Bibliography		259
Endnotes		265
Index		276

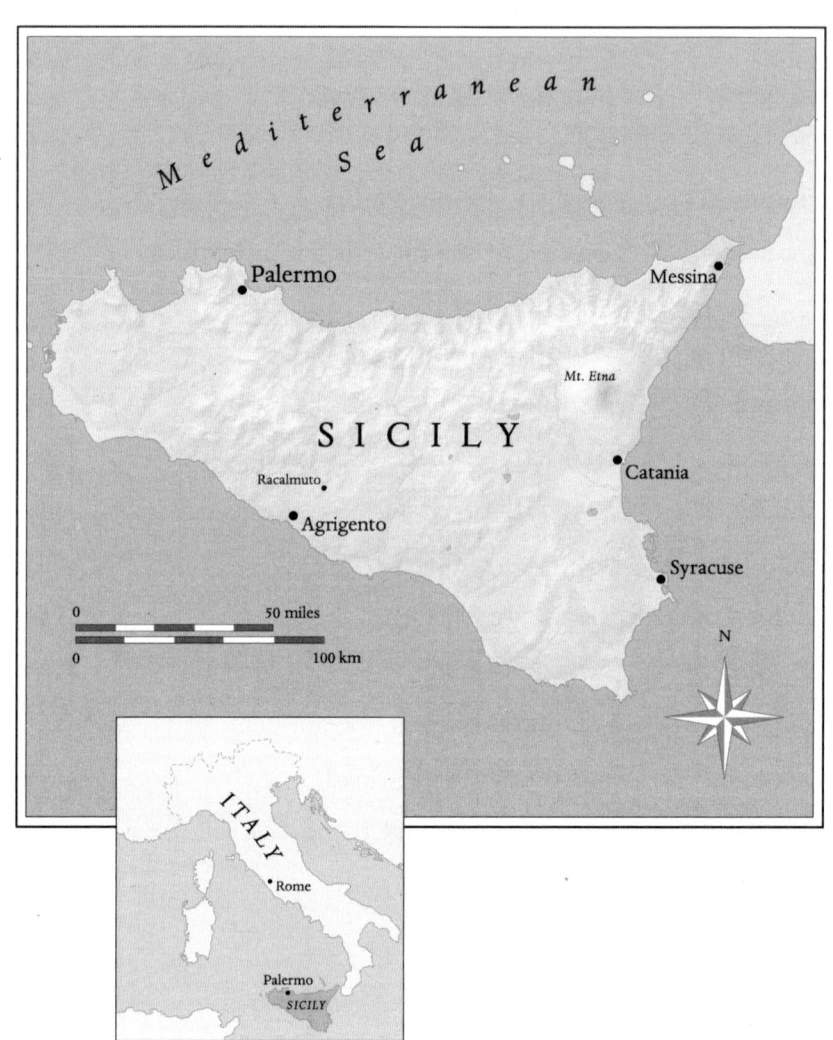

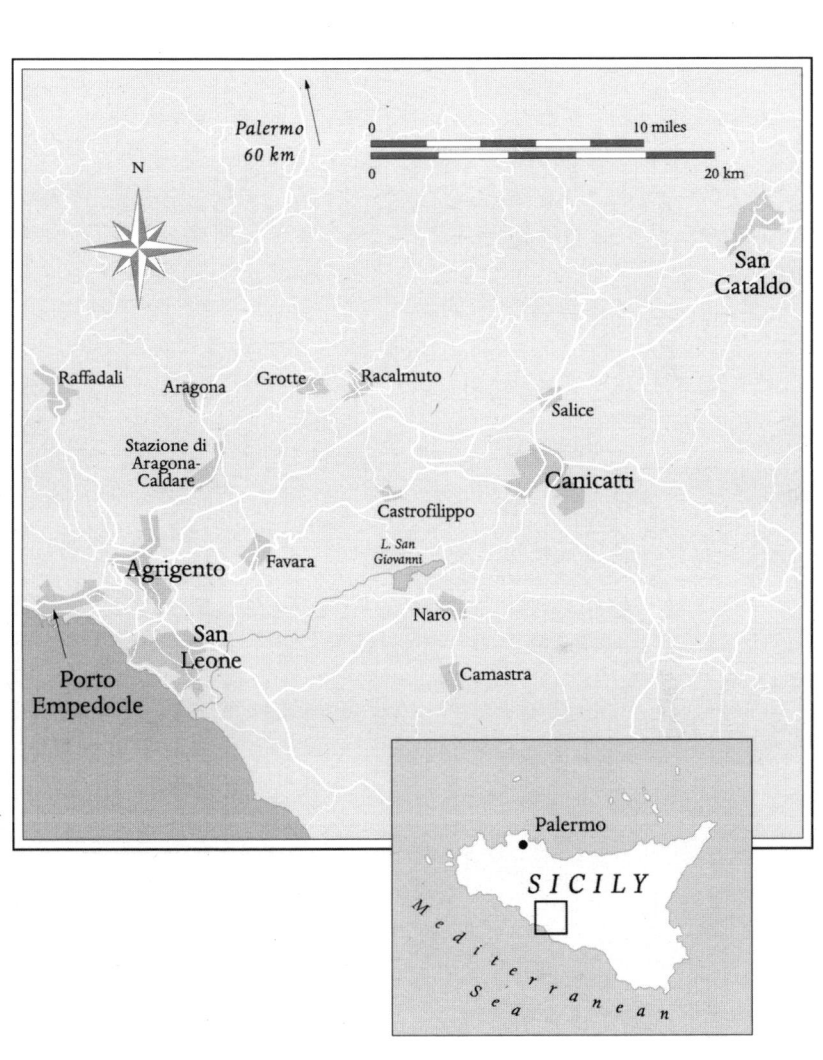

Foreword

A man walks down the main street of Racalmuto, a small town just north of Agrigento in Sicily. He has a cigarette in his left hand and he looks weary, resigned but full of curiosity. He is not tall, perhaps no more than 5 foot 7 or 8 inches, and he wears a crumpled suit; his tie has been blown askew by the wind. This is Leonardo Sciascia, one of Italy's best-loved writers, several times nominated for the Nobel Prize, who died in 1989. The walking man is cast in bronze. Racalmuto is where Sciascia spent most of his life, and Sicily is the area that has given Italy some of its finest writers: Pirandello, Brancati, De Roberto, Verga and Lampedusa.

Sciascia was born in 1921, shortly before Mussolini took power. The span of his life coincides with the most troubled years of Italy's history, when social turmoil and corruption were endemic and the Mafia's reach came to extend to all corners of the country. In his books – his detective novels (known as '*gialli*'), non-fiction historical investigations ('*inchieste*'), plays, essays, reviews and journalism – he explored and defined the malaise that gripped not just Sicily but Italy. He became a crusader against State malfeasance and corruption, and above all against the Mafia and its deep-rooted and intricate connections to politics and State institutions. His heroes grapple with truth and lies in a world in which everything is fleeting and equivocal, and they are invariably defeated by malign forces.

For Sicilians, through these turbulent years, Sciascia became their moral lodestar, a lethal critic of the inefficient, tainted system of Italian justice, never afraid to take positions that put his own life in danger. In a country given to verbosity and hyperbole, he was succinct and full of irony. He never ceased to be fascinated by the treacherousness of relations between the State and its citizens. *The Day of the Owl*, his first *giallo*, translated into forty languages, is universally accepted to have been the first serious portrayal of the Mafia in fiction and an uncannily prescient warning of the perils of ignoring it. But when it appeared, in 1961, no one listened. In Italy today, Sciascia enjoys a fame seldom accorded to modern writers.

In 1986, the Sicilians built an octagonal reinforced concrete bunker inside the fortress-like prison of the Ucciardone in Palermo. In it, they staged the *maxi-processo*, a trial of 471 men, and four women, accused of belonging to the Mafia and of having committed untold numbers of murders, along with kidnapping, extortion and drug trafficking. Cages were built in a semicircle along the back wall for the accused; in the gallery above there was room for many hundreds of journalists and spectators. The courtroom was the size of a small sports stadium. Outside were parked three tanks with soldiers.

Sciascia attended the trial and wrote about it for the *Corriere della Sera*. He was curious not just to see the men in the dock but to assess the quality of justice, a question that had obsessed him all his life. He heard the testimony of Tommaso Buscetta, the former Mafia boss turned State witness, who painted the first authoritative picture of Cosa Nostra, the name given to the Sicilian Mafia, and the way that it had dug its claws into the very fabric of Sicilian life. It confirmed everything that Sciascia had spent his life saying.

I never met Sciascia, but I knew his books; and I went to Palermo to write about the trial. I was there for Buscetta's testimony and watched the accused men, clustered in their cages, rattling their bars and shouting insults across the courtroom, and I saw Luciano Leggio, one of the most powerful Mafia bosses, sitting in a cage of his own, wearing a canary-yellow cardigan. I met Giovanni Falcone, one of the leading magistrates at the trial, in his office in the Ministry of Justice, a wry humorous man, somewhat like Sciascia, protected and isolated behind a series of coded doors, and I saw him again, sitting in a restaurant surrounded by twelve bodyguards, not long before the Mafia murdered him. Like his colleague Paolo Borsellino, he became one of many '*cadaveri eccellenti*' – excellent corpses – the lawyers, judges, policemen and journalists assassinated by the Mafia in those years.

Sciascia was not well and did not have long left to live. He had always courted controversy, and often outrage, by using his novels to describe an Italy peopled by rogues, corrupt politicians, self-serving magistrates and manipulative Catholic priests. And he had infuriated the establishment with his best-selling attack on the government for allowing Aldo Moro, the kidnapped former prime minister, to die at the hands of the Red Brigades. He was to provoke considerably greater hostility soon after the trial, with an ill-judged attack on Borsellino, a misadventure that would sadden the last months of his life.

I thought then that one day I would write about him, intrigued not just by the solitary voice of this small, obstinate man who became a major European intellectual and moral force, but by the question that he spent his life trying to answer: what did it mean to be Sicilian? And not just Sicilian, for Sciascia saw Sicily's ills as a metaphor for the political and social troubles that afflicted Italy during his lifetime. He believed that these had to be understood and their truths laid bare, for only then would it be possible to address them. 'We have to understand everything,' he would repeat, quoting Hannah Arendt, 'especially evil. Only then will we have the weapons to fight it.'

1

Dancing to another tune

It all began with the aunts. There were three of them. Angela was the eldest, sentimental, firm, blonde with blue eyes, and the keeper of the family purse. Giuseppina, known as Nica, was an excellent cook. The youngest, Maria Concetta, was the only one to have received an education: she was married and taught at the local school. The two sons of the family, Pasquale and Salvatore, were of less account. Both the older women were unusually small, and all three, who were in their early thirties, wore only black, though Maria Concetta had worn white on her wedding day. She was the only sister who ever left the house to walk in the village. Angela and Nica, having decided that they would never marry, on account of the improbability that their modest circumstances would bring them worthy husbands, had declared themselves '*zitelle*', spinsters.

Since they never went out, they received visits, from neighbours, relations, friends, the boy who brought the food, the pedlars who came regularly to the village. All day they talked, gossiped, ruminated, reminisced, speculated and dissected the minutiae of local life. Clever, shrewd women, they were known for their ability to synthesise complex questions into a few caustic words. Their maid, Totina, was a source of rumour and superstition, rife in early twentieth-century Sicily, about witches, spirits, auguries and devils, and there was always something horrible in the tales. Sitting under the kitchen table, the young Leonardo Sciascia listened. 'If you want to be a writer,' he said later, 'you need to grow up in a house full of women.'

Sciascia was born in the village of Racalmuto, 30 kilometres north of Agrigento in Western Sicily, on Saturday 8 January 1921. His birth broke the monotony of the dark, cloistered house. His great-grandfather, Pasquale, had arrived in the area as a seller of tanned hides at the very end of the Bourbon reign, but both Sciascia's grandfather, Leonardo, and his father, also Pasquale, were employed in the office of the local sulphur mines. Until 1860, the name Sciascia had been spelt 'Xaxa', a common name in the Arab world. Leonardo had started down the mines at the age of nine, carrying heavy loads along tunnels no wider than a man's body, and had worked his way to the surface with the help of a priest, who taught him to read and do sums. The mines were inhuman and suffocating, with constant fires and floods. Pasquale had taken off for the US as a young man in 1912, hoping to make his fortune working in a laundry in New York and later serving in the army, but had returned unexpectedly to Racalmuto in 1919 to join his father in the mines, where he was known as *l'Americano*. Though he was occasionally seen in his US military uniform with

Leonardo with his wife and children

white puttees and a broad rimmed hat, he never spoke about America. Emigrants who returned seldom did: it was embarrassing not to come back rich.

Pasquale soon married dark-haired, delicate-featured Genoveffa Martorelli, eleven years younger than himself and a friend of his younger sister Maria, whose family owned a small tile factory in the village. Sciascia arrived nine months and seventeen days later. When the boy was two, he and his parents moved into the aunts' house in the Via Regina Margherita, on a corner by steep steps leading up to Racalmuto's second largest church, Santa Maria del Monte. From the balcony, you could eavesdrop on the women squabbling at the fountain below. Racalmuto had no running water. Carts brought snow, packed in straw and salt, from the high mountains, with which Nica made granita with blackcurrants. The town lamp-keeper did his rounds morning and night with a ladder, a tin of petrol and scissors with which to trim the wicks. The aunts called the little boy Nando.

The house, with its thick stone walls and brown and green tiles, had three floors. The *zie* – the aunts – shared the ground floor with their brother Salvatore, who was a tailor and ran his business from a little room giving on to the street. Maria Concetta and her husband had the first floor with the elderly Leonardo, now somewhat frail and partially paralysed, who spent his days in a chair by the balcony, observing village life and tapping his stick impatiently when he wanted elucidations. Sciascia and his parents lived at the top, at least until his brother Giuseppe and sister Anna arrived, in 1923 and 1926, after which he was moved down to join his aunt Maria Concetta. Slowly extricating him from his parents, the *zie* made the little boy the reason for their existence. There was a marmalade cat called Gesuele.

Genoveffa was a retiring woman, happy to leave the management of the house to Nica, who ran up and down the steep stairs to each floor delivering meals. Pasquale was a contrarian and, as a father, severe, and the little boy felt closer to his grandfather. There was no heating. In the cold, damp winters, when snow settled on the nearby hills and rain and wind turned the roads into mud, the large family crouched round a charcoal brazier on the ground floor, shawls over their shoulders. In the summers, the heat was stifling. On religious festivals, of which there were many, the aunts

Leonardo, Anna and Giuseppe

peered down at the procession below, as the priests chanted, the drums thudded, the women shrouded in black sang and keened and the statue of the Madonna swayed on the shoulders of hooded monks, an image of the suffering mother in perpetual mourning and the pain of being alive. Under the Saracens, in the ninth century, Christians in Racalmuto had been forced to wear pictures of pigs on their shoulders; Jews those of monkeys. On the *Giorno dei Morti*, 2 November, Racalmuto's richer families had marzipan animals, made by the nuns, and sugar spun into the figures of ballerinas and huntsmen; the poor children had cakes of flour and honey, known as the bones of the dead. Of the aunts, only Angela was devout. Through the other women ran a vein of impiety, a critical, ironical screen through which all speech was filtered.

At home, the family spoke only in dialect, a Sicilian rich in metaphor and proverb, in which a '*biddina*' was a terrifying sea snake which chased its prey on land and water, and a '*cattiva*', a widow captive to the rules of mourning. An infant was a '*picciriddu*', and diseases were known by the villagers to be delivered by God, while the living could send messages and petitions to departed loved ones via the dying on their death beds.

When Goethe passed this way in 1787, he described a 'wilderness of fertility', an ocean of wheat and barley swaying in the wind. But by the time Sciascia was born Racalmuto lay at the heart of sulphur and salt mining country, its name derived from the Arabic *Rahal Maut*, or dead village, from the days of the plague of 1624. Half the population had died, leaving the survivors, it was said, preferring silence to speech. On one side of the village were the mines, stretching over the mountains into the distance, where the sulphur, on which its economy depended, had reduced the land to barren, bleached earth. From its smelters, out of which oozed a brown liquid then left to dry in the sun, rose blue vapours of smoke, giving off an acrid, cloying stench. At dawn, convoys of mule-drawn carts carried the sulphur to Porto Empedocle, from where it left for America. Greek mythology had given Pluto a throne of sulphur. Liquid sulphur, said the local people, flowed in their veins.

Many small boys like the elder Leonardo, and especially the orphans, had given their health and their childhood to the mines, nearly all of them in the hands of just a few families, who treated their workers as indentured labour. Some, in fact, had been sold by their families so that the other children could eat. Leonardo and Pasquale, as '*zolfari*' – demonic people – who risked their lives every day, regarded themselves as bolder and tougher, with greater ambitions and broader horizons, than the small-minded, avaricious but industrious peasants. But by the time of Sciascia's birth, the sulphur industry was in sharp decline, many of its 271 mines closed or soon to do so, its mismanagement and failure to modernise losing out against new methods in Louisiana and Texas. Both the mines themselves and their closure had a devastating effect on Racalmuto, already very poor and now much poorer.

On the other side of the village, tucked beneath a bluff, was a land of vines, olives, almond trees and prickly pear. It was here, far from the smell and poison of sulphur, that in the eighteenth century the local barons, a family called Matrona, had built a summer

Sulphur miners

house with fountains and rare imported shrubs and trees, to which they brought their friends in carriages with liveried footmen to picnic on linen tablecloths. There were scented magnolias, and visits to artificial grottoes of stalactites and the sulphur crystals the miners called diamonds. It was here, too, that Sciascia's grandfather had built a small whitewashed stone house called *La Noce* with exposed beams and four rooms on a rocky strip of land overlooking the mansion. The Matronas had fallen on hard times and the *zie* enjoyed telling people that an earlier baron had murdered a Sciascia cousin, a young forest guard whose wife he coveted.

La Noce, the nut, so called after the groves of almonds that surrounded it, lay six kilometres from Racalmuto. The elder Leonardo regularly walked backwards and forwards to tend his fruit trees, and in the summer the aunts shrouded themselves in enveloping black shawls, packed up the house and hired a cart to transport

La Noce

linen, plates, even small bits of furniture, and settled in for several months. Water was brought by donkey in an amphora and there was a wood oven, used to make bread. There were other similar small houses, built brick by brick by their owners, and Sciascia and his friends roamed freely, paddling in the nearby river Azzalora and prowling around the Matronas' abandoned gardens, a magical place of ferns, rose bushes, oleanders and the palm trees which later became for Sciascia 'a kind of heraldic symbol'. Sitting on the rough terrace as the light faded, Leonardo told Sciascia about the English, who had come to Racalmuto in the nineteenth century and left behind an expression, 'he looks English', to denote blond, rosy, blue-eyed looks and slender, honest people; and about the Germans and their brutality in the First World War.

In April, the hillsides were covered in pink velvety honeysuckle; July brought apricots and melons and figs; September the almond harvest, their shells kept for firewood. On clear mornings, the blue sky looked touched with violet; on moonless nights, the lamps were like fireflies, scattered in a huge and empty blackness. It was at *La Noce*, Sciascia said, that he learnt to talk, and later to write, in 'that landscape, those people, those memories, those things'.

By local standards the Sciascias were well off. The men were employed and none worked the backbreaking days down the mines where the heat was such that the miners went naked; nor did they belong to the category of day worker for local landowners, who gave employment only during sowing and harvest time and often paid just in wheat and vegetables. While the sulphur workers lived on raw onions, bread and salted sardines, and the day labourers and their families on soup and beans and what could be found growing wild, Nica kept the Sciascias well fed. But they understood precariousness. Sciascia, all his life, referred to the 'knot of fear . . . that people of my blood can return at any time to misery, to watching their children suffer and become bitter'. Life had dealt his father, and himself, a good card; but it would take no more than a very small shove, as he instinctively knew, for them to tumble down the flight of stairs back into the mines.

Neither Pasquale nor his father had served with the Italian army in the First World War. But 299 young men from Racalmuto had died in the fighting, some of them in the icy trenches above the Isonzo valley and many of them wearing a medallion from the church of Santa Maria del Monte. Those who survived came home, as did men all over Italy, to find themselves denied the jobs and land that they had been promised. A sense of frustration and desperation was palpable in the village, and there were outbreaks of violence. Most days, somewhere in the neighbourhood, a killing was reported. Bands of disaffected veterans fought each other. They had come back from the war savvy, having learnt about justice and equality, and they understood better the age-old disparity between the Sicilian feudal landowners and the landless poor.

The Versailles Treaty and the end of the First World War had left Italy politically in turmoil, its people sour and disenchanted with the old liberal governing elite and their incompetent handling of the war. Some now turned towards the Socialists and the newly forming Communist Party, which promised reform; others sought a strong clear leadership to impose order on the growing chaos.

In 1919, a group of angry men, and a couple of women, calling themselves Fascists had come together in Milan's Piazza San Sepolcro, turned themselves into a movement and brought Benito Mussolini to prominence. Mussolini offered not just order, but fairness, a more equal society, an end to the lawlessness and turmoil, albeit one imposed by force. Not long after the March on Rome, on 29 October 1922, when Victor Emanuel III handed the government of Italy to the former crusading Socialist, soon to become dictator, Mussolini paid a fleeting visit to Sicily. Sciascia, aged four, was taken to join the crowd that turned out to greet him on his train, which paused briefly at the station above the village. Racalmuto's dignitaries, in their heavy sombre clothing, stood sweating for several hours in the hot sun to catch a glimpse of the man most believed would bring some kind of justice to the poor. There were no protests: the police had taken the precaution of locking up all potential troublemakers. What Sciascia would remember was the intense heat and a stain on his white clothes from a spilt fizzy orange drink.

Sciascia's own family was politically divided. His grandfather Leonardo, by temperament anarchical, refused all commitment either to the left or to Mussolini. Pasquale, seeing the way the wind was blowing and the strength with which it blew, joined the new Fascist Party. As did Maria Concetta's husband, who welcomed it with considerable enthusiasm. The March on Rome in October 1922 had brought Fascist youths from nearby villages to join Racalmuto's young supporters and march down the main street before setting fire to the new offices of the Communist Party. But in the little house in the Via Regina Margherita, at least one aunt

Sciascia, aged four

encouraged rebellion. When the mutilated body of Mussolini's opponent, the Socialist Member of Parliament Giacomo Matteotti, was found in a narrow grave on the outskirts of Rome in the summer of 1924, Maria Concetta cut his picture out of a magazine, rolled it up and hid it in her sewing basket. The subterfuge fascinated four-year-old Sciascia, as did the sight of his aunt crying. When no one was about, Maria Concetta took out the picture and put her fingers to her lips. What Sciascia would remember was a man with a wide forehead, a thoughtful look, a 'serene and severe expression ... profound and tragic'. The brave Matteotti, his *zia* said, had been murdered by 'him', though she gave no name. Totina was more outspoken. Mussolini was a '*musso-de-porco*', a pig snout. It was Sciascia's first lesson in subversion.

But there was more afoot in Sicily than Fascism. To be Sicilian was to feel different, apart, separate, both connected to the mainland of Italy and at the same time divorced from its concerns. Tunis, after all, lay closer to Palermo than Rome. Garibaldi's thousand men, in their red woollen clothes and felt hats, climbing off their paddle steamers on the beach at Marsala on 11 May 1860, had indeed helped drive out the Spanish Bourbons and merge Sicily into the new united Italy. But their successors had done little to make the Sicilians feel they belonged.

Much of this sense of alienation and exclusion came from the island's particular history. Perfectly placed at the crossroads of the Mediterranean between Europe and Africa, Sicily could never have remained undisturbed, not least because of its exceptional fertility. For longer than 2,000 years, foreign invaders had landed on its shores to plunder, occupy and rule. Some, like the Goths and the Vandals, swept through leaving only death and destruction. The Byzantines established monasteries, the Greeks Doric temples. The Romans turned the island into their granary of wheat and barley, the 'nurse at whose breast the Roman people is fed'. The Arabs introduced lemons, bitter oranges, sugar cane, cotton, mulberry trees, pistachios and melons; and also goats, who stripped the new shoots off the fruit trees. The Normans brought enlightened despotism along with literature, the arts, astrology and astronomy and fine cathedrals. The Spanish and their viceroys lasted four centuries, enriched the Church, imported the Inquisition and the burning of heretics and left behind magnificent palaces and a pyramid of privileges. The Piedmontese, briefly, introduced frugality, undyed wool in the place of gold and lace; the British, even more briefly, an attempt at liberal parliamentarianism. Napoleon never crossed the Straits of Messina, thereby denying the island the benefits of the Enlightenment. All who ruled came with little regard for Sicily's own identity.

These many centuries of foreign invasion and occupation fashioned Sicily. Unwilling and unable to govern effectively, the occupiers relied on feudal landowners and barons for their policing, who in turn built vast fortified farmhouses and worked their labourers as slaves, paying taxes to support a weak central government and leaving the interior of the island wild and neglected. Feudalism, which disappeared in the rest of Europe by the end of the eighteenth century, hung on in Sicily, where the owners of vast estates moved one by one to Palermo and Catania and used their money to buy titles and privileges. To run their farms and fields and provide the money for their sumptuous new palaces, they left behind them a new class of powerful, greedy middlemen, the '*gabellotti*', who made themselves rich as intermediaries between the landless peasants and their distant overlords. Feeble attempts at land reform did little to lift the peasants out of constant debt. While the price of wheat fluctuated and taxes were levied on everything from silk to salt, a great game of evasion, corruption and dishonesty, enforced by brutality, settled stealthily over the island. While in Palermo, the 142 princes, 788 marquises, 1,500 dukes and barons enjoyed the fruits of the island's wealth, the *gabellotti* learnt all about the subtleties of true tyranny and the peasants the meaning of true poverty.

Whether or not the Mafia existed as a criminal organisation, or was only a state of mind, is a question that has exercised historians since long before the unification of Sicily with Italy. Even the origins of the word remain uncertain. Some have argued that it came from the Arabic, *mahia*, bold, arrogant; others that it took its meaning from *mu a fa*, strength and 'to protect'. Sciascia later drew attention to a witch named in a list of heretics in 1658, '*nomata ancora Maffia*'.

As public order steadily worsened during the eighteenth century, so the barons had turned to the *gabellotti* for the protection of their lands. Private militias, 'companies of armed men', took shape. When travellers on Grand Tours ventured further south than Naples they used the services of such men to keep them safe. Patrick Brydone, tutor to a Scottish nobleman, wrote to his friend William Beckford while touring Sicily in 1770 that he had been offered an 'honourable' group of ruffians, 'most respectable people' without whom it would have been foolish to travel. Brydone was a keen observer of all things Sicilian, noting that the morena eels were not as 'fat and luscious' as other eels. He added that he greatly preferred Sicily to Switzerland, with her 'cold and stagnating humours'. 'Adieu,' he ended most of his letters, 'the heat is intolerable.'

It was the commander-in-chief of English troops in Sicily, Lord William Bentinck who, in 1811, persuaded the Sicilian Parliament to approve a constitution based on the British one, thereby abolishing baronial jurisdiction and privileges. The bill that went through the following year, obliging the barons to sell uncultivated property to landless peasants, appeared progressive on paper. The peasants were too poor to buy, and so the land went to the *gabellotti*, who sublet it to the peasants for short periods at great profit, creating, in years of bad harvests, endemic poverty. Many families were driven to begging and cattle rustling, while the newly enriched *gabellotti* themselves turned to brigands to help safeguard their new estates. Taking advantage of the weakness and corruption of the Bourbon State, a web of collusion between venal landowners, accustomed to unimpeded power, dishonest mediators and capricious bullies deepened. Where people protested, justice came swiftly: their bodies were found, their genitals in their mouths, their tongues cut out.

When, in October 1860, Sicilians voted en masse for unification under Piedmontese rule, neither side understood the wishes and needs of the other. The northerners who arrived in the wake of Garibaldi and the annexation of the island in a plebiscite had been led to believe that Sicily was rich, a paradise of wheat and fruit. Comprehending nothing about the confusions and complexities of the island, intent mainly on moving wealth north, they imposed obligatory military service for their wars, introduced Piedmontese law and with it exorbitant taxation and protectionist tariffs. After six years of mounting discontent, the citizens of Palermo rose up.

The Italian navy killed five hundred rebels in a bombardment from the sea, declared draft dodgers and deserters to be outlaws and sent in twenty battalions to subdue an island they described as a 'bottomless well of filth', filled with 'self-centred and dirty' savages 'more like Africans than Europeans'. Two thousand young men, 'with the faces of assassins', were arrested, a small number of them from Racalmuto, and summary executions followed. For their part, the Sicilians complained that they were being treated like 'conquered and bartered sheep'. They retreated further into what became known as '*Sicilianismo*', a sense of intense local patriotism, hostility towards northern arrogance, a conviction that private justice was more effective than what was offered by the new Italy. Unification got off to a bad start. *Sicilianismo* was a concept Sciascia was born with.

By now, on mainland Italy, criminologists and sociologists had become fascinated by people one described as having 'little facial hair, large jaws and ears and canine teeth' and reported to be exceptionally violent. Enquiries were launched in order to try to understand the character of these rebellious islanders. Romualdo Bonfadini, a member of the Chamber of Deputies in Rome, was commissioned to explore further. His conclusion was that there was no such thing as a 'mafia' as such. Delinquency on the island was no worse than you found elsewhere, but it was made to appear bloodier by the 'tendency to excess of the Sicilian people in all things'. What were needed were more public works and especially more roads. In 1860, a play by two Sicilians, Giuseppe Rizzotto and Gaspare Mosca, set inside a prison and describing an association of criminals they called the Camorra, with its own rites, hierarchies and hidden power, *I Mafiusi della Vicaria*, was an enormous hit. The enquiries and reports on this so-called mafia continued.

Then, early in 1876, two Tuscan aristocrats, Leopoldo Franchetti and Sidney Sonnino – later Prime Minister of Italy – set out on a leisurely tour of Sicily, taking with them camp beds and revolvers. Riding through mile upon mile of uninhabited land, they noted 'silence everywhere and a desolation that wrings your heart'. Before long they had reached the conclusion that a mafia indeed existed, that it had deep, ancient roots in the very fabric of the island; that it was closely linked to feudalism and to the absence of

State order and that it had effectively wormed its way into all private and public affairs. 'All that scent of orange and lemon,' they wrote, 'begins to smell of corpses.' In Western Sicily they watched *mafiosi* riding around the hills and valleys like lords, because no one 'desires the dangerous glory' of opposing them. This 'industry of violence', run by a new class of mafia men had become a 'social force in its own right', dispensing its own crude form of justice in the case of quarrels and vendettas and relying on '*omertà*', a 'universal agreement about silence'. These people were 'dedicated to blood feuds, ready to kill for whoever paid them', and in return they expected money, power, privileges and obedience. Whether Sicilians were or were not more immoral than other Italians, they were certainly 'dancing to another tune'.

The Tuscan aristocrats caused a sensation, not least in Sicily where outraged liberals accused them of trying to ferment civil war. The next to weigh in was a scholar of folklore from Palermo, Giuseppe Pitrè, who devoted his life to producing twenty-five volumes on the customs, superstitions, proverbs and riddles of the island and ended up full of admiration for the noble ideals of the *mafiosi*. These he described as men of honour, possessed of 'beauty, grace, perfection, excellence', whose 'awareness of self' included a form of pride that demanded satisfaction. Pitrè chose to overlook the more criminal aspects.

His report found many admirers. However, an incident that contradicted his glowing words took place soon after. It put the Mafia and its connections to people in authority in a new light, one that would resonate down the years. On the evening of 1 February 1893, a former director of the Bank of Sicily and Mayor of Palermo, the Marquese Emanuele Notarbartolo, a man renowned for his probity, was stabbed twenty-seven times in his first-class carriage travelling between Termini Imerese and Palermo. Notarbartolo had been reporting to the government on corrupt practices in the bank, and in particular on the political machinations of its new governor, Raffaele Palizzolo. A warrant went out for Palizzolo's arrest. Notarbartolo was the first of the *cadaveri eccellenti*, the excellent corpses who would play such a grim role in Sicilian modern history.

But Palizzolo had powerful protectors in the police and the judiciary. The trial stalled. Then, pushed by Notarbartolo's family, it was moved to Milan, where it quickly became an indictment on Sicilian politics in general. Amid much talk of corruption, collusion and cover-ups, Palizzolo was given a thirty-year prison sentence. But this was not the end of the story. People began talking about another Dreyfus affair. Pitrè had set up a Pro Sicilia Committee to defend the island against 'sinister and malevolent' chatter and volunteered to give evidence at Palizzolo's appeal. In 1904, Palizzolo was acquitted after a new trial in which witnesses retracted their stories and he returned a hero to Palermo. The then famous novelist Luigi Capuana once again denied the existence of any 'social octopus, that monster of encircling, suffocating, viscous tentacles' squeezing the island, and Sicily was proclaimed a place of sunshine, beautiful skies and women with 'splendid eyes'. All suggestion of menace, illegality, bribery and string-pulling was declared to be absurd and illusory.

Other writers were quick to agree that the Mafia itself was nothing but Sicilian rebellion against the abuse of power. The year that Sciascia was born, Giovanni Alfredo Cesareo staged a successful play in which the Mafia was described as exercising 'just' law, as distinct from the 'unjust' law of the impotent State, and that it was fulfilling a valuable role in redressing the social imbalances of Sicily. During a campaign for re-election, the future prime minister Vittorio Emanuele Orlando went as far as to say that if by mafia what was meant was a 'sense of honour taken to extremes, an intolerance of arrogance and oppression', protection of the weak and loyalty to friends, well then, he was happy to be called *mafioso*. These were things that were 'linked to the Sicilian soul'.

And there, for the moment, shrouded in contradictions, the question of the Mafia rested. Imbued with the original sin of Sicily's reactionary history which flowed in the veins of its inhabitants and coloured the air they breathed, Sicilians were different, with a sense of pride that could, admittedly, come across as brutal and an unshakeable conviction that something malign and malicious lay over everything. The fact that very little had changed in Sicily since unification, that the vast feudal estates continued to be run by absent barons and their Mafia enforcers, that in the cities favours, bribes, extortion and threats were all becoming the order of the day was conveniently forgotten. In any case, the First World War had put a brake on further reports. The war had proved an excellent time for illegal affairs, and it had weakened public order and promoted the growth of private justice.

The military demobilisations in 1919 of some 400,000 Sicilian men had led to what was described as a 'hailstorm' of violence, much of it carried out by resentful men returning from the war to witness the new prosperity of the old *mafiosi* and unable to find work. The *gabellotti*-turned-Mafia had grown very rich and powerful and had stopped paying feudal dues to an increasingly ineffectual landowning nobility, itself impoverished by the wartime closure of export markets after 1915. Mafia families had become feudal lords, taking over the properties the landowners could no longer afford, dispensing patronage, mediating in disputes and choosing public servants: no Sicilian was now elected to the Italian Parliament without the Mafia's stamp of approval. A new balance of power was taking hold.

Much of the island desperately poor at the time of Sciascia's birth, Sicily was violent, backward, lawless, its people most often illiterate, its roads no more than mule tracks and sheep runs, though in Palermo and Catania a rich culture flourished. Western Sicily, where he grew up, was the poorest, most Mafia-ridden area on the island. Whatever its origins, the word 'mafia' was now being used to define a particularly Sicilian relationship between State, Church, landowners and middlemen, the *gabellotti*. A shadowy and subtle power at the service of landowners against peasants, these figures embodied a sense of private justice in a country with no strong central government. The men they used to enforce it were sometimes described as 'bandits', outlaws, willing to lend their arm to anyone in exchange for money.

Even as a small boy, Sciascia knew about the Mafia. It was in the air, the daily transactions of village life; but in the aunts' house it was not mentioned. At election time, strangers arrived in Racalmuto and made their preferences plain. He watched and noted them. They were nameless but obviously bore some special power and he was intrigued by the way that no one seemed to question their presence. The Mafia and its history lie at the very heart of Sciascia's story.

Many writers make their homelands the heartbeat of their work, but none more deeply than Sciascia. He never forgot where he came from. Sicily was his stage, with its tumultuous history, its anguished present, its unruly, unhappy inhabitants. He identified with the exploited, their class hatred, their sense of being beaten, weighed down by history and with their sharp feelings of rancour. He knew what centuries of domination, Inquisition, lack of an Enlightenment, Mafia and Fascist violence had done to them, how it had reduced them to inertia and resignation, made them cynical, sly, open to corruption, with an atavistic fear of death heightened in Racalmuto by generations of sulphur miners. The reality of Sicily was, for him, a state of constant fluctuation, an unceasing, losing battle against insecurity, trouble distinguishing reality from unreality. Insecurity coloured everything, bringing with it unease, mistrust, hidden passions, secrecy, fatalism and pessimism, all easily translated into arrogance and pride. In a world in which everything is fragile and shifting, only people and what Sicilians call '*roba*' – things, possessions, real or metaphysical, often accumulated over the generations – provide any security. '*Il sangue mio*' meant family, my blood; but it also meant people with particular power.

To be a Sicilian was hard: to be a Sicilian writer even harder, particularly if you refused to shy away from the role of perpetual dissident. It was, Sciascia said, to be a heretic, slightly despised, a sort of spy, saying things better left unsaid. Having become the most famous and the most controversial commentator on the Mafia in Italy – perhaps in the world – he later said that he could write about it precisely because, as a child growing up in Racalmuto, it was part of him. He understood in his very bones what it was to be *mafioso*, even if neither the aunts nor the combative Leonardo ever mentioned the word. Just what it meant to be Sicilian became the question he grappled with all his life.

2
Iron and fire

Maria Concetta did something even better than warn Sciascia against the abuse of power: she taught him to read. The *zie*'s house was full of books, though none, interestingly, by Sicilian writers. Victor Hugo was there, and Diderot and Stendhal. Everyone in the family read. Maria Concetta started her nephew on *I promessi sposi* (*The Betrothed*), Alessandro Manzoni's dark tale about seventeenth-century Milan and the plague that killed half its population, with its overtones of cowardice and scapegoating. Generations of Italian children, obliged to learn passages by heart, had been alienated by its sombre, grave tone, its interminable paragraphs, but Manzoni's voice, worldly and ironical, pessimistic, respectful of the '*umili*' – the defeated – struck a chord with the young boy. Later, he would often return to the words of the *Innominato*, the Unnamed One: 'Back and back he went in time from ... bloodshed to bloodshed, crime to crime ... They all belonged to him; they were who he was.' Sicily's ills were what Sciascia himself was.

At the age of five, Sciascia was taken to see the sea. Sicily has over a thousand kilometres of coastline, looking out towards Africa and Europe. But over the centuries, turning their backs on invaders and pirates, Sicilians had chosen to look inwards, clinging to the mountains and high plains, with their arctic winters and summers that brought the moist, hot sirocco wind from the Sahara. They pretended that the sea was not there. When mentioned in songs and poems, it spelt horror and bitterness. The Sciascias felt no differently. Though Agrigento and its shore lay just 25 kilometres from Racalmuto, visits were rare. When Sciascia saw the water, he did not like it. Neither then nor later was he prepared to learn to swim. But on this first outing he discovered what became and remained a great love: the train, with its unfolding vision of a moving world.

On 1 October 1926, when he was not quite six, Sciascia was sent to school. His teacher was a cousin of his mother's, and since his father Pasquale was a mine administrator and not a miner or labourer, he dressed differently from many of the forty-seven other boys in his year. He wore shoes, even in summer, and clothes that fitted him, not the handed-down and ragged jackets that drowned the poorer boys. Even at six, he was aware that he was privileged; he felt both fortunate and uneasy. He collected cards with footballers on them and fashioned bows and arrows with elastic bands to become Robin Hood. There were no bought toys other than a spinning top. The school had no proper building of its own, and classes were held in three separate places: a former governor's mansion, an old infirmary attached to a convent and a carabinieri barracks. All the rooms were unheated and in the winter the ill-fitted windows rattled and damp and mould seeped through the walls. Sciascia was enchanted by everything to do with writing, the pens and nibs, the ink delivered by tin can into a pot on the desk, the lesson books, their touch and smell. Physically small and neat, his hair carefully combed and parted by Nica before he left home, he was a timid boy. He smiled but seldom laughed. His brother Giuseppe, now nearly four, had a more gregarious, outgoing nature. As soon as summer arrived, the heads of the boys were shaved. The hillsides around were covered in pistachio trees and their resin stuck to the children's hair. They were told never to go near a bearded, sweaty, gloomy monk who arrived every summer on his mule, peddling prayers against catastrophes for oil and nuts.

In 1928, during the Christmas holidays, Leonardo died, an unrepentant anti-Mafia and anti-Fascist to the last. Sciascia had been very fond and proud of his grandfather and he liked it when people compared them. Leonardo, he said later, had possessed great honesty, 'that suffocated virtue of many Sicilians', though the aunts complained that he was foolish and pigheaded to refuse to make deals and earn proper money, whatever the incentives and threats. He was, they declared, a '*cretino*', an idiot, and as Sciascia would later say, 'I too am a *cretino*, and I am proud to be one.'

While the aunts and a priest gathered round the dying man, Sciascia sat in the next room, making an airship out of cardboard. Death was ever present in Racalmuto. Funerals were important moments, reflecting in their grandeur the status of the dead. Like all Sicilians, the Sciascias were strongly attached to death and its rituals, and reported that the dead often appeared in their dreams, sometimes bringing lucky numbers for the lottery. Calling a doctor was regarded as a purely social convention, for doctors were not thought capable of achieving cures; their presence was a mere ceremonial, a prelude to the theatre of death. A priest, on the other hand, was crucial since he could save the dying a lengthy sojourn in purgatory or an eternity in hell.

In his third year of school, when gentle women teachers were replaced by harder men, Sciascia learnt about Garibaldi and the First World War; he was taught about original sin and divine providence and sang patriotic hymns. He had become a '*balilla*', one of Mussolini's vast army of small Fascists, turned out in a shiny black shirt, blue neckerchief held in place by a pin with Mussolini's head on it, khaki trousers and a black beret with a tassel known as a fez. Every Saturday afternoon, cohorts of boys marched up and down carrying wooden replicas of rifles. The children staged an operetta about bread, and in the summer he joined other boys in a summer camp in the hills, stripped down to his pants, Mussolini having decreed that sun was good for Fascist boys. They were given bread and jam, which some had never tasted. Sciascia was a poor *balilla*, hopeless at keeping pace or shouting orders. He thought his fez made him look ridiculous and staged an act of rebellion by substituting it with a wide-brimmed felt hat. Membership was compulsory and, at 5 lire, expensive; but if a boy died, his family got 15,000 lire. Fascism, intolerant, controlling, was everywhere. It was, Sciascia wrote later, hidden in unexpected places, behind reassuring phrases, 'rather as if, in the corner of a chemist you saw something labelled bicarbonate of soda when it fact it was arsenic'.

Year four brought a harsh teacher who kept a switch on his desk and sometimes came to school drunk. The entire world, he told the boys, envied Italy. Before Mussolini, all had been confusion, misery and violence; the Duce's devotion to his people was exemplary. Napoleon, he added, was a man in the same mould, and this, Sciascia was inclined to believe. He began to collect Napoleonic memorabilia. Among his friends, with whose homework he helped, he had a reputation for solving problems and writing good essays. History was his best subject.

Year four brought another lesson. Sitting in his classroom in the carabinieri barracks, Sciascia listened to a captain beating up prisoners considered disrespectful of Fascism. Blows, moans, cries resonated through the classroom walls. It filled him with horror, he wrote later, and it 'sowed the first seed of my intolerance towards all violence carried out in the name of the law'. When Maria Concetta's Fascist-leaning husband became head of the local chapter of the *balilla* movement, a very reluctant Sciascia was promoted and given white gloves with which to carry a pennant during a parade. But Sciascia begged his aunt to get him released, and his uncle finally agreed: it was, Sciascia said later, a perfect, albeit benign, example of the Mafia code of friends, family and influence. From that moment on, he said, 'it was as if Fascism did not exist'; in any case, it was literature that filled his mind. In his school book at the end of the year he signed himself: 'Leonardo Sciascia: author, editor'.

Fascism had not, of course, disappeared; and nor had the Mafia. They were about to join battle.

As Sciascia was making his way through elementary school, all over the island, and especially in the west, with Palermo at its apex, the Mafia was making the orchards their fief and was moving stealthily into fruit and vegetable markets, water, butchery, mills, ports, fishing and much else. 'Respect' and 'contacts' ruled. No one, any longer, could regard their men as mere bandits. Powerful bosses had emerged – '*capi*' – men acknowledged to think and act with gravity and authority, and also quick to mete out justice, most of it violent. These *capi* were '*pezzi di novanta*' – pieces of ninety – from the name of the largest firecrackers on the market. They conversed mainly by gesture, moving their eyes, hands and heads, though a whole vocabulary of terms had been coined: a rich man was a '*sutrutu*' (an armchair), someone arrested by the police a '*pizzicatu*' (struck by a blow). Though there had never been the same level of popular protest by war veterans in Sicily as in the north – the years of the so-called Bolshevik 'red peril' – what there had been had been put down largely with the help of these men.

The first *capo di tutti i capi* – boss of all bosses – lived in Palermo. Don Vito Cascio Ferro was a tall, distinguished-looking man with a bushy white beard, elegantly dressed in a frock coat and pleated shirt. He ran a flotilla of fishing boats, some transporting stolen cows to North Africa, and others that he used to carry men wanted by the authorities to America, where they went to join the '*Mano Nero*', the Black Hand, in St Louis and Chicago, making illicit liquor under the guise of philanthropic activities and social clubs. Don Vito specialised in '*u pizzu*', the word taken from the beak of a little bird, with '*bagnare il becco*' meaning wetting the beak with a modest sip. Under Don Vito, *u pizzu* was a cut on every commercial activity in Palermo; those who did not pay up found their premises set on fire, their stock ransacked. When Don Vito did the rounds of his 'zone', mayors kissed his hand. He was rumoured to be responsible for twenty homicides and fifty-three violent assaults.

Racalmuto had its own neighbourhood boss. Villalba, which lay not far to the north, was a bleached, dusty village, surrounded by

Don Calò

feudal lands rolling away to the horizon. By the early 1920s, a watchful, paunchy, lizard-like man called Don Calogero Vizzini – Don Calò – had cornered the market in mediation between landlords and peasants. When he appeared in Racalmuto, people became wary. He was the illiterate son of a day labourer, who had got himself exempted from military service and been indicted many times for various crimes only to have evidence against him retracted in court. In the *zie*'s house the Mafia continued not to be discussed; but its existence hovered over everything and Don Calò was known to all of them. Sciascia would write surprisingly little about this period of the Mafia, as if it was as enclosed within him as it was in his family. But one chilling episode he always remembered. One day, he watched a man visit a shopkeeper known to be behind on his payments. The man tenderly stroked the hair of the shopkeeper's small daughter and said, 'She seems almost alive.'

Mussolini, who had other priorities than the prosperity of the distant south, was nevertheless eager to see his own form of social reform on the island, and he recognised that the lawlessness that pervaded Sicily had to be crushed first. He dispatched to Sicily a former police chief from Bologna, Cesare Mori, a man who had risen to the top through zeal and a total absence of scruples, with orders to put down the bandits, pacify the peasants, crush their demands for land, and then impose a strong central government, that is to say, his own.

Mori remains a somewhat perplexing figure. He was authoritarian, profoundly conservative and vainglorious and firmly believed himself to be a hero, a devoted husband and a spartan adventurer. His speeches were full of rhetoric and he wrote poems about sunsets. He disliked weak people but enjoyed the company of children and animals. In appearance, he was a good-looking man, with regular features, cropped hair and rather thin lips. What he lacked, however, was political shrewdness. Arriving in Palermo in October 1925, he moved into the sumptuous Palazzo dei Normanni. The weather that greeted his arrival was suitably apocalyptic: the worst storms in living memory had caused rivers to overflow and houses to collapse. Mori was, noted a newspaper columnist, somewhat like a cat, arriving among a group of mice busy eating delicious cheese.

At this point, Mussolini was still prepared to collaborate with the Mafia bosses, who, having become rich and powerful, were pleased with their new prestige and now had their eye on political futures. A visit to Palermo changed his mind. Having expressed a desire to see more of the island, a trip was arranged to Piana dei Greci, an hour from the city, where a small colony of Albanians had preserved their culture and customs. But Piana dei Greci was also controlled by a Mafia family headed by Don Ciccio Cuccio. Anxious about Mussolini's safety, Mori arranged for him to be accompanied by a cavalcade of armed police motorcyclists. Don Cuccio, insisting that there was no need for such protection, 'since I command the whole area', tried to dismiss them. Mussolini refused. To punish him, when he arrived in the main square to give his usual rousing speech, Mussolini found it deserted. There was no one there to listen.

On his return to Rome, Mussolini declared war: there was just one power in Italy and it was his own. There was no question of tolerating a state within a state. A plot against his life had recently been uncovered in Rome and tough new laws were being introduced to erase all vestiges of democracy. The Sicilian criminal Mafia, 'pus sacks of the bubonic plague', would be 'cauterised by Fascism with iron and fire'. This was a 'paradise inhabited by demons', a cancer at the foot of Italy.

Mori was ordered to act. With rapid, ruthless and clumsy brutality he began rounding up the Sicilians. The first to be arrested were sixty-two men from Cefalù, quickly followed by 142 from Piazza Armerina and 200 from Racalmuto. Sciascia watched them go. The new police chief cast his net wide: mayors, *gabellotti*, minor politicians and businessmen deemed too independent and tainted by the Mafia were soon to be seen stumbling their way in handcuffs on to boats bound for the penal islands of Lipari and Ustica. The Mafia, Mori announced, was a 'single guiding thread' bound together by a 'degenerate form of *omertà*', and bandits and *mafiosi* were just two sides of the same coin. To defeat what had clearly become a parallel state, outside the remit of the legal government, the Mafia had to go. High on his list of targets were the newly powerful *gabellotti*. The marginalised landowners whose lands the *gabellotti* had taken over were delighted. Never having known efficient democracy, they were not overly concerned with Mori's repression of liberty.

Cesare Mori

But Mori's brutality soon became excessive. Confessions were extracted under torture, supposed *mafiosi* subjected to forms of waterboarding, the soles of their feet burnt, their genitals crushed. A new instrument was introduced, a '*cassetta*' or little box, to which victims were attached and then flogged or given electric shocks. Hostages were taken. Every legal norm was flouted. Since it was very hard to say for sure who was a *mafioso* and who was not, many innocent people were denounced in cold-blooded vendettas. Don Vito, who was widely acknowledged to have murdered an American investigator come to explore the connections between the Sicilian and American mafias, but who had never been charged with the crime, was arrested on trumped-up smuggling charges. In court, he was silent and disdainful. In jail, he set about behaving as Mafia bosses behaved: he imposed order, did much to help the men arrested with him, including giving their daughters dowries, and allowed the other prisoners to take it in turn to make his bed. And there, in due course, he died of heart failure. Don Calò, from Villalba, whose dossier included thirty-nine murders and who also fell into Mori's clutches, pronounced himself honoured to have shared Don Vito's cell.

As the number of arrests mounted into the thousands, a cowed Sicily looked on appalled. But cattle rustling, extortion and kidnappings dropped dramatically and the number of murders fell too. In the province of Palermo alone, three hundred estates were 'freed' from Mafia control. By abolishing elections and replacing elected mayors with Fascist *podestà*, the Mafia had effectively lost much of its power and leverage. 'Mussolini,' declared *The Times* in London, 'has strangled the monster in its native lair.' Then, in 1927, Mussolini began to worry about the growing number of prominent men, some of them committed Fascist supporters, now being targeted by Mori. He pronounced the war on the Mafia over and declared that Mori, a 'pure white flame of Fascist justice' had performed 'heroic' surgery. The Mafia was no longer of any interest, 'because on the whole we have solved it'.

He was, of course, wrong. He failed to understand that behind the *mafiosi* Mori had rounded up lay important people, the real powers in this infinitely unhappy, corrupt island. Many Mafia leaders had prudently joined the Fascist Party, or gone into exile. The only beneficiaries of the purge were the nobility, now able once again to exploit their vast estates. None of Sicily's real problems had been addressed, neither the crushing poverty nor the profound social inequalities, nor the fact that the Mafia's form of justice, with its codes and *omertà*, was more real to most Sicilians than a toothless government. The Mafia, sensibly, had gone underground, to bide its time and wait for better days. As Sciascia later put it, a monkey could have done a better job. The Mafia had been anaesthetised, but it had not gone away.

As for Cesare Mori, brought back to Rome in 1929 and made a senator, he complained about being forcibly retired. He took to writing his memoirs, boastful and grandiloquent, along with short stories about witches and demons, and vanished into obscurity.

In March 1929, when Sciascia was eight, a national plebiscite was held on Fascism. In Sicily, as in the whole of Italy, the results were overwhelmingly in favour. Of the 190,797 votes cast in Palermo, only 320 were against. On election day, the voters – all men, women had no vote – were marched to the booths by cohorts of young Fascists while bands played. In Racalmuto, the electoral booth was just below the *zie*'s house and Sciascia, perched on the balcony, watched the voters filing past: not one negative vote was cast. In the *Popolo d'Italia*, which Mussolini's brother Arnaldo edited, he wrote that now that Sicily had crushed the Mafia it was time to develop the island. Plans were made for land reclamation, new roads, drainage, an anti-malaria campaign. But plans were what they largely remained.

Mori's successor as Prefect of Palermo was a capable, flamboyant playboy called Umberto Albini. Under his rule, the city itself remained poor and dilapidated. Landless peasants with no source of income arrived to live in dark, damp hovels in the decaying centre, where tuberculosis spread. Private contractors continued to exploit political connections. What had changed was not that the Mafia had been destroyed but that no one was allowed to mention it. Silenced, its men of honour had learnt how to play the Fascists, how to appear to support them while remaining a force and a power apart.

Mussolini's crusades, known as Battles, included one for Grain, which by the mid 1920s had brought some marginal lands back across Italy into cultivation. Together with the new fertilisers and some mechanised farming, yields in Sicily had risen. But nothing was done to address antiquated methods of tenure, management and production; though experts were consulted, no one listened. Herds of livestock were reduced and pastures were ploughed up in order for more wheat to be planted. Dust bowls spread. Olive oil and fruit crops, on which many farmers depended, were cut back. And the sulphur mines, one by one, were closing, no longer competitive with the sulphur being produced more efficiently in the United States. It took all Nica's resourcefulness to keep the Sciascias fed. In any case, Mussolini had lost interest in Sicily. The budget for the whole island was just one fifteenth of that for the northern province of Reggio Emilia.

In Racalmuto, Fascism thrived. The local elections of 1925, with Fascists as the only candidates on the list, had brought to the fore Enrico Macaluso, the village chemist. Macaluso promoted his friends, persecuted his enemies, encouraged vendettas and kept a small black notebook in which to record the names of those he suspected of harbouring anti-Fascist sentiments. As *podestà* and Fascist Party secretary, his rule, a subtle merging of Fascist might and Mafia tactics, was absolute. The women he pursued found his predatory ways hard to escape. Sometimes, now, Fascism and the Mafia could look like two variants of a common oppression.

Racalmuto had several barbers' shops. In one of these, and in the haberdashery near by, a little cabal of surreptitious anti-Fascists met not so much to plot as to lament. The single copy of *L'Unità*, the Communist Party paper, that arrived by post came in a wrapper improbably marked 'Perfume' and was slipped silently from hand to hand. In the *zie*'s house, Fascism was a topic to avoid. On the first floor, Maria Concetta continued to look secretly at Matteotti's portrait with tears in her eyes, while her husband strutted off happily to march with the *balilla* centurions. Below, in his tailor's shop, Salvatore kept up a low-level rebelliousness: whenever Mussolini's name was mentioned, he muttered, 'He's a devil' – by which he meant both crafty and corrupt. When he refused an apprentice's request to attend a Fascist camp, Macaluso called to deliver a severe reprimand. Salvatore's workshop had become another useful source of rumour and gossip. Salvatore, whose main interest in life was hunting, had taught the boy to shoot. Sitting quietly, Sciascia learnt more about the intricate webs that bind people together. Giorgio Agosti, later a renowned resistance leader, would write that those who refused to identify with Fascism in the 1930s felt like tortoises inside their shells, sometimes, very anxiously, sticking their necks out and catching sight of another tortoise head, equally circumspect.

Macaluso was capricious and fanatical but he was also generous with his money. He paid for water to be pumped up to the village and then for electricity to be installed in street lamps all along the Via Garibaldi. The Centrale, the vast new electricity plant, purred like a cat. For Sciascia, the coming of the electric light was a moment of delight, a feeling of being flooded with luminescence. Little by little, Racalmuto, enclosed, poor, dark, where after dusk no one stirred, was opening to the world. Radios arrived, on which Mussolini's speeches blared out; electricity brought fridges.

Not all Macaluso's schemes worked out. He wanted to introduce a kind of paving he had encountered in Tripolitania to replace Racalmuto's dirt streets, but the rocky terrain proved incompatible; the winters remained muddy and the summers dusty. But he loved trees and many were planted. And, best of all, he brought the cinema.

Racalmuto

When he was eight, Sciascia discovered films. It opened a new world. In the 1860s an enlightened local administrator had built a charming little theatre, the Regina Margherita, just above the Sciascia house. All plush and gold, with frescoes of Apollo and the muses in a luminous blue sky, it had 250 seats in a horseshoe and two levels of boxes. A production of *Rigoletto* had been staged here by a Sciascia forebear on opening night in 1880, and from time to time travelling theatre companies arrived to put on plays. Macaluso decided to introduce film shows on Saturdays and Sundays. Charlie Chaplin was shown, and Harold Lloyd and Buster Keaton. In the summer of 1929 a white sheet was hung in the main square and people gathered to watch Umberto Nobile's flight over the North Pole. Between Monday and Friday Sciascia and his friends talked of nothing but the films they had seen. He thought of them as shadows and of himself as a shadow watching other shadows and merging with them.

Performances in the theatre were rowdy, with much booing and spitting at villains and traitors, and loud whistling at love scenes, and a policeman was on hand to deal out cuffs when the children became too rowdy. As Maria Concetta's husband ran the projector, Sciascia watched from the privileged position of the box and was occasionally allowed to take home unused snippets of celluloid. He saw the actor Mosjoukine with his 'lively melancholically neurotic face' in the film of Pirandello's *Il fu Mattia Pascal*, encountering a writer whose work would soon enchant him. A horizon had opened, he later wrote, 'of books read, things seen, events lived, of loving, of pain'. It was as if life itself had begun to clear, to 'unveil' itself.

Early in May 1931 a Sardinian anarchist called Michele Schirru was arrested in a hotel in Rome, accused of plotting to kill Mussolini. After loudly proclaiming his hatred for Fascism, he was executed on 29 May by firing squad. Ten-year-old Sciascia was overwhelmed with horror. He could not sleep but lay in his bed in the Via Regina Margherita agonising at the thought of the shots, a death imposed so coldly and traumatically. The adults in the house had no desire to discuss it; he pondered and fretted.

In his fifth year at school, on an outing to the country, Sciascia caught malaria, endemic in many parts of Italy, as did Giuseppe and one of the *zie*. It was sufficiently bad to keep him out of school for most of the year. He filled the days listening to the aunts and reading the books from their shelves. Though he and Giuseppe were close, he saw how much his mother preferred his younger brother. Coddled in the *zie*'s house, he felt different, particularly

Sciascia with Giuseppe

after Pasquale berated him for spending so much time reading, when he should be 'living more'.

During Sciascia's eleventh summer, his maternal grandmother, Rosalia Fantauzzo, an intelligent and cultivated woman who had married at sixteen and was now a widow, took him for his first visit to Palermo.

When Goethe arrived in Palermo in the spring of 1787 he was overcome by the beauty of the ancient princely palaces bathed in sunlight, the traces of Arab, Norman and Byzantine in the architecture, the magnificence of the groves of lemons and oranges in the Conca d'Oro, the golden coast stretching east, and the air scented by oleander and anemones. To have seen Italy without seeing Sicily, he wrote, 'is not to have seen Italy at all. For Sicily is the key to everything.' A hundred years later, Palermo enjoyed its *belle époque*, every bit as glorious as that of Vienna. Both Sicilian and foreign aristocrats would remember and write about the days when the nobility squandered the last of its patrimony on elegance and frivolity, on balls, tableaux vivants, horse racing and carriages, with landau, phaetons and victorias parading down the art nouveau Via della Libertà, the men in top hats, the women tightly corseted. The Trabia liveries were yellow and gold; those of the Marquese d'Ajeta dark purple. Writing of his Palermo childhood, Fulco di Verdura described 'lace parasols against a background of palm trees and cypresses and long tables covered with white cloths spread with pyramids of strawberries and every kind of ice cream'.

In 1895 the Teatro Massimo had opened, not much smaller in size than the Paris Opera and the Scala, and drew Puccini and Sarah Bernhardt. Ignazio Florio, whose family had made their fortunes out of foundries, ship building and armaments, presided over a social galaxy that attracted dukes and barons from all over Europe to spend the winter months in the balmy climate of Palermo. Many came by yacht. Florio travelled around Europe in his own railway carriage. By the turn of the century, Palermo was the fifth largest city in Italy.

By the time of Sciascia's visit in 1932, the *belle époque* was long since over, Sicily's nobility impoverished, the foreign royalty gone. The Marsala that had created several dynasties of businessmen was no longer in fashion and America, once an importer of Sicilian oranges and lemons, now exported them. Uncontrolled spirals of prices and shortages had provoked strikes. Cholera had reduced the population and the phylloxera blight destroyed the local vines. Admiration for the city had been replaced by fear of corruption, violence, poverty. Mori's heavy hand, and the idleness of his successor had done little to restore the city's fortunes. The Mafia had merely shrunk back into the shadows. But Sciascia was fascinated. He had never seen trams or imagined such faded glory. His grandmother took him to see his first talking picture: Cecil B. DeMille's *The Sign of the Cross*. It starred Claudette Colbert and Charles Laughton.

Enrolled in his last year of elementary school, Sciascia was now also apprenticed to his tailor uncle. And, since Racalmuto had no secondary school, there he might have stayed, a village tailor, had it not been for the fact that Pasquale was offered a job in a mine at Assoro, not far from the town of Caltanissetta, home to several excellent schools and to Genoveffa's brother. In any case, Sciascia was bored with tailoring and thought he might like to study more. The family prepared to move, taking Nica with them. Before they left, Sciascia spent a month with Pasquale at his mine. He liked watching the sulphur flow like oil from the ovens, then left to harden before it was loaded on to carts to wind its way slowly between the eucalyptus trees to the coast. His relationship with his father was awkward, and he felt estranged by Pasquale's severity.

Yet later, Sciascia would say that his childhood had been happy 'shut up in that little place'. Between the ages of eight and fourteen he had read three hundred books, some of which he would read and reread all his life. Here he had learnt the importance of family, a closed world from which it is almost impossible to extract oneself, always right even when wrong, though he had sometimes felt suffocated by his aunts' love. Racalmuto had been a microcosm in which he had learnt to read the contradictions in life, the endless battle between good and evil that would later fill his books. He had learnt that friendship was the glue that held the world together, permeating and suffocating everything. Life with the aunts had left him with a sense of the terrible power of Sicilian women, a matriarchy condemned to silence and deference in public, but all-powerful and sometimes malign in private. 'I find it restful', he wrote in one of his first poems. 'To a village left behind', to 'remember your grey days/ Among those men I learnt heavy lessons about land and sulphur' . . . 'a yellow and deep red world, arid and smoky'.

Everything, Sciascia would say, that happens in a man's life has already happened in the first ten years, all the 'presentiments, premonitions, prefigurations, seeds. We become in our beings what people, places and objects have fixed on us', framed often not by the big things, but by the little, long-forgotten ones. Racalmuto had been his island, a family island, inside a small town island, itself an island within a province, within the island of Sicily. Its people, he would write, with Pirandello in mind, were intelligent, 'characters in search of an author'. He would give them one.

3
A society doubly unjust

For boys like Sciascia, who came from villages without running water, connected to the outside world by mule tracks, where the women were always in black and the summers filled with clouds of flies, Caltanissetta was exhilarating. There were at least a dozen cake shops and ice-cream parlours and the streets smelt of coffee, maraschino, cloves and freshly baked bread. Iron-pronged chandeliers lit the main streets. When the Sciascias moved there in 1935 it felt like freedom.

Caltanissetta had been a modest feudal agricultural town, built around a monastery and a castle, living to the rhythms of the wheat fields that stretched for mile upon mile all around, until sulphur was discovered in the middle of the nineteenth century. Realising that they had come upon something needed by every industrialising country, the newly rich and close-knit mining aristocracy had poured money into handsome mansions; clubs and hotels had opened; newspapers were printed; the railways arrived. Caltanissetta was made a bishopric. Though the spring brought flowering almonds and fruit trees which looked like 'puffs of smoke', the ferociously hot summer burnt the countryside all around into a yellowish dust bowl.

It was only in the poorer parts of the town, where peasants and miners continued to live in dark, damp windowless houses with their sickly and hungry families, bound together by deeply complicated rituals of friendship, that the old superstitions survived. And it was here, in the years after the First World War, that peasants and miners had joined forces to demand better lives. Six large estates had been occupied and held for forty-five days. By the time Sciascia arrived, Mori's repressions had put men in prison and there was a palpable feeling of mourning. But also one of rebellion and lively debate: Caltanissetta, people said, was a 'little Athens'.

Young Sciascia with his family

Since he would need to find regular employment as soon as he left school, Sciascia was sent not to the prestigious Liceo Ruggero Settimo, but to the recently opened Magistrale, where he could begin studying to become a teacher. It could not have been more fortuitous. The Magistrale 1X Maggio, which occupied a former convent on the edge of a small square, had attracted a collection of remarkable teachers. Its headmaster, Luigi Monaco, stood and greeted the boys one by one at 8.30 as they milled about waiting, eating their bread and mortadella. Monaco would become Sciascia's model of a cultivated, fair, calm man, good hearted but intolerant of stupidity; when he scolded his pupils, they felt remorseful.

Sciascia flourished, and having learnt to churn out five or six equally competent essays on any topic, became the boy to whom the others turned for help in Latin and literature. He made two inseparable friends, Stefano Vilardo and Lilly Bennardo, who regarded him as 'breezy and wild as a young colt' but elegant in ways the other two admired. The boys took long walks in the almond groves, discussing books and poetry. Sciascia liked to play practical jokes, but looked so innocent and candid that no one ever suspected he was the culprit. They were always penniless; Vilardo lived on money made by selling eggs laid by his family's hens. A friendly newsagent with a tiny kiosk let them look at the newspapers and even sometimes peer into the dark corner where he kept scabrous books. His friends found Sciascia disarmingly modest, full of curiosity and irony and though timid and reserved, capable of flashes of not always gentle sarcasm. They protected him, watched over him. His memory was prodigious and he never corrected or altered anything that he wrote. They said to him: 'When you're famous, remember us.'

One of Sciascia's first pieces of luck came with a young teacher of literature, Giuseppe Granata, not much older than the boys he taught and not yet fully qualified. Sciascia had arrived at his new school already intrigued by other people, their 'feelings, thoughts, preferences and failings peculiar to the Sicilian man'. Granata was quick to feed the fourteen-year-old boy with his own enthusiasms, poets such as Montale, with his quiet, yearning despair, and Leopardi, the asthmatic hunchback whose diaries concluded that human beings are nothing, achieve nothing and that there is nothing after death.

Perhaps most importantly, Granata loved the range of earlier Sicilian writers, who from Verga on had been exploring the ambivalences and ambiguities of life on the island. Giovanni Gentile, Mussolini's Minister of Public Education, had declared that Sicily's culture was dead, disappeared into the 'twilight'. But he was wrong. More than anywhere, Sicily by the 1930s had become a place where writers defined themselves and even those who left never quite freed themselves from its contradictions, its intense light and its obsession with death. Borrowing their books – Federico De Roberto's great family saga, *The Viceroys*, Luigi Capuana's *Cronache Letterarie* – from Granata, and getting others from his teacher aunt, Maria Concetta, Sciascia read without cease. The books fed his sense of unease and his growing curiosity about the past.

No Sicilian writer has delved more deeply into the Sicilian sense of constant insecurity, betrayal, futility, resentment and a fanatical concern for *roba* – possessions and the terror of them being stolen – than the writer and playwright Luigi Pirandello. In

Caltanissetta, Sciascia began a relationship with him that shaped his entire writing life, though he never actually met him. He both loved and hated him, like a son with a father, overwhelmed by his 'mysterious, chaotic and incandescent' prose, but repelled by his ardent early espousal of Fascism. And there was another important link: Pirandello had been born in 1867 in Grigenti – then the name for Agrigento – not far from Racalmuto, into a prosperous sulphur family made destitute when a rockfall destroyed their mine. Pirandello was a writer, as he would be, from the indelible world of sulphur, and in the pages of his books Sciascia discovered the 'reality into which I was born and grew up'. He was memory: 'of things that happened, people I knew, revelations, upheavals and terrors I went through'.

Luigi Pirandello

Pirandello was also a bleak master. In his books, love has the odour of death and putrefaction and few characters are not touched by madness. No woman, however attractive, is not also repulsive.

Life is a tunnel of nightmares and unreality, a vast disturbing place of paradox and contradiction. Destiny is cruel. But Pirandello, Sciascia would say, taught him the religion of writing, 'of writing being life', of 'writing instead of living', even if his world of mirrors and shadows drove him to 'the point of madness'.

Having written forty plays and seven novels and received the Nobel Prize in Literature, Pirandello died in 1936, quixotic to the end. He had insisted on signing his own book of condolences and in his will had asked for his naked body to be wrapped in a sheet, then burnt and the ashes scattered in the winds of Sicily. He had long since turned his back on Fascism and was now at odds with everything that Mussolini stood for, but fearing that the Fascists would claim him, wished to be naked to avoid the authorities dressing him in Fascist uniform. Not long before, he wrote that 'without the adventure of sulphur, there would never have been the adventure of writing, of telling stories'. Sulphur, Sciascia would later say, had formed them both.

Then, at fifteen, Sciascia discovered the French Enlightenment: eighteenth-century France, in which 'sensitive and lively men' had woken Europe up with their music of desire, 'their joyous and playful spirit, amused, ironical, mocking, light, subtle'. After the madness of Pirandello, it all felt weightless, reassuring. Though Sciascia did not understand all he read, he felt profoundly drawn to the *Encyclopédistes*. The idea that the weak might be perceived not as failures but as good, that war could be seen as stupid, feudal justice unjust, and that hard work might be rewarded by pleasure, suggested that there was after all some hope in life. He was seduced, he said later, by their form, their style, their rhythms and dialogue. Most of all, he warmed to the earlier Montaigne's benign scepticism and his phrase '*Je ne fais rien sans joie*' – 'I do nothing without pleasure' – which became his lifelong mantra. It all made a welcome change from Sicily's deep pessimism.

Diderot, in particular, captivated him, with his light and shadows, the fierceness with which he sought the truth and painted his work as provisory, a house permanently untidy, in which the doors did not fit properly. And there was Voltaire, who taught him to check everything before deciding whether it was true, and the political writer Paul Louis Courier, who used his pen like a sword to battle for justice in his village. Casanova he admired not for his amorous amoral conquests but for the fact that he wrote about them as if he had principles. Anyone who had not read Stendhal, he suggested, was to be profoundly pitied. Sciascia thought: How wonderful if this is what literature is. The French Enlightenment became his model of perfection, of richness of thought, and France the place where enlightened men had had the courage to reveal hidden truths. In Diderot he saw the kind of intellectual he dreamt of becoming, taking everything seriously but with such lightness of touch that he gave the impression that he took nothing seriously. Reason, he was beginning to think, would act as a counterbalance to the chaos all around him.

Not all his reading reached this level of profundity. Sherlock Holmes had been a familiar character in translation since well before the First World War. But as part of Mussolini's increasing stronghold over the media, censorship now extended to include books supposedly damaging to national morale. Crime fiction, he declared, was too decadent to be a 'genuine product of the Italian soul'. A quota was put on foreign books and an edict issued that the culprits and villains in fiction must never be Italian. All reference to suicide was forbidden. However, in 1929, Mondadori had begun to publish British crime fiction – Margery Allingham, Agatha Christie – under the rubric *'libri gialli'*, from the yellow colour of their jackets. *'Gialli'* became the popular term for police thrillers. Sciascia delighted in these battles between murderers and detectives in which criminals were eventually brought to book. He considered Sherlock Holmes too rigorous and technical and found the Americans on offer, such as Dashiell Hammett, 'dissolute', and their hard-boiled sleuths ambiguous. Most of all, he warmed to Simenon, saying that the world inhabited by his detective Maigret, who relied on knowledge of the human heart and his own powers of intuition, was one he knew and recognised. He liked Maigret's peasant-like qualities of stubbornness and astuteness.

Sciascia, who was very silent in class, did badly at science, but he excelled in other subjects. A day came when Granata, reading yet another impressive essay that he had turned in, became convinced that the boy was copying things out. He took it home, consulted books, and finally showed it to the headmaster. Monaco, who had been watching Sciascia carefully, reassured him that the essay was certainly the boy's own work. Granata was not convinced. At the next essay session, he placed Sciascia by his side to keep an eye on him. The essay that he turned in was impeccable.

By his second year, Sciascia had become the leader of a small group of boys who, like him, were avid readers and loved the cinema, to which they went whenever they had money. Jean Gabin brought them a breath of France's *Front Populaire*, a vision of Europe from which Mussolini's all-embracing Fascism seemed to exclude them. Hollywood continued to export its films to Italy – soon to be banned by Mussolini on account of competition with the new Italian film industry – and the boys fell in love with Irene Dunne and Myrna Loy. Sciascia himself preferred his stars less glamorous, more domestic: 'real women' for him were mothers, sisters, wives. He gave the films asterisks and wrote lengthy reviews which he sent to a friend in Racalmuto. He was enchanted by a local girl with blonde pigtails who looked like Simone Signoret, though there was of course no question of speaking to her. A boy in his class had pictures of women dressed only in tights, obtained from an uncle who had a friend in Paris and shown surreptitiously under the desk to a few chosen boys. They were, wrote Sciascia, 'rosy-skinned, sly, plump' and like an animal in spring, he felt a faint sense of delirium. He came across the words '*crêpe Georgette*', a kind of material worn by women in magazines, and they sounded to him erotic and suggestive. He began to smoke, a habit he never gave up.

Then, in this fortunate boyhood, came another piece of luck. Vitaliano Brancati, born in Catania in 1907, had been a successful journalist and devoted Fascist in Rome in the 1920s. Just when Fascism might have been most useful to him, he turned against it. Mussolini became for him the epitome of sexual indulgence and moral ugliness. He returned to Sicily and began to write novels in which he painted a grotesque and comic picture of Italy under the Fascists. Fascism, he said, had for a while given him the comfortable feeling of belonging, as to a flock of sheep, but it had been 'a drunkenness of stupidity'. Soon after Sciascia arrived in Caltanissetta, Brancati took a job as a teacher at the Magistrale.

Though Sciascia was never in his class, he was acutely aware of Brancati. He watched him every morning as he arrived at school, a morose, surly, scowling figure with a slight limp, defying anyone to approach him. Every week, in a literary magazine called *Omnibus*,

Brancati wrote a column on life in Caltanissetta – which he called Nissa – and Sciascia often forfeited a cinema ticket in order to buy the magazine.

Brancati had also written what later became one of the most admired novellas about Fascism, *La noia del '937*, about boredom. Arriving by chance in a town in which the wind never stops blowing, where people close their doors at dusk and dogs try to bite their own tails, a man takes a room in a hotel. And there he stays, thinking that this is the very essence of the boredom and claustrophobia of small-town Fascist life. He sends a telegram to a friend describing it and is soon visited by a local policeman, who demands that he withdraw it. He chooses to take his own life instead. Brancati's work made Sciascia think and laugh; he was not put off by reading his *gialli*, even though Brancati declared thrillers to be 'horribly mediocre books' somewhat like pornography. Sciascia never dared to approach him. But, he wrote later, 'he gave me the idea that I too could become a writer and be like him'.

These years in Sicily were little marked by Mafia violence. But Mori's draconian measures had merely driven them underground, to wait and watch while sinking their roots deep into the fabric of Sicilian life, ready to emerge as the good times they confidently expected returned. Among Sciascia's schoolfellows, there were the boys without the luck that he was always conscious of having, and some of these, he knew, were drifting in bad directions.

In the evenings, in the little house in Caltanissetta, Sciascia regaled Giuseppe, Anna, his mother, Nica and his young cousin Maria with talk of the books he was reading and the movies he saw. Genoveffa was a private but affectionate woman, much loved by everyone in the family. The three children looked very alike, with their thin faces, dark hair and deep-set round eyes. Sciascia had taken over one of the small rooms, filled it with his books, which he loved to touch and stroke, saying that they contained the secret of life. 'I want to die,' he said, 'before books disappear from the world.' Giuseppe was growing up very different from his brother, less bookish and more outgoing, though pulled down sometimes by anxiety.

Whenever he was able, Sciascia returned to Racalmuto to visit the *zie* and catch up on local gossip. Every summer, the family migrated to *La Noce*. Sciascia took with him many books – the

Sciascia, aged fourteen or fifteen

summers were his time for reading the Russians. Along the banks of the Azzalora, people had planted vegetable gardens, with special onions known for their sweetness, eaten raw or with the strong local pecorino or caciocavallo. At dusk came flights of swifts and swallows, and Sciascia and his friends caught frogs, roasted them over a fire, sucking the flesh out of the legs. He went shooting with his uncle, and the warblers they brought back were wrapped in greaseproof paper and placed in the cinders to roast. Stefano Vilardo, who came to stay, always remembered Nica's meals, huge plates of spaghetti with basil and tomatoes, sardines or roast chicken, eaten outside the house at a long chestnut table under the almond trees.

In August 1937, soon after his conquest of Ethiopia and proclamation that Italy now had its empire, Mussolini paid another visit to Sicily. The war in Ethiopia – barbaric in ways kept from the people in Italy – was the pinnacle of Fascist glory. Even Sciascia and his friends stopped on their way to school to look at the maps of their new empire, placed prominently in bookshops. They were not unsympathetic to the idea that Italy had defied other countries, themselves imperialist, who opposed and condemned her actions. It was a question of class, they agreed, of belonging to a poor people which rich nations wanted to suffocate. There were photographs of Mussolini everywhere, smiling, laughing, certain of victory; while those of Anthony Eden, the British Foreign Secretary, made him look, thought Sciascia, 'like a nervous sort of man, one who bites his nails'.

During the Ethiopian campaign, Fascism demanded of its writers that they celebrate what it meant to be Italian, vital, full of Christian purity, in language that was exhortatory and robust. What was known as the 'Fascist style' was martial and austere. The persecution of Jews was increasing. In Palermo, a city rich in the sciences, two prominent Jewish professors, the physicist Emilio Segre and the physiologist Camillo Artom, were sacked from the university.

Mussolini's trip to Sicily was meticulously orchestrated. Holes in the crumbling streets were filled in and houses whitewashed. At the Magistrale, as in all other schools in Sicily, pupils were ordered to perfect their marching for the coming parades. One Saturday afternoon, Sciascia was caught sneaking off to the cinema by a patrol scouring Caltanissetta for truants; he was locked up in a warehouse with other miscreants. When midnight came, the boys forced the heavy doors and slunk home to anxious parents.

The Duce's performances, before immense crowds, were legendary. Addressing 100,000 people in Palermo's *Foro Italico*, a vast green park along the sea front, he told them that Sicily had become an 'imperial island' with a bright future as the bridge between Italy and its African empire. He promised Sicilians generous funds. ('What an impostor!' declared the ever-sceptical Maria Concetta.) Sicily, Mussolini announced, was 'Fascist to its marrow'.

He was wrong. Sicily had never shown the same level of Fascist fervour as much of the rest of Italy. In any case, belief in the Fascist dream was shrinking. The Spanish Civil War, which followed so closely after Ethiopia, and to which Mussolini dispatched many thousands of so-called volunteers, would feed a growing sense of disenchantment with the regime. In Sicily, young men, driven to enrol by acute poverty and the lure of good wages, began to arrive home wounded, with stories of brutality and hardship. People began to doubt.

For Sciascia, the civil war in Spain proved shocking. He was disgusted by the triumphalist articles that filled the Fascist papers and by Mussolini's boast that he was *'padrone'* – master – of the Mediterranean. He felt revulsion when a boy in his school refused to wash his face where he had been kissed by the Duce during his visit. And if not only Hemingway and Dos Passos, but also the Hollywood actors he most admired, such as Gary Cooper, were supporting the Republicans, then, surely, something was wrong. And the fact that Pirandello had rejected the Fascists meant that he no longer had to qualify his admiration for him. The shooting of Federico Garcia Lorca by the nationalists was an act of treachery, carried out by 'imbeciles'. Poetry, the boys agreed, was on the Republican side. And Sciascia had found another mentor, José Ortega y Gasset, whose writing convinced him that one needed, always, to return to the facts, however obscure, and then establish causality and consequence. As he would soon write, in one of his most powerful short stories, *L'Antimonio*, the Spanish Civil War was the moment in his life when he knew with absolute clarity exactly what he felt.

Salvatore Sciascia – no relation – was one of 'little Athens's' most interesting figures. He owned a bookshop and a small publishing business on the Corso Umberto, and produced a number of literary magazines. It was here that Caltanissetta's intellectuals gathered, and here that anti-Fascism quietly flowered. Luigi Monaco, Sciascia's headmaster, was a regular visitor, as was his teacher, Granata. There was Pompeo Colajanni, soon to become a partisan and who kept repeating that Italy had been 'morally drugged' by the Fascists; and Giuseppe Alessi, a future left-wing journalist; and a young trainee lawyer, Gaetano Costa. Sciascia's brother Giuseppe was friends with a boy called Antonio Macaluso and his elder brother, Emanuele, already active secretly in left-wing politics, was also to be found there. Nervously, silently, Sciascia and his friends began to drop in. They had a new acquaintance, Luigi Cortese, who sported a large moustache and smoked cigars, who made no secret of his political views. In the Caffè Romano, the boys exchanged banned literature in plain wrappers. They bought the *Osservatore Romano*, the Vatican paper, the only one that did not trumpet unadulterated Fascism. The talk was cautious, veiled, exciting, a hunt for the nuances of rebellion. In Salvatore Sciascia's bookshop, wrote Vilardo later, 'you breathed the oxygen of freedom'. Long after, Sciascia would say that never before those days or since had he felt such intensity and purity, such love and such hatred, and that never would friendship, sincerity and trust burn so brightly in his heart.

When Pasquale came back on his fortnightly leaves from the mine, he urged Sciascia to be prudent. Giuseppe was afraid of his father and tried to please him; but Sciascia was not. In school he had begun keeping a list of his friends and teachers, describing their characters and their tics by expressions taken from the titles of films. He called the girl with the pigtails Primavera, saying that her hair smelt of spring. He and Vilardo would sometimes skip school to lie in the grass reading or to wander the streets when intense heat drove people indoors. They told each other that they would grow up to be engineers, poets. Sciascia, said Vilardo, calmed him; he gave him 'certainties, a sense to my days'. The boys had discovered the work of Alberto Savinio, the Greek-Italian writer, musician and painter who increased their feeling that they could 'emerge into light and air from somewhere enclosed and dark'. Savinio, said Sciascia, painted for him a world far more complicated than he imagined, governed not by a single truth but many truths, which had to be sought 'freely and fearlessly'.

Elio Vittorini, the son of a railway worker from Siracusa, was one of Sicily's most promising young writers. Thirteen years older than Sciascia, he was already describing Sicily as a land in which people lived in dark hovels, existing on snails and chicory, their children coming home famished, like wild animals, to chew on pieces of wood to stave off hunger. It was what he called '*un mondo offeso*' – an offended world – traduced by Fascism and the cancer of absolute power. Like Brancati, he had in his youth been a Fascist, but was now disenchanted, saying that since he could not shoot, he would write. He had started to contribute to the underground press and travelled around Sicily with suitcases full of clandestine material. Salvatore Sciascia's bookshop was one of his ports of call. These mostly young, clever, frustrated men were just a very small pocket of resistance in a great sea of indifference. But things were beginning to change.

In the summer of 1939, Mussolini signed a 'pact of steel' with Hitler. As Europe went to war, Italy remained on the sidelines, neutral. Like the rest of the country, Sicily was getting poorer, hungrier.

Genoveffa's brother worked on the railways and was able to buy wheat and pasta for the Sciascias.

On 10 June 1940, as the Germans advanced steadily through France, Mussolini, fearing that Italy would lose out on the spoils that German victory would surely soon bring, took Italy into the war. Sciascia and Vilardo saw the news on the headlines of a newspaper in the Caffè Romano: the world, they told each other, 'has exploded'. In Racalmuto, the women waiting at the pump outside the *zie*'s house stood listening to Mussolini's call to arms over loudspeakers positioned all around the village. They asked Maestro Pietru, a blind man known for his shrewdness and wisdom, what he thought. 'Even though I am blind,' he declared, 'I see it black.' '*Lo vedo nero*' became the local synonym for deep pessimism about the state of Italy.

Around the province of Caltanissetta the sulphur mines closed as men were called up. Racalmuto gave its iron railings for the war effort. Orders went out for public employees to wear black shirts or their Fascist uniforms: those who refused were sacked. Every day, at one o'clock, the radio broadcast a bulletin: it was always about Italian victories. Listeners had to stand up and remove their hats. In the windows of shops and on walls were posters with the word '*Vincere*', to win. The magazine *Omnibus*, with Brancati's iconoclastic articles, was closed down by the censors. The island, as Sciascia put it, 'went dark'.

Sciascia and his friends received their military summons. They had been listening secretly to Radio London, learning the truth about Italy's disastrous war, in which losses of ill-equipped, ill-trained and badly led men were growing steadily, though in theory to do so risked death. After their terrified families begged them to stop, a lawyer, an officer in the militia but also a clandestine anti-Fascist, invited them to listen in his own house. When Sciascia was called up, he was passed as unfit for military service, on the grounds of low weight and extreme thinness. This happened again at his second call-up; the third time he was declared fit only for 'sedentary service', and then he heard no more. Many of his friends were making their way to the Russian front; others had joined a cavalry regiment in Parma. He felt relieved – but uneasy – not to be with them.

Having left school and got his teaching diploma, Sciascia won a place at the University of Palermo with an essay on Thornton Wilder, but gave it up after his first poor exam results. He was already writing, filling lesson books with poems, stories, fables, art criticism, and he had an article on American politics published in a local paper. Hearing about the London Blitz, he read Virginia Woolf's *To the Lighthouse*, both because he wanted to pay homage to her, and because he needed an antidote to the horror and repugnance he felt for the triumphalist Fascists. Casualties on the Eastern Front kept mounting; some of the dead were boys from Racalmuto and Caltanissetta.

Everyone was hungry. Rations kept dropping. There was no meat or fish; then no soap, coffee or sugar; then no potatoes. Food shops and markets closed. Fleas and scabies spread. There were no more shoes, only clogs. One day a cat was spotted leaving the house of the Fascist Party secretary in Racalmuto. It had in its mouth a large piece of salted cod, with which it retreated to a rooftop, ignoring the frantic calls from its owners. Perhaps, people said, it was a fifth columnist, or even a Socialist. Salt cod, *baccalà*, was an unimaginable luxury, not seen for many months. A military post was set up in the village with a canteen for officers. Hungry children stood at the door, sniffing. Among the soldiers was a young lieutenant, educated and anti-Fascist, and he and Sciascia exchanged books. The summer of 1941 was exceptionally wet. Heavy rains were followed by intense heat then more rains and wild winds. The oranges fell early and rotted, their sweet, nauseating smell, wrote Brancati, was like that of 'blood, labour, misery'. In Racalmuto, Sciascia and two friends put on a play in the Regina Margherita to raise money for local men at the front.

Early in the war, quotas had been set for a certain amount of wheat that farmers had to deliver to the authorities. Turned down by the military, Sciascia was taken on by the *Consorzio Agrario* in Racalmuto to help enforce the ruling. He had grown up knowing in his bones about the precarious world of sulphur; now he learnt about peasant life. Around Racalmuto were many sharecroppers, forced to give half of all they produced in return for their rents. There were also smallholdings, few larger than 20 hectares, their owners rivalrous and litigious over their boundaries. Many, by this stage of the war, were barely surviving: the demands for wheat were often more than could be borne. Everyone was lying, cheating, dealing clandestinely.

The Allies began to bomb Italy. Palermo was hit so repeatedly that people spoke of it as mutilated. Then Caltanissetta was hit and many people died, among them one of Sciascia's friends, killed while trying to save books in the library. Genoveffa, Maria, Anna and Giuseppe stood on the balcony to watch the incoming planes, then fled to the countryside to take cover. Part of the town centre was flattened. Pasquale, hearing of the raids, came home to find the house empty; he set out to walk the 20 kilometres to Racalmuto. The King visited Sicily: to Sciascia he looked so grey that he seemed to be carved out of dried clay, 'a poor old man from a hospice'. Germany had sent 30,000 troops to Sicily and a division had been posted to a spot along the railway leading to Racalmuto. As the trains went past, the passengers peered through slits in the blinds at the blond, healthy-looking young Germans among the trees, bare chested in the sun. All over Sicily, refugees were moving inland to escape the heavy bombing of the coastal areas.

While at Messina, taking his diploma, Sciascia had caught sight of a young teacher, Maria Andronica, whose father was a *maresciallo*, a senior officer in the carabinieri, serving in a village some 15 kilometres from Racalmuto. He was at this point going out with a local girl. Almost painfully thin, and overly neat in dress, he was not exactly good looking. But his eyes were watchful and intense and he was known to be unnervingly clever. After Maria took a job teaching in Racalmuto, she became friends with his aunt, Maria Concetta, who invited her to visit them. As was seemly at the time, she came accompanied by the school janitor. The aunts had promised to introduce her to their nephew who, like her, was a 'great reader'. Maria was dark haired and comely, a year younger than Sciascia, and she was sharing a flat with three other teachers. Her visits to the aunts' house became more frequent, with Sciascia happily talking literature to the little group of women. When alone, he and Maria discussed books and films. 'I would like you to read this,' he would tell her, giving her his copy of Virginia Woolf's *To the Lighthouse* and Willa Cather's *Death Comes for the Archbishop*. Bit by bit, their encounters became more public, but it was a long time before he switched from addressing her with the formal Fascist '*voi*' to the more intimate '*tu*'.

A SOCIETY DOUBLY UNJUST

The war was getting closer. Mussolini had promised that there would be no Allied invasion of Sicily – 'here, no one will land, not one single soldier' – even when his generals feared otherwise. The island was not mobilised for defence. No air cover was put in place and there were virtually no bomb shelters. The bombings continued. Palermo had become a ghostly shell. General Roatta, in charge of the island's Italian divisions, announced that there was nothing to fear, and that in any case Sicily would be protected by Italian soldiers. Everyone was waiting. No one was careful any longer about what they said. Fascists were beginning to court former anti-Fascist friends. German vehicles covered in camouflage came and went. No one knew what was happening. The harvest was ready, but enemy planes were rumoured to be strafing peasants in the fields, and the crops were left to rot. Sciascia's lieutenant friend disappeared from the village; next day a motorcyclist appeared with a copy of *Moby Dick* for him.

Meditating on the importance of the past, both his own and Sicily's, the 'subtle and long tentacles' that led back to the 'galaxy of memory', Sciascia reflected that he had spent his first twenty years in a society doubly unjust, doubly unfree, doubly irrational, a 'society-non society', Sicily as described by Pirandello.

Like everyone else, he was waiting; but for what, he was not sure.

4

Terrified of the present and uncertain of the future

Late on the evening of 9 July 1943 the inhabitants of Racalmuto, standing out on their balconies to catch the faint breeze, saw the horizon above the coast beyond Agrigento lit up by flashes of brilliant yellow light. It was as if, Sciascia wrote later, the moon had fallen on to the shore and cast its beam along the length of the island. After this came explosions, clearly audible in the still night air. People emerged from their houses. From the darkened streets and alleyways could be heard chatter and excited laughter. The Americans and the British had landed.

Six months earlier, at Casablanca, on 18 January, Churchill and Roosevelt had approved Operation Husky, an assault on Sicily as a prelude to an invasion of the Italian mainland before a rapid advance up Italy and into Slovenia, Austria and Hungary. It was to be the largest amphibian invasion in history and all through the spring a vast armada had been assembling along the coast of North Africa, from Egypt to Algeria, together with stockpiles of tanks, armoured cars and weapons. A plot was hatched to fool the Germans about Allied intentions. The corpse of a supposed army major was washed up on the coast of Spain with a briefcase full of papers stating that the Allies planned to land in Greece and Sardinia, with only a very small, irrelevant sideshow in Sicily. It was believed.

There were two German divisions stationed on the island, but its coasts remained poorly defended, manned by ill-trained and ill-equipped soldiers, many of them Sicilians too old or unfit for active service. They wore sandals or went barefoot. In a few places, a single line of barbed wire separated the beach from the shore. There were some bunkers made of cardboard. General Roatta, who had pleaded in vain for cement with which to build proper defences, had been pronounced defeatist and his replacement as commander-in-chief of Sicily was a sixty-one-year-old veteran of the Italo-Turkish war of 1911. Alfredo Guzzoni had never been to Sicily before.

In Racalmuto, at dawn on 10 July, the church bells began to ring. An Allied plane flew over, letting off several rounds of fire and killing a carter and wounding a child, but people agreed that it had undoubtedly been a mistake. A state of emergency was declared. The *podestà*, his interpreter and the village priest readied themselves for the arrival of the Americans. They waited. Sciascia and his friends loitered in the main street, determined not to miss the glorious moment when the Allies arrived.

The first people they saw were a group of twenty wounded Bersaglieri, riflemen in the Italian army, many from the Veneto, who limped into the village. They had their wounds bandaged and were given civilian clothes in order not to be captured as soldiers. Since there was nothing for them to eat, the call went out for food. The richest man gave an egg; the poorer people were rather more generous. Everyone was thinking about American corned beef.

A travelling salesman appeared, breathless and agitated, from the coast, bringing with him a packet of Chesterfields and a few lumps of sugar, somewhat like Noah's dove, bearing an olive leaf. A respectful group gathered round him. 'So many boats, so many boats', Sciascia heard him say, stretching to the horizon and beyond, so densely packed that there was no water between them. The villagers decided to use the time waiting for the Allies to get rid of all signs of Fascism: posters and photographs were torn down, flags put away, insignia and membership cards thrown into the sewers.

Another day passed. Two armoured cars, full of silent, sweating Germans appeared; they did not stop but pressed on north. They were followed by two German officers, and while they sat at a café table eating and smoking their cigars, the silent villagers gathered round their car radio to listen to the news from Rome. The electricity was cut. Flour ran out, then vegetables, because no one dared leave the village for the kitchen gardens on its outskirts. Racalmuto felt so silent, so dead, that Sciascia and his friends worried that the Americans would not bother to come.

A SICILIAN MAN

Sciascia was standing just inside a doorway when, on the hot and sultry afternoon of 16 July, five American soldiers wearing dark glasses suddenly appeared at the top of the main street. Fanning out, with one in the middle and the others hugging the walls, their rifles slung loosely by their sides, looking somewhat like cowboys in a Hollywood western, they advanced towards the piazza. The carabinieri sitting at the café tables froze, before getting, very slowly, to their feet. It made Sciascia feel that he was watching a film, magically turning into reality before his eyes.

Circling behind the carabinieri, the Americans removed the guns from their holsters. Suddenly a villager called out, asking for cigarettes. One of the soldiers threw over a pack. There was an explosion of cheers, shouts, applause. People emerged from their houses with bottles of wine. The school janitor produced an American flag. The villagers who had been able to build their houses with remittances from their relations in America started to talk to the soldiers as if they were old friends, which in many ways they were since the US army had included many Sicilian Italians in the first wave of landings. Some of the young people began to dance.

Sciascia noted that the loudest cheers came from a lawyer called Calafato, who, not so very long before, had leapt on to the running board of Mussolini's train to shout, 'Duce, I give you my life.' Not even the unfortunate shooting of a man seen running away – he was in black, in mourning for his father – dampened the good spirits. By nightfall, more American soldiers had arrived in jeeps, pulling cigarettes and sweets from their pockets, speaking the local dialect, looking for wine and women. As the Racalmutesi told each other, '*Quasi Americani siamo*', we are almost Americans. It was a 'festival of liberty'. Most had never tasted the peppermint in chewing gum or seen a tin of orange juice.

And then the spies, the men with grudges, those who feared they would be overlooked and so miss out on the spoils, began sidling up to the American soldiers. They had lists of names in their pockets. It was, Sciascia noted, 'a masked ball of informers'. Next day, the *podestà*, the *maresciallo* of the carabinieri and the Fascist Party secretary were all arrested and driven away, not to reappear for many months. The party secretary, as Sciascia remarked later, had in fact been a good man, but someone had to go to prison to show that a new life was beginning. Even at this delightful moment, no one could quite forget the vast and poisonous legacy of the Fascists, their 'spies, thieves, hatred'.

The Sicilians, desperately poor, some of them on the edge of starvation, short of everything, expected abundance from their new occupiers. In Palermo, people had been reduced to a diet of oranges. There would be not just corned beef, but all manner of good things. Among Sciascia and his friends there was a heady feeling of hope. Furthermore, their war was now over, while the Italian mainland faced a further 594 days of fighting, a country at war not just with the Allies but with itself, Italians fighting Italians in a bitter civil war. A final message from King Victor Emanuel, who would soon flee south from Rome with his entourage to set up a tiny ineffectual *Regno d'Italia* in Brindisi, exhorted the islanders to 'love their homeland' – that is to say, Italy. It was greeted with suitable derision. The Sicilians were now free. They had plans for the future of their island, though not all shared the same dreams. The Mafia, too, had plans. With the Fascists gone, and mainland Italy otherwise occupied, the moment had come for serious political and financial gain.

Despite their many Sicilian immigrants, the Americans knew very little about Sicily. There was a deeply held conviction that it was filled with lazy, untrustworthy, excitable and cowardly people, prone to cold-blooded violence. For much of the spring of 1943, the military in the US and the Foreign Office in Britain, with the help of a special unit of sociologists and anthropologists at Oxford's Balliol College, had been putting together a picture of the island. They drew from newspapers and interviews with émigrés, but much of it was shaped by gangster films and the memory of the disastrous Italian defeat at Caporetto in the First World War. It was both ignorant and out of date.

By 1931, Mussolini, anxious about having enough soldiers to compete with other European countries, had made emigration illegal without a special permit. An earlier wave in the late nineteenth century had taken many men to France and Tunisia, and in the years leading up to the First World War, one and a half million Sicilians, driven abroad by misery, had made their way to the United States, Argentina and Brazil. Most of these were men, and many left wives behind them, known as 'white widows', who seldom left their houses. Remittances had contributed injections of capital into agriculture, and those returning on a visit after some years with money to invest had brought with them not just higher standards but an expectation of greater equality. The '*Americani*', proudly strolling down the streets of their native villages, showed less resignation, less deference.

Like Sciascia's father Pasquale, however, there were many who had failed to make their fortunes and were unwilling to discuss what had gone wrong. As a result, the Racalmutesi had become ambivalent about emigration, looking on America both as an exhilarating land of plenty and as a bitter, negative destiny, a place where people did not really know how to live, were ground down by merciless labour and learnt to dress and speak in peculiar ways. Among the children Sciascia played with were boys dressed in second-hand American clothes sent by relations in New York, Boston or Chicago. Relatives who suddenly returned were looked on, wrote Sciascia, with scorn, 'as if they had become even stupider than before'. For their part, the *Americani* complained that nothing had changed and that Racalmuto was as dirty as it had ever been.

The expectations of the Allied soldiers now making their way across the island were further warped by a *Sicily Zone Handbook* issued to officers. This devoted more space to folklore and superstition and the many perils from malaria, dysentery and hookworm that the Sicilians, themselves immune on account of their primitive state, would undoubtedly transmit to the soldiers, than to the people or their politics. It was also much concerned with the nobility. Aristocratic Sicilian women, it claimed, who seldom did anything more intellectual than read French novels, 'are sometimes charming, petulant, witty and gay, with more than a soupçon of orientalism'; the men were incorrigible gamblers and not inclined to work. As you moved down the social scale, you found loafers and bounders, who were also somewhat effeminate, in the sense of being duplicitous, capricious and vain. The peasants were altogether more agreeable and came in a 'patchwork of colours'.

Caltanissetta and Agrigento were singled out as having 'among the roughest and least attractive people on the island'. Everywhere the soldiers would find many goats. In Siracusa, people used sarcophagi as beds. Sicily was, in short, 'an oriental or African' country, and its culture was a far cry from the humanism of the rest of Europe. The message was unequivocal. The Allied campaign in Sicily would liberate cowed and illiterate children from the treacherous Fascist yoke. It would bring with it a benign and civilising mission, and help build a new and better world from its very foundations. Occupation would be redemptive. It would also, very possibly, be brutal. 'When you meet the enemy,' General Patton, commander of the US 7th Army, had instructed his soldiers, 'do not forget to strike and strike hard . . . Kill him. Have no pity. Kill, kill and kill some more.'

Having been told to expect a lush and verdant land, the soldiers climbing out of their landing crafts were dismayed to find a barren, arid landscape, made worse by a raging sirocco which blew yellow dust into their eyes. The sudden storm witnessed by Sciascia in Racalmuto the night before had thrown the gliders off course, and sixty-nine had crashed, but the men were pushing on. In temperatures of 40 degrees, their tin helmets scorched their heads. The mosquitoes were murderous. But as the men advanced into the interior they found orchards, olive trees, fields of broad beans and ripe tomatoes. They had been warned that they would have to fight their way through a wall of mines, machine guns and barbed wire. In the event they encountered nothing but a few light wooden roadblocks and half-hearted resistance from the Italian defenders, unshaven and unkempt, happy to throw down their weapons and surrender. There were soon so many Sicilian prisoners that orders went out to release them to go home to their harvests. By the second day, phone lines had been laid. The local population also proved friendly, with villagers offering wine, though they kept getting in the way 'just like Arabs'. The Italians, noted General Montgomery, commander of the British 8th Army, 'are a rotten crowd. They lie among their grapes and lemons and breed. Far too many of them.' What struck the Allied soldiers most was the utter poverty, people living in caves and threshing with mules.

The Germans, caught off guard, rapidly regrouped. The Hermann Göring Panzer division was dispatched from Calabria. There were now some 150,000 Allied soldiers on the island, their numbers growing with each new wave of landings, facing just over a quarter of a million Italians and Germans, but the Allies had superior airpower and many more tanks. Within a few days, the Germans lost 323 aircraft. But as General Montgomery and the 8th Army pressed up the east of the island, and General Patton and the 7th Armored Division turned west, towards Caltanissetta and Racalmuto, through outcrops of volcanic rock and deep gulleys, they began to meet stiffer German resistance. The advance stalled as engineers went ahead to clear the mines and rebuild bridges that had been blown up. Bulldozers became essential.

Sicilians were used to being occupied: they had known nothing else. They had hated the Germans, and hated them even more when a troop of soldiers opened fire one early morning in the village of Castiglione di Sicilia, aiming at the inhabitants who, hearing the sound of trucks, had emerged on to their balconies: sixteen people died and many more were wounded. Now the Allies had arrived they expected better treatment. A former governor of New York, a lawyer called Charles Poletti, had been parachuted into Palermo before the invasion to start preparing for what would follow. He had set up his headquarters in the vast Abbey at Monreale. The British had wanted to administer the island, to affirm their hegemony of the Mediterranean, but Roosevelt argued that with such a large Sicilian population in the US, the task should be shared. Under AMGOT, the Allied Military Government of Occupied Territories, the British and American civil and military officers were to have a joint command. A slew of orders, prohibitions, warnings and threats poured out, but in their badly translated Italian many were incomprehensible. American military currency – the 'am-lire' – were printed and put into circulation. Written on them were the freedoms President Roosevelt had promised the Italians before Congress – of speech and religion and from fear and want; but these were written in English. The am-lire led to a rapid rise in inflation.

Sicily had nine provinces. The Allies had planned on installing six hundred officers to administer them, one for every ten thousand inhabitants. In theory, these men all spoke Italian and had some knowledge of the island. In practice, the British had backgrounds in colonial affairs or were diplomats and businessmen, and among the Americans only a few had any experience of government. Most were over fifty and had been given crash courses in special schools in Wimbledon and Charlottesville. One of the Englishmen knew

Latin. They were told by Patton that Sicilians were cheerful people, seemingly 'contented with the disorder they live in', and that there would be little point in trying to elevate them to American standards. Their orders were to dismantle Fascism from top to toe, avoid chaos, help the military to advance, scotch any sign of Communism, 'bury the dead and feed the living'. It was immediately clear that they needed not six hundred men, but six thousand. The British agreed to send an extra fifty policemen.

No one had been prepared for, or been told about, the disastrous lack of food, nor the degree of destruction caused by the heavy Allied bombing, nor the sheer number of homeless refugees wandering around the island. Sicily seemed to the invaders so poor that it belonged to another age. A quarter of a million houses lay in ruins; 2,300 kilometres of roads had been destroyed, along with bridges, aqueducts, sewage plants, stations and hospitals. Agriculture had collapsed and straw, beans and chickpeas were being used to make bread. People marched, shouting, 'Bread! Bread!' In some villages, offal and excrement lay about waiting to be washed away by the rains. Unexploded mines lay everywhere. City centres had been reduced to squalor and desolation. Looting was rampant, the retreating Germans carrying off food, mules, bicycles and even hearses. Absurd rumours abounded: that the American fighter planes were piloted by naked blonde women, and that the Allied soldiers were given special tablets to make them brave as lions.

With the invaders had come 13,000 tons of flour, 94 tons of soap and 150 tons of medicines. It was nothing like enough. There were food riots. The *'ammasso'* – the food rationing system that Sciascia had been helping to run in Racalmuto – was kept in place and though the village was relatively prosperous, he was again conscious of the acute poverty of some of his neighbours and of his greater good fortune. When their requests to the Allies for shoes, petrol and bicycles, often written in the florid prose of village scribes, were ignored, the Sicilians, at first so welcoming, turned mistrustful and resentful. As the rations of bread dropped further, they continued to starve, in dignified silence. Why were their friends, the Americans, refusing to give them more?

The Allied intention had been to sack all the authorities tainted by Fascism and to appoint new, uncontaminated, men. '*Epurazione*', the cleaning out of the Fascists from public office, began. A committee for *'defascistazione'* was put in place. The old Fascist-appointed *podestà* were removed, along with civil servants, senior policemen, university professors and judges. Some, as Sciascia noted with sympathy, were men who had simply tolerated Fascism in order to keep their jobs. Others were victims of vendettas. They were soon making their way to prison camps in North Africa. But there had never been a proper plan for who to put in their places. It would soon prove to be a terrible mistake.

There is a story, much beloved by historians, which may or may not be true, or even partly true.

In 1943, a *mafioso* called Salvatore Lucania, known as Lucky Luciano, was serving a fifty-year sentence in an American prison for drugs and running prostitutes. Sometime early in the year, he had been moved to the Great Meadows Penitentiary, conveniently close to the Office of Naval Intelligence, and had agreed to help protect, through his excellent contacts, New York's harbour from enemy sabotage. Luciano had been born not far from Racalmuto; his face was scarred from a rare form of smallpox and his back was bent from a tubercular spinal ailment. He had good friends back in Sicily, not least Don Calò, the paunchy boss from Villalba. On the morning of 14 July, an American fighter plane circled over the village and dropped a packet with a yellow flag and the letter L. Since it missed its target, a second was dropped the next day. This one landed on Don Calò's doorstep.

That evening, a messenger on horseback left for the nearby village of Mussomeli with a letter for 'zu Peppi', Giuseppe Genco Russo, a fellow Mafia boss. The area around Mussomeli was crucial for Patton's progress towards Palermo. The letter contained instructions to Genco Russo to look after the Americans while Don Calò himself went north with Patton's soldiers. On 20 July, three American tanks arrived in Villalba: one flew a yellow flag with the letter L. The officer in charge spoke excellent Sicilian. Don Calò, now in his late sixties, with his vast belly and eyes that swivelled slyly like those of a lizard, waddled out, in shirtsleeves and braces, a cigar in his mouth. Producing his own little yellow flag, he was hoisted on board the Sherman tank; orders went out to his followers to make the passage of the Americans easy. Italian soldiers serving in the neighbourhood deserted en masse. The Americans reached Palermo in seven days, with barely a shot fired, in what Patton called the 'fastest blitzkrieg in history'. The British, pursuing the Germans fleeing towards Messina to embark for the mainland, took somewhat longer to reach the coast.

Don Calò, returning to Villalba in an American jeep, was soon handsomely rewarded. He was made the new Mayor of Villalba and presented with two Fiat trucks and a tractor, and American officers arrived to present him with a scroll at a ceremony attended by his brother, the local priest. The new Prefect of Caltanissetta sent a gift of fifty pairs of shoes. Magisterial and gnomic, Don Calò was now truly a feudal lord. When Sicilians were ordered to hand in their weapons, he convinced the Americans to allow his friends to keep theirs. Even better, he was invited to compile a list of suitable candidates for the position of mayor across the whole of Western Sicily. Whether or not this was true, half the towns on the island soon had men in place with close ties to the Mafia.

In Palermo, Charles Poletti was following much the same course. Instructed to appoint new men to positions of authority, he took as his interpreter Vito Genovese, another friend of Lucky Luciano's, who in 1937 had fled to Sicily from New York where he was wanted for drug trafficking and murder. Who better to govern, said Genovese, than the proven anti-Fascists, the men who had been imprisoned as *mafiosi* by Mori in the late 1920s? Before long, among Poletti's interpreters, consultants and new Sicilian friends were many old *mafiosi*, who were able to produce documents showing how much they had suffered under Fascism. 'Poletti, fewer promises, more spaghetti' became a catchword for the distortions of occupation. It was not as if nothing had been known about the Sicilian Mafia. In the Sicily handbook there had been explicit references to a 'complex social phenomenon, the consequences of years of bad government', and a vice consul called W. E. Scotten warned AMGOT that it was being hoodwinked and used. But Poletti found it more expedient to listen to Genovese, while Lord Rennell, the British senior civil administrator, concluded that the paternal guidance being offered by the Allies was now working well. Sicilians, he said, were being transformed from 'whipped dogs and fawning puppies' into 'thinking, emotional, decisive human beings'.

Lucky Luciano was freed from his American jail and allowed to come back to Palermo, where he lived unmolested until his death in 1961. The Mafia was now back in business. The Allies had profoundly, disastrously, misunderstood the reality of Sicily.

Not surprising, the first thing the Mafia did was to organise a vast black market. Don Calò, enjoying his protected status, was able to use his new trucks to take control of the market in olive oil. Vito Genovese set up a flour, oil and salt business with the *gabellotti* in charge of the large estates. When stopped by the police, he said that he was working for AMGOT, and when later arrested, he was able to produce a clutch of laissez-passers from the military command. The Sicilians stole from the Allied soldiers; they in turn when drunk prowled in search of women. But the Allied soldiers were also happy to sell the *mafiosi* their cigarettes, tyres, blankets, shoes, matches, nails, travel permits, railway tickets, petrol and medicines, especially quinine and insulin. Sicily became an enormous, chaotic, illegal market; and the Mafia grew very rich. In Racalmuto children wore sweaters with Mickey Mouse on them and men ties with naked women. As Sciascia later described it, the arrival of the Allies had been like that of the Arabs, in June 827. They had seized an island without defences, 'crushed by a greedy and corrupt administration, terrified of the present and uncertain of the future'.

The Allies had believed Mussolini's boast that Sicily was one vast granary. In Racalmuto, however, as elsewhere, there was almost no grain, and Sciascia remained in his job in the *Consorzio Agrario*, trying to enforce the quota asked of farmers to feed an island on the edge of starvation. There were heavy penalties for those who failed to deliver the wheat, barley and other cereals, with special patrols of carabinieri detailed to make spot checks and arrest anyone found illegally holding or selling more than their share. In a single month 880,000 kilos of grain were confiscated. It was not made easier by the Sicilians' age-old skill at subterfuge. A British officer with the Allies drew up a list of sixty-two ways that people were using to get around the rules. Sciascia, ever attuned to the idea of what was fair and just, was outraged when one day the carabinieri arrested a priest and a peasant, the former for having squirrelled away 200 kilos of illicit wheat, the peasant for having concealed a few sackfuls. The magistrate who heard the case allowed the priest to go free; the peasant was given a two-year prison sentence. In the evenings, Sciascia filled lesson books with poems and short stories.

Immediately after liberation, an American officer arrived to oversee matters in Racalmuto. After the initial euphoria and the delighted reunion with the émigré Sicilians who accompanied the US forces, a hungry apathy had settled over the village. Everyone was wary, uncertain, looking for food. The Allied soldiers had been ordered to stay away from the women, but there was an elderly prostitute, Zi Peppina, who took a cartload of famished girls every week to a nearby military camp. It seemed as if the war was over; but it was not.

In the village, the young teacher Maria Andronica was greatly admired. Vilardo noted that five young men were courting her and that she was 'timid, tender, sweet but as tenacious and hard as steel'. On 19 July 1944 she and Sciascia got married; she was pregnant, and Sciascia had managed to extricate himself from his earlier liaison. It was all very quick. The *zie* did not attend and there was no honeymoon. Father Alfonso, who had taught Sciascia at school, officiated. After the church ceremony they had a granita in a café. Vilardo had made them a present of a rabbit and two pigeons; later he complained that whenever Sciascia described his wedding, he left out the pigeons. Sciascia then went off to meet his friends.

The couple moved up to the top floor of the *zie*'s house, and the aunts went down to what had been the tailor's shop. Maria was quiet and soon much loved by the aunts, whose authority she was careful not to challenge, sensing, rightly, that they had no intention of relinquishing their hold on their nephew. In this shuttered, inward-looking house, their writ remained absolute. Sciascia chose new art deco tiles for the floor and hung a picture of Pirandello on the wall. There were four small rooms and a balcony overlooking the rooftops, from where he continued to eavesdrop on the women gathered by the fountain below. Pasquale and Genoveffa had stayed on in Caltanissetta with Anna and Giuseppe, but Nica had returned and once again cooked for the entire household. Maria, like her mother-in-law, was content to let the aunts reign. They remained excessively proprietorial about Sciascia, feeding him the best bits of their very scanty meals. Marriage suited Sciascia perfectly and Maria watched over him assiduously. He found it restful and unthreatening, which was how he planned to spend his life. 'My family life begins serenely,' he wrote to Vilardo. 'I am beginning to feel affection towards people and also towards things that my fickleness of yesterday prevented. Unhappiness is a condition necessary for intelligence. But serene I am.' He was, he added, 'ready, and true to myself'. A daughter, Laura, was born in 1945.

Sciascia with wife Maria and daughter Laura

He had decided to stay on in Racalmuto where everyone knew everything about each other: it was a 'rich' field for a writer. It was made richer when he became a member of one of Racalmuto's clubs, the *Circolo Unione*, with its premises on the main street. Clubs had been a feature of Sicilian life since the mid nineteenth century. Under Fascism they had been renamed '*dopolavoro*' – afterwork – and membership had often been regulated by the degree of Fascist fervour of a candidate. But with the Fascists gone they had reverted to their earlier state, with one club for hunters, another for salt and sulphur miners. Locally known as the *Circolo dei Nobili*, for its past connections with the gentry, the *Unione* had a big room on the first floor with faded furnishings and dark leather chairs, three smaller rooms for card players and a reading room, with newspapers, where the radio was kept permanently on. On balmy spring and summer evenings the club servants carried chairs out on to the pavement for the talk to continue late into the night.

Of its 150 members, Sciascia worked out that some two thirds were former Fascists, two of them '*fascisti furiosi*', rabid believers; there was a single Communist, who sensibly never came; and three 'normal lunatics', one of whom, when first taken to see a train travelling through the valley had insisted that no one could fool him: it was obvious that it was being powered by horses, tethered inside. As one of the younger members, Sciascia listened but said little. Club life provided him with a feast of gossip, scandal, exaggeration, bragging and competitive memory and there were crude references to sex. Many of the more singular members would later make their way into his books, as wily priests, venal civil servants, scheming *mafiosi*. He saw Brancati and Pirandello in them all.

On the evening of 15 November 1944, Sciascia and several friends were in a bar when they heard shots. Racalmuto was full of people milling about, who now took cover in shops and doorways. When they looked out, they saw the body of the new mayor, Baldassare Tinebra, lying on the rainy pavement. He had been shot in the neck. Tinebra was the manager of a sulphur mine and, more importantly, a friend of Don Calò, and as such another *mafioso* appointee, showered with AMGOT am-lire. He was much hated in the village. There were rumours of a falling-out with Don Calò, but earlier in the day Tinebra had had an altercation with an unemployed sulphur miner who had come to him for help. The man was immediately arrested and given a twenty-four-year sentence for murder. Sciascia never really believed in his guilt and the incident fed into his growing mistrust of the law.

As, slowly, mainland Italy was being liberated by the Allies fighting their way north, so disbanded soldiers began to return to the village, exhausted, hungry, in search of work that did not exist, bringing with them tales of defeat and civil war. Racalmuto was rife with ill-tempered exchanges, profiteering, reinvention, the true anti-Fascists sometimes accused of being Fascists and the true Fascists deftly changing sides.

The Allied troops pulled out of Sicily after thirty-eight days. They had expected to cross the island sooner but the Germans, retreating towards the Straits of Messina where ships waited to carry them the three kilometres across to mainland Italy, had fought unexpectedly hard. Some 62,000 Italian soldiers, abandoning most of their equipment, crossed first; the Germans followed, taking most of theirs, looting and vandalising as they went. Between them, they had lost over 9,000 men; the Allies had lost 5,500, but they had taken 120,000 Axis prisoners. Twenty thousand of the Allies had caught malaria.

They left behind their AMGOT officers to oversee the return to peace; but it was a wretched peace, discontentment and misery fuelling chaos. The Sicilians felt betrayed by everyone. Calls for young men to cross to Italy to fight the Germans as they withdrew towards the north were met with derision. A poster went up: '*Non si Parte!*' – We're not leaving. One graffiti read: 'Sicily for Sicily and Italy for any whore who wants her'. Barracks were set on fire; students rioted. Of the 76,000 men estimated to be eligible, only 14,600 were eventually tracked down and coerced into signing up, many of them in handcuffs.

On 8 September 1943, the Allies had signed an armistice with Italy; five weeks later, Italy declared war on Germany, but was not accepted, as it had hoped, as a 'co-belligerent', after Churchill refused to grant it Allied status. Mussolini, who had been imprisoned by the Italians after a successful coup against him, had been rescued by the Germans and installed in a puppet government on Lake Garda. A government of national unity, made up of all the different democratic parties, was waiting in the wings, but it would be many months before Rome was liberated.

Overwhelmed by its task of provisioning an island on the brink of famine, struggling to control epidemics and venereal diseases and trying to sort out the banks and the economy, AMGOT remained in Sicily for another seven months. Often it seemed to be steered chiefly by the Sicilians who spoke the best English. Poletti was known to have links with the '*ex-fascisti rabbiosi*', dangerous and excitable former Fascists. No attempts were made to understand the complexity of Sicilian society. The landowners turned to the Mafia and their *gabellotti* for help; the Mafia, delighted by their new veneer of respectability, made ever greater fortunes on the black market, while the newly installed Mafia mayors became custodians of local justice and protection.

When the last AMGOT officers pulled out, in February 1944, they left behind them the worst winter in living memory, thick snow covering much of the island, soup kitchens, dead bodies in the streets and a record number of murders. Even the Allies had done their share of looting. From France, Yugoslavia, North Africa and Albania, disbanded Italian soldiers were coming home, often on foot, after terrible journeys. They brought with them weapons and anger. That April, the police chief in Agrigento noted that his province had the 'sad honour' of having the highest number of kidnappings and theft of animals on the island. Beyond a need to keep the Communists at bay – there were fears of the kind of civil war that had followed liberation in Greece – and remove the most egregious former Fascists from their posts, the Allies had not been greatly concerned about the political mess they had helped to create. They had promised to be above politics, but what they had achieved was to provide a great boost to the Mafia and the speedy return to the ruthless exploitation of the rural poor. The extreme poverty to which many families had been reduced was made apparent when an elderly man was murdered and a list made of his possessions: two terracotta plates, one fork, two green glass bottles, a mattress, a blanket full of holes, one towel and one oil lamp. Sciascia knew just how fortunate he was.

When restrictions on political campaigning had been lifted, some sixteen different parties had declared themselves: there was barely one in which the Mafia did not have some kind of presence. The politics of the island became chaotic, and in any case completely incomprehensible to outsiders from the north. The party for which the Allies had felt some sympathy was the long simmering separatist movement, who were vowing to turn Sicily into an independent country. Keen to redeem centuries of penury, rancour and a sense of profound inferiority, the separatists came in several different hues, but they brought together the middle classes, the large landowners, some dukes and princes, a sprinkling of romantics and idealists and, inevitably, the Mafia, to provide strong-armed tactics and quell all nascent Communism. Popular discontent would be their leverage.

At a meeting in Palermo, attended by twenty-eight important 'friends of Sicily', Don Calò among them, plans were put in place to crush social reform, by whatever means. The *'vento del nord'*, the strongly left-wing northern wind from the partisans now flowing through mainland Italy, had failed to cross the Straits of Messina. The separatists had found a persuasive leader in Andrea Finocchiaro Aprile, a member of Sicily's pre-Fascist elite, a brilliant orator and an idealist who genuinely believed in the possibility of a free and independent Sicily. He spoke of Churchill and Roosevelt as his friends; but he said the same about the Mafia. Don Calò, conferring on him a cautious seal of approval, ensured that his speeches were well attended. Don Calò's writ now extended to parts of Palermo, where he was courted by men with their eye on the future and where he kept a permanent room in its only standing luxury hotel.

What the separatists were demanding was self-rule, a Sicilian republic, even perhaps linked to the United States and appearing on its flag as its 49th state. Even before the men from AMGOT left, pro and anti separatists were lining up to do battle. In Racalmuto, Sciascia and his friends put together a *'movimento antiseparatista'*, renting a room in which to hold meetings and write their manifesto. 'In separatism,' Sciascia later told an interviewer, 'was everything I most hated: Fascism, the landed right-wing, "*Sicilianismo*", the obsession with the worst side of Sicily.'

The anti-separatists, who called themselves *'unitari'* – united with the mainland – were in fact growing in number, recruiting from among miners, peasants, the landless poor, the 'perennially disinherited' and the political left. Not long before, Palmiro Togliatti, the leader of the PCI, the Italian Communist Party – which, like the left generally, was firmly against secession – had sent down a number of men to organise the Sicilian branch and take charge of the peasant movement. Among them was a brave, honest and much-loved former prisoner of the Fascists, Girolamo Li Causi, who possessed, said the writer Carlo Levi, a gift for oratory 'touching people's hearts with understanding and love'. Though older than Sciascia and his friends, Li Causi was a man they greatly admired. At twenty-three, Sciascia was a watcher, a thinker, a reader, his thoughts more about literature than politics, and not yet quite ready to enter a world he was beginning to perceive as infinitely complicated and irrational.

The anti-separatists had a clear cause and it was one that was dear to Sicily's vast force of agricultural workers. When the provisional government had finally taken power in Rome, one of their first decrees had been that land left uncultivated, or badly cultivated, on the big estates in Sicily be divided up among cooperatives representing the island's quarter of a million landless peasants. Similar associations had flourished for a while in the late nineteenth century, but they had been ruthlessly suppressed. Neither the big landowners nor the Mafia however, had any intention of letting this happen; what they hoped for was to see a speedy return to pre-Fascist rule and their own comfortable exploitation of Sicily. The Gullo Decree – so named after its architect, the Minister of Agriculture, Fausto Gullo – was ignored. Frustrated peasants began to occupy neglected land; there were violent clashes and once again they were brutally put down. The *'lotte contadine'* – the peasant battles – became Sicily's war of liberation, its own form of resistance, one of its founding myths.

Liberation had seen a flowering of independent, largely left-wing, newspapers. Articles began to appear attacking Mafia power. Li Causi decided that the moment had come for a more formal challenge. He chose his target with care.

Of all Sicilian feudal landowners, those around Villalba were among the most entrenched and unyielding. The history of the village was full of rebellions against the local barons and their *mafiosi gabellotti*, none of them successful. Long after other areas had adopted some small measure of land reform and justice, Villalba remained obdurately feudal. The Gullo Decree had already resulted in several local murders. More important, perhaps, Villalba was Don Calò's fief. He had become extravagantly rich with his black-market affairs, a friend to many Mafia families, the *capo* of his own.

On the morning of 16 September 1944, Li Causi and his supporters arrived in the main square of Villalba to speak about peasant rights. Don Calò, who had agreed to the meeting, invited the speakers for a coffee in the bar, where he told them that he loved peace and quiet. They should think of his village as an abbey.

When Li Causi began to address the villagers, describing what they could do to improve their conditions, Don Calò shouted out:

'It's all a lie!' It was a signal. Shots were fired; grenades thrown. The crowd fled, leaving eighteen people wounded and lying in the dust in the main square, among them Li Causi. Don Calò was one of several people charged with the attack, but the case against him soon sank underneath conflicting testimonies and witnesses who changed their stories. It would run on, year after year, while Don Calò remained at liberty on bail. It had been a message, crude perhaps but effective: public meetings were not safe places and labour organisers should not try to radicalise the peasantry.

There was another force now at play. Bandits, as the historian Braudel described them, had flourished across the whole Mediterranean in the late sixteenth century. They were a form of revenge against the ruling classes, righters of endemic wrongs. Post-war Sicily became a paradise for these latter-day misfits, disbanded soldiers, landless peasants, escaped prisoners, men caught between landowners and speculators, unable to make ends meet, and those with grievances. Because they had secured modern weapons from the departing armies and possessed good horses, they were hard to catch. Theft of animals, kidnapping and extortion overwhelmed much of the island. Racalmuto had its own gang of bandits, just one of many across the island preying on travellers and the rich, and the atmosphere in the village was often tense. Sciascia was very conscious of an unspoken resolve among the villagers to provoke no one. What had started out as an expression of need and poverty now became a matter of politics, the guns for hire useful to those in power for suppressing dissent. In many places, these bandits acted in harmony with the Mafia and the separatists.

The Italian State and the politicians in Rome had no desire to see Sicily secede. Concessions were made to the separatists, offers for a limited autonomy, more local say in the governance of the island, under a legislative assembly of ninety deputies and a cabinet of ministers. The elections of April 1947 for the first Regional Assembly brought many new men into politics, the *mafiosi* among them forging strong links with deputies and civil servants. The Mafia tactics were simple: the offer of large numbers of votes – secured by bullying, bribes, intimidation – in return for promises of contracts and preferment. The new Christian Democrat Party, backed by the Vatican, looked certain winners. Priests warned against the depravity of the left. However, the results saw surprisingly large gains for the Socialists and the Communists and their plans for agrarian reform, and in those areas where they did best, the peasant protests and occupations gathered fresh steam.

It was now that Sicily's most famous bandit took the road that would cost him his life, as it had already taken the lives of so many. Salvatore Giuliano was a showy, bright twenty-year-old from Montelepre, just above Palermo, with boyish features and dark hair slicked back, and a taste for finery. One day his cart, with several sacks of black-market grain, was stopped by two carabinieri. Giuliano pulled out a gun and shot one of the men dead and wounded the other. Having organised a break-out of friends from the prison in Monreale, he recruited them for a gang in the mountains above Montelepre. A few months later, he shot another carabiniere. Quick to share any spoils with needy villagers – including the widow of a Racalmuto carabiniere killed by his men – he soon became something of a celebrity. A glamorous Swedish journalist with whom he was said to be having an affair paid a visit to his hideout. In Racalmuto, where Giuliano's exploits were minutely followed and discussed, Sciascia watched small boys playing at being the famous bandit; the travelling storytellers added his exploits to their funds of tales about daring youths and arrogant barons.

Salvatore Giuliano

The separatists, seeing support draining away from them, had set up a military wing, EVIS, the *Esercizio Volontario d'Independenza Siciliana*, with which to continue to intimidate the reformers. It had its own uniform and yellow and green flags and appointed Giuliano lieutenant-colonel in its new ragtag army. By the age of twenty-three he was known as the King of Montelepre; he called himself not a bandit but a political fighter and boasted that he punished spies, traitors and extortionate money lenders. But he was getting more violent; as were the police. Curfews and roadblocks were set up and the men taken into custody told of torture with electric shocks. The police were reported to be 'terrorised'.

1 May, Labour Day, was a popular holiday all over Sicily. For many years the neighbouring villages of San Cipirello and San Giuseppe Iato had shared their feast day, meeting halfway on the high pass of Portella della Ginestra, between two craggy peaks. Arriving in wooden carts painted with epic historical scenes, waving banners and flags, they brought with them picnics, packs of cards and bread baked in decorative shapes. There were ballad singers, with guitars. The mood was cheerful: the war was over, the Germans had gone and the recent elections had brought hope of real agricultural reform. There was much to celebrate.

Soon after ten o'clock, just as the speeches were beginning, short, sharp cracks were heard. At first it was thought to be fireworks. Then, around the edges of the crowd, people began to fall over. Bullets ricocheted off the rocks. By the time the firing stopped, eleven people were dead, several of them small children; fifty-five others were wounded. A stampede of frantic families began to flow down the hillside.

Giuliano, in his white raincoat, and eleven of his followers, in stolen American army uniforms, had been waiting behind the rocks since before dawn. Long before the police arrived, they had fled back to the high mountains. There was much talk of the Mafia, but the finger of blame seemed to point at the separatists, intent on terrifying the peasants into silence and using Giuliano as their messenger. Lucrative kidnappings, with the captives treated with great courtesy, kept him and his men in funds. He continued to harass police posts and attacked a Communist headquarters with dynamite and Molotov cocktails.

It took another three years before Giuliano was caught; and his fall came not through police efficiency but treachery. After the 1948 elections, which brought increased autonomy, the separatists lost their voice and agreed to abandon their armed struggle. Giuliano was no longer a useful tool for those in power, especially not one as uncontrolled and narcissistic. When an ambush left eight carabinieri killed, executed one by one, a team of anti-bandit specialists was formed and 2,000 men sent out to scour the mountains. Giuliano and his remaining followers retreated towards Trapani. Then Giuliano made a fatal error. On 5 July 1950, he descended from the mountains to spend a night in the village of Castelvetrano. It was here that his cousin and second-in-command, Gaspare Pisciotta, shot him dead as he slept, having been bribed by a substantial sum of money, a false passport and eventually a total pardon. Since the police wanted the glory, Giuliano's body, in white vest and khaki trousers and a gold belt, was dragged out into the courtyard, more bullets were fired into it, and photographs taken of policemen in heroic poses. In Rome, the government announced triumphantly that he had been shot trying to escape. It was only later that a beady-eyed reporter from Rome noticed that the bloodstains, and the way they appeared to flow uphill, bore no relation to the official story.

As for Pisciotta, he was not fated to survive for long. Caught after five months on the run, he was eventually brought before a court in Viterbo. What no one had anticipated was what he would say. While the witnesses changed their stories and the police contradicted each other, Pisciotta was clear, articulate and accusatory. He named high-up political figures and policemen complicit in the assassination, spelt out the bribes Giuliano had been offered, and the fact that even as they railed against the bandits, the police had not really intended to wipe them out. They were too useful. 'We were,' he told a bemused court, 'a single body, bandits, police and Mafia, like the Father, the Son and the Holy Ghost.' He then produced safe conduct passes from police forces all over the island.

Pisciotta thought that he held a trump card: he claimed to have a copy of a long memorandum written by Giuliano, naming names at the highest level. He promised to produce it. Sentenced to life in prison for his part in the Portella massacre, despite the promises of a pardon, he would eat only the food brought in by his mother or that he tested first on a tame sparrow. Shortly before he was due to give evidence in a new trial, he was moved to the Ucciardone, the main prison in Palermo, renowned for being under the control of the Mafia. One morning strychnine was slipped into medicine he had been prescribed for tuberculosis. Realising what had happened, he tried to drink olive oil from a bottle he kept in his cell. It was no good: half an hour later he was dead. The memorandum was never found. No one ever discovered exactly why Giuliano had carried out the massacre or who precisely had ordered it, though many theories were advanced, and the men who might have been able to answer soon died themselves, in mysterious circumstances. All denunciations were shelved. The events at Portella della Ginestra became the first '*buco nero*' – black hole – in a chain of unsolved mysteries; there would be many more.

But the legend of Giuliano and his men lived on. Later, Sciascia would say that the lies told at Castelvetrano marked the moment when Sicily became a 'place without truth'; and that Sicilians knew it. It was a terrible warning; and one more element now feeding into his sense of an island betrayed by its rulers and vulnerable to every kind of predator.

For a while, as Sicily stumbled towards a better peace, the battles between peasants and landowners continued and trade unionists and lawyers went on dying. A left-wing activist, Placido Rizzotto, who had led a march of landless peasants, refused to stay silent despite repeated threats to his life. In May 1949 he was kidnapped and disappeared. A distraught eleven-year-old boy went to the police saying that he had witnessed Rizzotto's murder. Taken to the head of the local hospital, Dr Navarra, who was also a local Mafia boss, the boy was given a calming injection. It turned out to be a bubble of air in his veins and he died soon after. In a single year, three socialist trade unionists, along with forty-six carabinieri were killed, while 734 more were wounded. Thirteen pitched battles between protestors and police were recorded. A spirited 'march on Caltanissetta' – a long line of peasants supported by the sulphur workers and carrying banners with the words '*Terra! Terra!*' – did win some concessions of land, and, bit by bit, a fairer distribution began to be enforced. The murder of Rizzotto – and thirty-eight others like him – put a brake on most peasant protests but they did not cease altogether.

In any case, Sicily's political world was changing. The Americans had moved on, lost interest in the separatists or the fortunes of the island. The Second World War had ended; the Cold War was beginning. Italians had voted, by a narrow margin, to replace their monarchy with a republic. The Christian Democrats had played only a small part in the liberation of Italy from the Germans, but, backed by the Vatican, they had managed to overthrow the immediate post-war government of Ferruccio Parri, the veteran partisan leader. Parri was a mild, modest, clever man but he was no match for Catholic politics. By 1948 the Christian Democrats were firmly in power in Rome, heavily backed by the Americans with their Marshall Plan, there to remain for the next thirty-five years, steered in the early years by an aloof, dignified, canny anti-Communist, Alcide De Gasperi about whom it was said that he inspired the respect of the left, while denying them all their objectives.

The Mafia, seeing a new wind blowing, wisely shifted their support from the separatists to the Christian Democrats. They had understood that the anarchy had to stop and they played their part in rounding up the remaining bandits. '*Ora basta*,' announced Don Calò. 'Sicily must have peace.' In any case, regional autonomy, agrarian reform and the lure of industrialisation seemed to promise vast new riches. The *pezzi di novanta* began to turn their attention towards far greater profits in the cities.

Sciascia's brother Giuseppe was always known in the family as Peppino. He was lively, outgoing and affectionate, but prone since early boyhood to bouts of depression. With Sciascia rebellious and going his own way, Pasquale had wanted his second son to follow him into the administration of the sulphur mines, even though the brutishness of the miners was singularly ill-suited to his gentle nature. The two brothers were close, but Peppino was somewhat in awe of the more assured Sciascia. Reluctantly, he agreed to take a diploma at the Regia Scuola Mineraria in Caltanissetta and went to work at the Assoro mine, where Pasquale was now the accountant. Pasquale was a conscientious worker, taking very little time off. One day, the miners at Assoro went on strike. Pasquale and Peppino could have gone home, but Pasquale insisted on staying at his post and Peppino stayed with him. The countryside around was lonely, grey, with rocky hills made barren by the sulphur. Peppino had told Sciascia how much he hated the rocks and crows that lived there, but no one in the family quite understood how wretched they made him.

A SICILIAN MAN

On Monday 5 May 1948, at around seven in the morning, Pasquale knocked on Peppino's door and asked him what he wanted for breakfast. The boy replied that he would like two fried eggs. Soon after, Pasquale heard a shot. Peppino had gone into his father's room, discovered his loaded revolver and shot himself. In the diary found in his pocket he had written: 'Monday, the day on which I was born, the day of my worst unhappiness. Wednesday, exhaustion, dejection. Sunday, a day of depression, no trust in tomorrow. I am ill.'

Sciascia was walking with friends down the road in Racalmuto when an acquaintance came up and drew him to one side. He turned very white and, saying nothing, went to find his mother, then got a lift to the mine. His sister Anna had recently married a teacher in Caltanissetta and had left for her honeymoon in Siena. The shock of Peppino's violent death scarred them all, reducing the family to even greater introspection and silence. The whispers became softer and the aunts seemed to shrink in size. Pasquale, overwhelmed by guilt, turned, almost overnight, into another man, angry, brooding, erratic. Having insisted on returning to Racalmuto, to be near Peppino's grave, Genoveffa became almost entirely reclusive. She spoke little and took off all her jewellery, saying she wanted nothing that shone. Very little was ever said: these were not things you talked about. Sciascia buried his brother's death deep inside him, where it lay as a black stain.

Twenty days later, Sciascia passed his last teacher training exams with a viva on Pirandello. Maria had given birth to a second daughter, Anna Maria, and they continued to live upstairs with the aunts. The household was quiet, dark and sad and Maria, as pliant as ever to the aunts, channelled her love and attention chiefly towards her husband. Sciascia was now appointed to teach in his old elementary school in Racalmuto, but with no great enthusiasm. He felt himself to be, as he said, more a writer than a talker. For his brother's tombstone he chose a verse by Catullus: 'Together with you is buried all our house, together with you have perished all our joys, once fed by your sweet love'. He wrote one of his own most poignant poems, 'In Memoriam', about death, poppies, roses, the sulphur valleys with the swallows on their evening flight on 'this, my sad evening that is yours'.

5
Sword thrusts

On 12 October 1949 Sciascia arrived to teach at his old school, a few steps from the *zie*'s house. He was given a class of thirty boys and a damp, dark classroom in the former convent to which, since there were not enough rooms for all of Racalmuto's children, the pupils came in shifts. Twenty were the sons of Communists; and one family had voted for the neo-Fascist Movimento Sociale Italiano. The sons of the salt and sulphur miners seemed to him more alert than those from peasant families, the poorest in the poorest of towns, but there was almost no child who was not poor. The boys came to school barefoot, or in their fathers' army boots with gaping holes, or in wooden clogs with leather straps. Some wore their mothers' woolly berets. Very few owned socks and in winter, when ice formed into crusts on the windows that the locals called 'cattle horns', their feet were covered in mud. Their sweaters were full of holes; the more fortunate wore overcoats made out of military blankets. One day there was a charitable distribution of shoes, but the donors had imagined 'little feet like those of Jesus' and the shoes went to younger brothers. The boys' hair looked like rooks' nests. They came from houses like hovels, whole families sleeping in the same room, a new baby every year. Their fathers got drunk, and one undersized boy with bandy legs told Sciascia that it was his task to make sure that his father got home safely at night. He drank too, he said, when he could get it. In the playground, the boys played at being Giuliano, the bandit who helped the poor.

In the mornings, the boys washed quickly, like cats. If the weather was beautiful they truanted, and if caught by the carabinieri, their fathers sometimes spent a night in jail. Some lived like vagabonds, going home only when starving. They stole, pilfered whatever they could find and spent half of the day when they were not in school working for richer families for a pittance. In his club, Sciascia heard his pupils described as animals. Walking home, he saw their sisters, little girls shivering in their short-sleeved summer dresses, with eyes of beasts confused by suffering. They looked, he thought, so insubstantial that they could be swallowed in a glass of water. Boys were more valued than girls. They provided extra hands for work. Only when someone asked for a girl in marriage was she taken to buy nylon stockings, an item of unimaginable luxury, a symbol of everything people wanted and did not have.

In class, Sciascia tried to teach the boys things that might interest them: he used clear, simple language and told them about the Risorgimento and America and set competitions with small prizes of pens and rulers. He read poetry to them, but its 'luminous echo' struck few chords. The two or three who seemed genuinely clever bent over their books; the others, pretending to do the same, watched to see whether they could copy. Sciascia understood why they did not want to learn: they preferred to play, to make paper rabbits, to swap insults, immersed in their own reality of rancour and poverty, dreaming of unattainable things, playing games to make the time pass faster, anything to forget the chores that awaited them. Like all the teachers, he kept a switch on his desk, but he used it only to point at rivers and cities on a map.

On religious holidays, he accompanied his pupils to church, a winding river of boys that made him think of a snake that had swallowed a sparrow. He knew that some did not go to confession: their families believed not in the Catholic Church but in the evil eye. Sciascia's own view of religion was complicated, more to do with humanism and behaviour than faith, and like many of his pupils he did not go to church. What he had seen of Catholicism's influence in Sicily had made him sceptical. Listening to the boys talk, he admired the richness of their expressions and the way that they used words and dialect so precisely. At Christmas their accounts were so pitiful that he could hardly bear to listen.

The boys were hungry, persistently, miserably hungry. The school provided for a small number of pupils to be given lunch every day, in turn, ten at a time from each class. When the bell rang, Sciascia led the lucky ones to a canteen which smelt of soap and rancid meat, where they fell on the food. He thought: these boys are so famished, so in need of everything, while my daughters read comics and fairy tales, have baths and eat as much milk and jam as they want. He felt a knot of fear, the fragility of destiny, his own precarious good fortune. 'I know,' he wrote, 'that if I adapt to this daily anatomy of misery, of instincts and raw human relationships, if I begin to see it as inevitable and fatal . . . then I will have lost that sense of hope . . . that I believe is what is best in me.' He hated being just another State employee, another oppressor, on the side of the 'unjust'. How, he asked, do you teach grammar to boys who are too hungry to learn?

At break, the teachers stood in the corridors, smoking and talking. Sciascia said little and came across to his colleagues as shy, embarrassed to speak. He listened as they complained about their pay and talked about radio programmes they had heard or life under Fascism, when on Saturdays they had worn uniforms with flashes on their berets. They never talked about hunger or the fact that the new school books were so inadequate that they seemed a 'diseducation'. The headmaster described the boys as donkeys, too stupid to follow lessons. Sciascia saw in them despairing and implacable poverty, 'donkeys who are always the very poor, who have spent centuries sitting on the benches for donkeys, dazed by exhaustion and hunger'. When summer came, those who failed to move up were forced to repeat their class. Sciascia passed as many as he could, knowing that without some kind of school certificate they would never get a job to lift them out of this life of misery; it was the one gift he could give them.

Increasingly, Sciascia felt alienated from his job, disgusted by those who seemed to take pleasure in it. Some days he felt trapped, as in a nightmare from which escape is impossible, and he told a friend that he felt he was gathering mould. He could imagine enjoying teaching, but in Racalmuto he entered his classroom 'with the same feeling that the sulphur miners felt when they descended into the dark tunnels'. He felt ashamed of his good clothes, his heavy shoes, his books, his 'harmonious days'. He had little contact with his pupils outside school, but he grew fond of them and they confided in him, told him about their families and their lives. And when he was ill, or away, boys came to his house to see when he was coming back, opting not to go to school unless he was there. Later, they would say that he had treated them as friends.

Sciascia was not the most conscientious of teachers, taking what were registered as 'forced absences' about which the school remained surprisingly tolerant. He had discovered a new love for editing and literary criticism, and Salvatore Sciascia, who ran the bookshop in Caltanissetta, asked him to help launch a new magazine, *Galleria*, and soon after to become its editor. It was his job to find authors and collaborators, and he selected them among the foreign writers, especially the Americans, he had long admired. He despaired when Italian university professors sent in articles 'like rivers of cement' and devoted much time to seeking out what he called forgotten 'jewels'. *Galleria* brought him a new world of literary friends and invitations to contribute to other literary magazines. He had started translating and was working on poems by Walt Whitman. The first issue of *Galleria* contained a review of Truman Capote's *Other Voices, Other Rooms*, an unpublished short story by Pirandello, a report on the dying sulphur industry and an article by Sciascia himself on the arrival of the American soldiers in Racalmuto in July 1943. *Galleria* was, as he saw it, a 'breath' of international culture in a small, backward Sicilian town and he modelled it on *Il Ponte*, a magazine launched in Florence in 1945, to which he contributed an article on the 'resurgence' of Fascism in Sicily. Whenever he could, he used pieces by Sicilian writers. Vittorini pronounced *Galleria* the best literary magazine on the island; sober, modest, free of posturing and provincialism.

Sciascia was also writing his own poetry, saying that for him it represented the raw matter out of which prose is carved, and that 'prose is a very hard affair'. A first collection, *La Sicilia, il suo cuore*, printed at his own expense, touched on summer, funerals, images of daily life in the sulphur villages, cicadas and poppies, which 'flowered like blood'. But, he told his friend Vilardo, who was also writing poetry, you succeeded only when you realised that finding the right word to use was the hardest thing in the world. He was beginning to see in literature a mirror to the world around him, trying to find his own voice, both as a Sicilian and in the wider world of Italian literature. 'It wasn't God who created the world,' he wrote to his friend Mario La Cava, 'but books.'

SWORD THRUSTS

One of Sciascia's enduring fears was that Fascism lay so deep at the heart of Italy that it would take little for it to return. The chaos of the post-war years made Italy, he felt, vulnerable to extremists, and he was more concerned at this moment with the far right than with the Mafia. Fascism remained an 'eternal possibility' and you needed to be ready to do battle whenever it raised its head. The question was how to make the generations of Italians who had not lived through the Mussolini years understand just what they had been like. A translation of George Orwell's *Animal Farm* had recently been published in Italy and Sciascia decided to use ridicule as the way to deliver his message. In the evenings and on holidays he was writing fables, very short and mordent Orwellian allegories in which foxes, rooks, weasels and lions incarnate the evils of Fascism, from pettiness to violence, injustice to tyranny.

In these twenty-seven fables, chilly and elegant and not always easy to understand, the words pared down to the minimum and few longer than a few paragraphs, there are no titles and no numbers and no context. A toad is squashed by a train; a cock is gnawed to death by a weasel. The mouse is the animal which appears most often. Into the fable of the cat who tells a friend that though he would prefer to eat the canary, 'his singing is delightful, and often assuages my endless boredom' could be read Mussolini's beady eye on dissenting intellectuals. The veneer of civilisation barely conceals a rule of primitive savagery. There are irony and satire in these fables of hunted and hunting, but no mockery. Rather, the reader is invited to contemplate a world in which the strong win, the weak go under and society, unconstrained by ethical considerations, is ruled by cruelty. When he read one of the fables aloud to his class, he was pleased to see that they listened intently. Enigmatic and suggestive, they laid the beginning of Sciascia's moral framework.

One of Sciascia's new friends was a poet, Mario dell'Arco, who had contacts with the Bardi publishing house in Rome, which printed the Senate papers. At Sciascia's expense, Bardi published 250 copies of *Fables from the Dictatorship*, and Sciascia kept back thirty to send to critics and editors. The little book was spotted by the writer and filmmaker Pier Paolo Pasolini who reviewed it for *La Libertà d'Italia*, where he praised the 'gnomic' nature of the work. The 'drops of blood' were so pure, he said, that a reader might end up thinking that the Fascist dictatorship itself had been a fable. Sciascia returned the favour by mentioning Pasolini when asked by an American encyclopaedia to provide names of the most promising new writers in Italy.

The two men, in temperament as in appearance, could not have been more different. Pasolini was an impetuous, dramatic, good-looking man, with a square face and a generous mouth. Born a year after Sciascia, he wrote with frenzied speed, pouring into his poems a diary of his fantasies and emotions. He liked to shock. He had recently been thrown out of the Communist Party after a boy told his priest that he had had sexual relations with Pasolini. This was something that the somewhat puritanical Sciascia chose not to dwell on. What he and Pasolini had in common was the violent death of their younger brothers, Pasolini's executed in error by partisans who were unaware that he was part of the resistance. They also shared a taste for polemics, a contagious delight in locking swords with opponents and a style that wove light sarcasm with erudition; and they deplored the way that the Italian language was being hijacked by 'bourgeois technocrats' who, declared Pasolini, were making it poor, limited, unsubtle and lacking in all humour. Sciascia and Pasolini now joined forces to help start up a new magazine in Bologna called *Officina*, and collaborated on a book about dialect, both of them fascinated by the way it had been used during Fascism by resisters to escape the wordy, plodding language

Pier Paolo Pasolini

of the regime. More crucially, the extrovert, noisy, sensation-seeking Pasolini and the quiet, modest, retiring Sciascia shared a common fear about the state of Italy and a desire, always, to ask awkward questions. As Pasolini put it, 'the intellectual courage to tell the truth and political reality are incompatible in Italy'.

When Alcide De Gasperi was made Prime Minister of Italy soon after the war, he promised a 'new equilibrium ... based on social justice'. But few signs of equality followed. To stay in power, the Christian Democrats reneged on their promises and were forced to search for political allies from the right as well as the left. The neo-Fascists became a hovering presence over Italian politics: the long reign of unstable coalitions, forming and falling, had begun. By the elections of 1953, there was fighting in Korea, the Cold War was at its height and Clare Boothe Luce, the outspoken and right-wing American ambassador to Rome, wife to the publisher of *Time* magazine, was warning of dire consequences if the Christian Democrats failed to win. But they did win, helped by American money and American pressure, called by *The New York Times* 'rough house diplomacy'.

In Racalmuto, families received letters from their relations in the US, instructing them to vote for the Christian Democrats and them alone, which they obediently did, though it was telling that some of the best results for the neo-Fascist MSI, Movimento Sociale Italiano, were in Western Sicily. By the time of his death in 1954, De Gaspari, stern, moral, devout, was recognised to have been a masterful politician, committed to European political unity, but he had not delivered on his promises for social reform and justice and he had devoted too much energy to virulent anti-Communism. But Italy had not, as many had feared, collapsed. Schooled by his aunts and his grandfather Leonardo, Sciascia remained firmly to the left, his instinctive sympathy for the losers in Sicily's profoundly unequal society sharpened by observing his pupils' lives, but he remained intensely wary of political parties. Though he 'profoundly' mistrusted the Christian Democrats and all they stood for, it was telling that he joined neither the Socialists nor the Communists.

Long after it became obvious that this was an ignorant mistake, Sicily continued to be viewed as rich. In practice, the island remained cut off from the mainland by a Maginot Line not of concrete and steel, but of something more fundamental and tenacious: ideas, culture, traditions, the very fabric of its people. Sicily suffered, wrote the journalist Guido Dorso, from a persistent sense of inferiority and it lacked 'sufficient strength to evolve'. A quarter of its inhabitants were illiterate; in the north of Italy just 5 per cent. Barely a third reached the top class in elementary school. There were pitifully few tractors, radios or telephones. Almost two thirds of the men lacked regular employment, and stood aimlessly around their village squares as if waiting for a funeral. In the village of Palma di Montechiaro, out of six hundred families, a quarter slept on the floor on bare earth and many shared their single rooms with pigs, donkeys, hens and goats. A recent scandal had broken out in what remained of sulphur territory when nine- and ten-year-old boys were discovered with deformed spines from carrying heavy loads. When *L'Espresso* sent a team of reporters from the mainland to replicate the Franchetti–Sonnino inquiry of 1875, they visited Caltanissetta and saw women and children lying on straw and mud, living on chicory and bread. It was, wrote one reporter, 'our Africa'. Sicily was not, of course, alone in its post-war poverty: in Rome, in 1952, there were still 93,000 people living in shacks, caves and cellars. But in Sicily it was all much worse. Compared to most of the rest of Italy, now turning firmly towards industry and progress, Sicily sometimes seemed to be going backwards.

In 1953 writers from all over Italy, among them Calvino, Vittorini and Pasolini, arrived in Palermo for a writers' congress. Sciascia was invited and spoke about Pirandello. Exhilarated by his new literary encounters, he returned somewhat disconsolate to Racalmuto, telling his friend La Cava that meeting them had left him feeling 'even emptier and more despairing' about his isolation.

After the regional government expropriated 700,000 hectares of uncultivated land, the large feudal estates which had dominated the island slowly began to die. The 2,000-year-old world of the *latifondi* was over. But scheming landowners and *gabellotti* continued to do all they could to stymie change, keeping back the more fertile olive groves and vineyards, and the reform boards set up to oversee the allocation of land to peasants were inefficient; the strips of land they handed out, after considerable delays, were often the most barren and stony, and in most cases totally insufficient to meet a family's needs. Luigi Einaudi, the economist made President in 1948, had called for reforms to be pushed through 'like a blow from a battering ram'. It was more like a prod from a twig. The *Cassa per il Mezzogiorno*, a state fund for the south, was set up to deliver public works – irrigation, land reclamation, roads and aqueducts – but old habits of feudalism and servility proved hard to eradicate. A fatal mixture of political intriguing and cronyism settled over Sicily. One after the other, regional agencies, set up in the wake of the *Cassa per il Mezzogiorno*, sank into bureaucratic inertia, infighting and corruption. Even the union organisers seemed to have forgotten their battles for a better world.

In 1953, oil was discovered off the coast of Ragusa. A large refinery was built at Augusta, with a petrochemical plant, terminals and jetties. Then important finds of methane gas and potash were made, which could have remedied some of the losses from the dying sulphur industry. Just sixty of the earlier six hundred mines were still in operation. But mistrust, reluctance to take risks and fear of the Mafia plagued Augusta from the start. Taking advantage of the generous subsidies, companies ploughed their profits from these new 'cathedrals in the desert' back to ventures on the mainland. Sicilian wealth did what it had always done: it travelled north, and Sicily itself remained what it had always been: a loose structure of centres of power, serving the interests of different factions. A new dominant class of mediators, the Christian Democrat bosses, bureaucrats, speculators and lawyers who controlled the *Cassa*'s purse strings, took over from the old landowning elite. Power, in the shape of jobs, perks and contracts, was now handed down from party bosses and politicians through the ranks of civil servants and local administrators to the ordinary people, who were expected to express their gratitude with votes. The Mafia, cannily, were moving ever closer to the centres of power. Kinship was what really mattered.

Sitting in his classroom in Racalmuto, Sciascia observed the steady drain of families leaving Sicily to seek work elsewhere. Some battled on until a sudden catastrophe, like the death of a mule, pushed them over into destitution. Boys, their hair neatly brushed, in clean clothes, came to tell him excitedly that they were off, leaving for the industrial cities of Milan, Turin and Genova, or to Liguria to grow flowers, or to the newly opened coal mines in France and Belgium, or to Emilia to take over the work of the sharecroppers who had abandoned the land. Between 1951 and 1953, some 400,000 people, almost a tenth of the population, left the island. In his neat, small handwriting, in red ink, Sciascia wrote 'emigrated' next to their names in the class ledger. In Racalmuto, those bound for the US chanted, '*Io sono più Americano di te*', I am more American than you are.

Sciascia had not enjoyed his class in 1952: he described it as 'literally a disaster' and thought that 1953 could only prove better. He was wrong: the boys who came to him were as poor, hungry and bored as their predecessors and he continued to lament that he was forced to spend his days teaching them things that would be absolutely useless in the lives they were condemned to live. By now he was writing all the time; later, his pupils would say that Sciascia set them tasks and then sat at his desk 'writing, always writing'. He published a long essay on Pirandello which won a prestigious Sicilian prize. He told Mario dell'Arco that his head was full of disorder, but that writing 'seems to be my way of finding consolation and rest. A way of finding myself in the contradictions of life.' But it was paying very little. His real 'illness', he told a friend, was a feeling that he would always 'live like this'. When Brancati suddenly died from complications during an operation, Vittorio Nisticò, the editor of Palermo's newspaper *L'Ora*, invited Sciascia to take over as its literary critic. Not long before, Brancati had asked him: when are you going to produce a '*real* and *proper* book'?

Every month, the teachers were expected to produce notes on their pupils. During his fourth year, Sciascia decided that instead of the usual banal and meaningless phrases that were customary, he would write a true, proper portrait. He wrote it very quickly, in just a few days, and he called it a 'scholastic chronicle'. He showed it to the writer Italo Calvino, who sent it on to Alberto Moravia, who in turn arranged for it to appear in a literary magazine called *Nuovi Argomenti* in January 1955. There it was read by Vito Laterza, a publisher based in Bari. Sciascia went to Bari and met Laterza, who suggested that he turn the pieces into a full-length book about life in a small Sicilian village. Sciascia hesitated, reluctant, as he told Vittorini, to return to things that had already been published because he usually felt 'disgusted' by them. But Vittorini chided him and Sciascia set to work.

He wrote about the scarred, swollen hands of the sulphur and salt workers and their rasping coughs when they gathered in the piazza on Sundays; he described the strangers with the faces of thugs who descended on the village at election time with bribes and threats and how the workers visited their employers to ask which way they should vote and then went off and did the opposite; and how 'patrols' of Jesuits arrived to hand out pasta and cheese and told people to vote for the Christian Democrats. He talked about the village priest who had been to the US and come back with loudspeakers to replace the church bells, and the way that on icy days the carts carrying the pale wood coffins of the dead covered with angels squeaked on the stone cobbles. He painted portraits of the old women whose families had emigrated sitting on their doorsteps waiting to die, and calculated that of Racalmuto's 12,000 or so inhabitants a quarter were so poor that they seldom left their houses. He remembered the men who had so arrogantly joined the Fascists and how afraid they had been when Fascism fell, and he regretted not having done something to help them. It was then, he wrote, that 'I discovered pity. A terrible thing, pity. A man must love and hate, but he must never pity. A man that is. I was just a boy.' And he described the day that one of his pupils arrived in a coat so enormous that his head poked out of it like that of a tortoise, so that all the other boys laughed at him and called him a clown, and how the boy, expecting a blow from Sciascia and with terrified eyes, told him that a former teacher used to spit at him. At Christmas, when the most fortunate among them told him that their mothers had given them a hot bath and perhaps a few sweets, he felt his heart as heavy as a stone.

Writing, Sciascia discovered a language that was dry, clear, pitiless, funny and full of compassion, and in which he laid down all the themes that would later fill his books: injustice, poverty, corruption, power and memory, driven by a strong sense of morality and the consciousness of being Sicilian. 'All my books,' he would repeat, many years later, 'are effectively just one: a book on Sicily which touches on all its saddest aspects', the single cry of a man alone against the cancer of power and poverty and all that flowed from it. As he wrote, he kept thinking of the words of the French polemicist Courier and his 'sword thrusts' on behalf of his French village. The pen, Sciascia decided, would be his sword: he would strike blows for the sulphur workers, the day labourers and the famished children. And in his introduction he laid down the credo by which he would live the rest of his life. 'I believe in reason and the liberty and justice that come from reason.' The writer, he declared, must represent truth; neither a philosopher nor a historian, he had to be someone who sought always for the truth.

Laterza was delighted with this *'ottimo lavoro'*, this excellent piece of work, and suggested a few small changes, along with something on 'ecclesiastical power'. There was much debate about the title, Sciascia wanting to call it 'Salt on the Wound'. They settled on *'Le parrocchie di Regalpetra'*, 'The Parishes of Regalpetra', a loose version of Racalmuto. '*E bellissimo,*' Sciascia wrote when he saw the finished copy. 'I am very happy with it.' He was right to be: his account of life in one of Sicily's poor small towns was indeed exceptional, touching but never sentimental. It was a quiet success, selling modestly but well enough for Sciascia to honour his promise to buy a fridge for the *zie*. In the club in Racalmuto, members argued about his characters, trying to identify themselves. They congratulated him warmly, and though he kept saying that he had invented many of the stories, the whole village seemed to smile at him with knowing expressions of complicity. Pasolini told him that the book was 'really beautiful'. Previously, he wrote, he had felt great affinity with Sciascia. But the book had turned this into a 'true, strong, heartfelt sense of brotherhood. How rare are hearts like yours.'

Sciascia was now in his mid thirties and had never travelled beyond the shores of Italy. Like all Sicilians steeped in the fractured history of their island, he was both drawn to and repelled by the thought of elsewhere, escape and return, the way that the very things that annoy you at home become objects of 'chronic' nostalgia when you leave them. Sicily was, as he put it, 'a place both loved and hated', to which you returned with a sense of 'burning defeat and vindictive mistrust'. As Nisticò, editor of *L'Ora*, said, there were two kinds of Sicilians, those of the shore and those of the open sea. The first left Sicily but on their second day away fell into a crisis of homesickness; and on the third day they went home. Those of the open sea were those who turned *Sicilitudine*, Sicilianness, into their credo and then adapted it to live a different life. They returned on visits to Sicily because Sicily remained in their heart, but their eyes were firmly set on new horizons. Sciascia was a man of the shore; but it made him no less curious to see at least a small part of the world.

For his first foray abroad, Sciascia ventured, with Maria, to Paris, home of the Enlightenment thinkers he loved and whose names and sayings he was already dropping into everything he wrote, confident that his readers would know and love them as he did. They travelled by train, Sciascia enjoying the fact that the passengers talked to each other. Paris, since boyhood, had stood for elegance, refinement and beauty. They arrived at night, when it was already dark, and woke to find the city brilliant with sun and full of flags flapping in the wind. It made Sciascia feel that he was in a painting by Utrillo. He paced the city and found himself in the Place Pigalle on market day, with stalls of spun sugar and nougat and festoons of lights. He wandered, visited the Louvre, sat in cafés and made pilgrimages to the streets in which Diderot, Voltaire and Pascal had lived. It all felt deeply familiar. For the rest of his life, he would return again and again. Paris, he thought, was a place of endless *festa*, but a *festa* that did not end in melancholy.

He had discovered that he had a real love for graphic art, for etchings and lithographs, and wherever he went he now sought out antiquarian shops. In Paris one day he saw an early painted map of Sicily and knew that he wanted it. Returning to their hotel, he counted the money he had left and decided that he had just enough. 'It seemed,' he wrote later, 'a sign . . . a sign that I would continue to decipher Sicily's past.' For him, as for Pirandello, Sicily had become a metaphor for the world.

Spain was also in his soul. He made it his second trip abroad, visiting Burgos, San Sebastian and Barcelona with Maria, travelling from Milan by bus, revelling in the names of towns he knew from the surnames of the viceroys, the Ossunos and Toledos, who had governed Sicily. For him Spain meant four centuries of Sicilian occupation, the poetry of Lorca and Cernuda, the country of the civil war. It was here that 'our personal story began . . . where we found reason for our instinctive anti-Fascism', where we 'encountered ideas and poetry . . . where we constructed our utopias'. In

Spain he recognised everything he saw and loved and also hated in Sicily, its splendour and pomp, its harsh climate, its smells, the arrogance and melancholy of its people. The owner of a parador they stayed in was wearing an insignia of the far-right Falange party in his lapel. Sciascia thought that for all Franco's victories he looked ashamed and 'walked with death'. Spain, too, became a place of repeated pilgrimages. Like Sicily it was more a way of being than a nation; to be Spanish was the closest thing to being Sicilian. He began to seek out and buy collections by the 'fraternity of Spanish poets' who had stood up against Fascism.

Maria

Sciascia's newfound taste for travel spread to Sicily itself. He visited the recently excavated Piazza Armerina and admired the girls in the mosaics dancing 'in the watery light filtered by the chestnut trees'. Increasingly, he was drawn to writing about the land, about the hard bare crust of Sicily's packed earth and its veins of deep cracks, and the 'sea of rocks that look like bones', with the damp grey houses clinging to the sides of mountains and the streets and villages in which the island's painters and writers had been born. He returned from his trips exhilarated by all he had seen but complained that his elation quickly faded to a 'cold distance', then 'annihilation', kept at bay only by reading and looking at maps.

Home quickly felt like a confinement at the hands of the 'family police'.

It was while standing at Racalmuto station waiting for a train that an idea came to him for a short story. A family of returning emigrants had just arrived, to be greeted by hugs, tears and joy by their relations. The man standing next to him said softly: 'And in less than a week, they'll be quarrelling.' Sciascia now wrote about the jealousy, the envy, the resentments between the people who left and those who stayed behind. *'Gli zii di Sicilia'*, 'The Sicilian Uncles', is about an aunt arriving home after many years, bringing with her a cowed American husband and sulky children, with trunks full of second-hand clothes which she distributes, together with $5 bills. No one is pleased. No one really likes the brightly patterned ties or the odd-looking hats. The family who stayed behind in Sicily feel they are being patronised. The aunt, who complains incessantly about the heat and the flies, cannot quite get over the ingratitude of the villagers, having expected to find them destitute and deeply appreciative of her handouts. *'Gli zii'* gave Sciascia a chance to explore his delight in irony and language, the 'linguistic promiscuity of Sicilians', reporting joyfully on some of the absurd renderings of English into Italian used by the emigrants – *'stora'* for store, *'orrait'* for all right, *'ciunga'* for chewing gum – and teasing out new meanings for expressions. He was in love with words. In a country of circumlocutions, sub-clauses and obfuscations, he used them delicately, even parsimoniously, making certain that not one contained a single note of ambiguity.

On its own, *'Gli zii'* was too short to make a book. It appeared first in a magazine with another story, about an old Communist who, after Khrushchev's reforms, visits his local party office every day to make certain that Stalin's portrait has not been taken down. When Calvino, who worked as an editor with the publishing house Einaudi, read *'Gli zii'* he said that he had never expected Sciascia to be such a skilled storyteller, with such a 'felicitous vein of caricature', though he thought that *The Death of Stalin* was a bit too like a pamphlet. While discussions were continuing about how to publish the stories as a book, they won the Libera Stampa Prize in Lugano. At the prize giving, a reporter noted that Sciascia had the 'laconic tones of an islander' and that he spoke in defensive monosyllables. To his friend Mario La Cava he wrote that while he was pleased with the money, he did not know what he would do with the 'echoes of glory'. Asked by his Swiss hosts whether he would like to place the money in a bank, he took it instead to spend in an antiquarian print shop.

Einaudi now pressed ahead with publication, adding two new stories, one about the Risorgimento, another a bitter tale about a young Sicilian returning wounded from the Spanish Civil War. Talking about his four stories, Sciascia said that they represented the collapse of four myths crucial to the Sicilian psyche: Fascism, the uprising of 1860, Communism and the great American dream. His skill lay in the true novelist's ability to transform reality into fiction. 'I believe,' he wrote, pleased with their success, 'in the mystery of words' and that however dark things seemed, the very act of writing was itself a form of optimism. Vittorini had successfully used humour as the best weapon against the *'mondo offeso'* – the wounded world; Sciascia preferred irony, a tone that sometimes seemed almost detached.

Later, Umberto Eco would coin the phrase 'a whisper of books', books whispering to each other. Sciascia was inviting his readers to listen in, to be drawn into a circle of kindred spirits, feeding on literature in order to face up to whatever challenges life brought them. *Le parrocchie* had allowed him, finally, to express his real feelings. He was now beginning to think about something longer, and considerably more ambitious.

Pasquale had never recovered from Peppino's suicide. Overcome by feelings of guilt, he became increasingly irrational and touchy. He had a slight stroke. One day, taking out his Beretta, he went to the office of his lawyer, Carmelo Burruano, who was a distant relation and who, he thought, had been betraying him in a complicated legal case. Aiming low, he fired three shots; none of them hit the lawyer, indeed they were most likely simply an expression of frustration. Pasquale then handed himself in to the carabinieri who took him to the prison of San Vito in Agrigento. Here in hospital, on 2 April 1957, he had a second stroke and died. It was something of a relief, for he might otherwise have ended up in a hospital for the criminally insane.

Pasquale had been a hard, authoritarian father and Sciascia had never felt close to him. But he had found his father's descent into paranoia and dementia extremely painful. What he could not bear, he told a friend later, was 'talking to someone who couldn't understand me, couldn't hear me ... like a wall'. For Sciascia, without understanding there was nothing but confusion. It was at Pasquale's funeral in Racalmuto, well attended by some of Sciascia's new literary friends, that the villagers said they first had a glimmer of his growing fame.

After Peppino's death, the *zie*'s house had become still more cloistered and silent; a permanent blackness seemed to settle over them all, broken only by whispers and constant, despairing weeping. Genoveffa refused ever to leave the house. Maria continued to teach, remaining obedient to the aunts. More than ever before, the aunts provided a cosy, safe shell which embraced them all, with Sciascia, the writer, at its very heart. For Anna Maria, though, who had just turned eleven, the gloom was oppressive and terrifying. When not at school, she wandered desolate from floor to floor among women in deep mourning, and she was jealous of her older sister Laura who was regarded as the more intelligent and talented. The two girls shared a small bedroom with no window; they had a marble chest of drawers held up by caryatids and a Deposition of Christ on one wall. At night she could not sleep and when left to cry, she waited desperately for the relief of daylight. The house was always cold. When Sciascia installed a gas heater in his study he was very nearly asphyxiated by its fumes. 'I felt,' wrote Anna Maria in a touching memoir about her childhood, 'different, as if I didn't belong.'

Everyone, even her sister Laura, took refuge in reading. When she interrupted, Anna Maria was scolded or told that she was quarrelsome. For hours on end, exactly as Sciascia had done as a boy, she crouched silently by the front door, looking out on the spectacle of village life, listening to the gossip, watching the women gathered around the pump. When an aunt discovered her, she would tell the little girl not to talk about anything upsetting to her sister, who was thought to be fragile. Anna Maria's real love was for her father. He read to her, in his warm, soft voice, made slightly rough by his constant smoking. When he went to Caltanissetta for the day, she watched him trudge through the mud to the station, and waited at the window for him to come back. He seldom expressed love, but his manner towards her was gentle and attentive. In a household in which literature was everything, the sound of the 'other life, the real one' seemed indistinct. What happens, she wondered, to people 'who enter the world and do not write'?

In 1957, to Anna Maria's dismay, her father was posted to the Ministry of Public Education in Rome, where one of his jobs was to contribute to the house magazine, *Prospettive Meridiane*. Sciascia took a room in the Hotel dei Portoghesi near the station, but soon gravitated to the streets around the Pantheon, home to many Racalmutesi. There were two kinds of Sicilians, he told a friend, those who, like Vittorini, went to Milan because they wanted something different, and those like himself who chose Rome because they really wanted to go on living in Sicily. Bored with his job, Sciascia did what he always did: he marked out a small area of bookshops and picture galleries and seldom ventured elsewhere. His new friends in the post-war literary world in Rome teased him about his interminable silences, when he would sit and say absolutely nothing, or pause so long before speaking that they had ceased to think anything would be forthcoming. At a conference on Pirandello, he spoke with filial admiration about the man he thought had written most profoundly about Sicily's refracted light, in which appearance and reality do not quite match. His voice, low and a bit quavery, carried a trace of Sicilian dialect.

In Rome, Sciascia was hopelessly homesick. It never stopped raining and he sat forlornly in cafés listening to the 'malicious chatter of the literati'. He wrote to Vilardo that he rather doubted that he would ever adapt. 'Pascal was right when he said that all problems arise from not knowing how to live in one's room . . . I cannot find any peace in my own thoughts.' He told Vittorini, who had become a friend, that in Rome he could neither think nor write, and that he needed his own 'despairing and violent village'. As soon as he could, he returned to Racalmuto. All that could be said about Sicily was that 'neither with you nor without you can I live'.

Laura had now finished elementary school. Since there was no secondary school in the village, the family needed to move. There were many discussions about where they should go: the aunts opposed them all, having cast, as Anna Maria later remembered, their claustrophobic embrace over the whole family. Every suggested destination was viewed as a betrayal. Zia Angela cried ceaselessly. But Sciascia insisted and they settled eventually on Caltanissetta, near enough for frequent returns to *La Noce*; they left behind the much-loved fridge. Once again, Nica agreed to come with them.

In any case, Sciascia was restless. He had been reading and thinking about Montaigne and Machiavelli, he told Vilardi, and was very pleased with a translation that he had just finished of Baudelaire's poetry. 'Spiritually,' he told his friend, 'I am ready and famished. What shall I do?'

6
The reluctant *mafiologo*

'This is a mafia village,' Sciascia had written in *Le parrocchie*, more, perhaps, in the sense of attitudes and behaviour than in actual deeds, though there were those too. Regalpetra, he wrote, had two *capi-mafia*, who strutted around, making their presence felt. But it was really only during election time that you observed the Mafia openly at work. A local politician Sciascia called Zorpi would arrive in the village square in a big American car, 'fat, flaccid and playful'. Villagers thronged round him like flies. He hugged some of them, greeted others with a handshake, assured a man whose brother had botched a kidnapping that the matter had been taken care of and the over-zealous carabinieri who wanted to arrest him transferred elsewhere. '*Onorevole*,' the villagers said, 'we are Sicilian orphans, we are in your hands. You won't lose a vote here.'

From time to time, fathers of his pupils appeared in Sciascia's classroom to tell him that their sons *had* to have free lunches and *had* to pass up into the next class. You knew, he wrote, that these men were 'friends of friends' and that it was a question not of hearing a dog bark but of knowing that it could bite. It was a 'very sad game'. A country could die of the Mafia, he said, exactly as a man could die of cancer. Mafia power was beginning to intrigue him.

Much has been written and said about how Mori crushed the Mafia and the Americans brought it back, but what the Allies really did, by appointing *mafiosi* to key positions and giving them money and power, was to facilitate the Mafia's resurgence. It had simply been lying dormant. In the late 1940s and early 1950s, the Mafia's Indian summer took off. Post-war Sicily, bankrupt, lawless and hungry, was in no position to defend herself. The obese, shambling Don Calò, who had kept peace of a kind between warring Mafia families, and done his best to preserve a feudal world infested by *mafioso gabellotti*, died in 1954 from a heart attack. Politicians, senior clergy and local dignitaries flocked to pay their respects as he lay in state in Villalba. On his memorial stone, Don Calò was described as chaste, temperate, forbearing, tireless in defence of the poor and the weak, a veritable '*galantuomo*' – a righteous gentleman.

The very nature of the Mafia had changed. The *Cassa per il Mezzogiorno* and its many offshoots had brought an ocean of money to builders and plumbers, drivers and craftsmen, purveyors of cement and steel and electrical fittings, contracted to construct apartment buildings, roads, bridges and new hospitals – and to the men who secured the deals. What soon became known as the 'sack of Palermo' saw art nouveau monuments and Renaissance palazzi torn down. The magnificent Conca d'Oro, home to orange and lemon groves, was cemented over. Palermo came to resemble Chicago, at the time of Prohibition. A '*borghesia di stato*', a parasitical world of middlemen, with strong roots in the Mafia, acquired power. What Carlo Levi called the 'heroic and creative' years of peasant rebellion were over: the miners had already gone abroad, now the peasants left too.

Drugs came next, and with them a new, younger Mafia, less respectful, more brutal, less inclined to settle their disputes through the *capi*. A number of 'undesirables' had been extradited from the US, bringing with them knowledge of the drug markets and gambling. Young men were trained in the ways of extortion, calling on shopkeepers in the guise of rubbish collectors and sellers of lottery tickets. At a meeting held in the art nouveau Hotel delle Palme in Palermo in 1957, where Wagner wrote *Parsifal*, Lucky Luciano, now back in Sicily from New York, and Don Genco Russo, who had taken over the leadership of the local Mafia from Don Calò, agreed to replace Cuba with Sicily as the transit country for heroin into the US. It was a summit for the two mafias and the launch of great things to come. Heroin began travelling to Sicily from Turkey and Syria in fishing boats, to be landed along deserted stretches of rocky coast, before being delivered for repacking into sardine tins and wax oranges, the exact size and weight of real oranges, and then boxed for export to the US. Mafia wars broke out, many of them centred around Corleone, north of Palermo, whose Mafia had flourished in the meat markets, even stealing and butchering nineteen rare breeds of cows and six hundred equally rare sheep belonging to an experimental breeding station.

In Corleone – which saw 153 murders in just four years – Dr Navarra, the doctor who had murdered the eleven-year-old witness to the killing of Placido Rizzotto, was now boss. Dr Navarra, like Don Calò, was corpulent and cunning; he was a keen hunter and a good card player, and had grown rich on abandoned US military vehicles and a petrol distribution business. A young and rising carabinieri captain, Carlo Alberto Dalla Chiesa, stationed in Corleone, began filing reports about the violent enforcers in the neighbourhood, though he had left by the time Navarra was machine-gunned and his young killer, Toto Riina, intent on thwarting the doctor's business interests, had disappeared into hiding. Riina had made his fortune in butchering stolen cattle and was running his own *cosca* – the word taken from the many overlapping leaves of artichokes.

Standing up to the Mafia was becoming highly dangerous. When, in October 1958, the crusading editor of *L'Ora* in Palermo, Nisticò, published an enquiry into the Mafia, along with names and photographs of the current bosses, including a long article on Don Vito Ferro, a *capo* of the old school and master of extortion rackets, his printing presses were blown up. No one was hurt, but the message was clear. A funeral director, deaf to extortion, received a package containing the head of his dead Alsatian dog. The owners of cars in Palermo, exhausted by losing so many to arson, parked them in garages opened by young *mafiosi*, where they were safe. Violent death became commonplace, with no witness, however close to the scene, ever seeing anything. Many of the attacks were brazen, and nowhere more so than in Sciascia's province of Caltanissetta. Alfa Romeos laden with dynamite picked rivals off. The geography and armoury of violence was changing, from feudal lands to city centres, from the *lupara*, the sawn-off shotgun, to the Kalashnikov.

The Mafia spirit was in the air. No corner of daily life seemed to be exempt. There was a Capuchin monastery at Mazzarino, the town near Caltanissetta which had given its name to France's great eighteenth-century cardinal. One day shots were heard in the cell belonging to thirty-nine-year-old Brother Agrippino. When the police arrived they found him wounded but not dead.

Getting nowhere with their investigations, they closed the case. But the Capuchin monastery was not a peaceful place; there were reports of extortion, intimidation and unexplained fires. Then it all became more complicated. The shots, it turned out, had been intended for a visiting friar, who usually occupied Brother Agrippino's cell, but just why this friar was a target was not immediately clear. Soon after, a threatening, anonymous letter was delivered to the Capuchin mother house: the entire monastery at Gela would be destroyed and all its friars killed unless two million lire were produced. The threats grew wilder. Then a local landowner, driving his family in his Fiat 600, was shot and killed. His widow told the police that he had ignored a series of threatening letters, even after being advised by an older friar at Mazzarino, Brother Vincenzo, to whom he went for confession, to pay up. Then a local chemist had his shop set on fire. The police decided to dig deeper.

What they uncovered was a vast web of corruption and extortion, organised by the friars during confession and carried out by Mafia enforcers, with local people obliged to hand over large sums of money to the monastery's gardener. In the monastery itself were found stashes of cash, guns and vast quantities of delicious food. The friars, who had taken vows of poverty, had set up bank accounts all over Sicily and were making loans at extortionate rates. They had become millionaires. Four monks were arrested, Brothers Agrippino and Vincenzo among them, but when they appeared in court, people rushed up to kiss their hands. A witness had his hand chopped off, then claimed that he had done it himself. At the trial, the friars pleaded innocence of the ways of the world. They were absolved, and three illiterate labourers, who would have been unable to write the carefully crafted extortion notes, went down for many years. Only much later, after several new trials, were two of the four monks given eight-year sentences. The people of Racalmuto had been right to warn Sciascia and his friends against the travelling monk with his donkey.

Sciascia knew all this, and more, as did most Sicilians. But it was little spoken about. Over the years, he had touched on the Mafia in various ways, going so far as to give it a formal definition in *Tempo*

Presente in 1957 – something that no one else had done. The Mafia, he said, was neither folklore nor a state of mind as people claimed, but rather a 'criminal association, set up to make illegal gains for its members, in the shape of mediators between property and work; mediation, it should be understood, both parasitic and imposed by violence'. Even so, he continued to circle round the subject until he had a chance encounter with a carabinieri officer, Renato Candida. Candida had been based in Agrigento for some years, working on Mafia crimes and growing increasingly alarmed at what he perceived was happening in Sicily. Having written a book about his experiences and his fears, he was introduced to Sciascia, who helped him place it with his editor friend in Caltanissetta, Salvatore Sciascia. They became friends and spent long hours discussing Candida's failure in Agrigento to make cases against the Mafia stick. There was no crime in Sicily, Candida told him, that did not carry, however tenuously, the stamp of the Mafia, and he provided a precise description of the successful *mafioso*, put together from his observations: violent by nature, unscrupulous, treacherous, mendacious, a man of few words, but with an expression of false bonhomie. When Candida's book was published, Sciascia reviewed it, together with a book on the American Mafia by a journalist called Ed Reid.

It was as if something suddenly became clear in his mind. Returning to his earlier definition, he now went further. The Sicilian Mafia, he wrote, was extremely powerful and would endure unless checked. And, were it to move from the countryside into the cities, manage to infiltrate the regional civil service and take hold in the new factories and enterprises, then 'the problem would be around for many years'. A year later, after his book was published, Candida was quietly transferred to the mainland. Sciascia's thoughts were beginning to take a prophetic turn.

Alongside his more serious readings of the French Enlightenment philosophers, Sciascia still found time for detective thrillers, which seemed to him the perfect vehicle for exploring the dangerous and disorderly post-war world. The characters he continued to admire most were Simenon's Maigret and Chesterton's Father Brown, men who knew how to listen, saw clues not in fingerprints but in gestures and who were not just kind and patient but respectful of the rights of their suspects. They could 'read the crime in the human heart'. He especially liked Maigret as he aged and grew wiser, and Chandler's taciturn inhabitants of the underworld. The *giallo*, he decided, was the most interesting vision of this underworld, this undergrowth, with its potential to offer 'authentic surprises'. In November 1958, he wrote to Calvino to tell him that he was thinking about writing something 'perhaps excessively modern', a tale involving the Mafia, the carabinieri and the politicians, possibly set in the sulphur industry. It would be a *giallo* in the style of the mirrored, fractured world of Pirandello. Calvino was the perfect literary friend for him: of the left, engaged with the foremost Italian writers of the day, and himself the author of a number of novels in which he was experimenting with different kinds of writing.

Sciascia with Calvino

It did not take Sciascia long to settle on his story. On 4 January 1947 a trade unionist, a giant of a man called Accursio Miraglia, had been murdered while coordinating peasant land occupations not far from Agrigento. Efforts to find the killers collapsed before a wall of silence, though it was widely known that the murder had been organised by local landowners and the Mafia. For his detective, Sciascia chose his carabinieri friend, Renato Candida, inspired by his accounts of the growing rift between the new and the old Mafia. In 1959 he set to work on the book that would change his life.

Salvatore Colasberna, Sciascia's victim, is an honest building contractor, a Socialist, who is killed at six thirty one morning as he runs to catch a bus. The case is given to Captain Bellodi, a former partisan recently posted to Sicily from the mainland, a firm believer in justice and the rule of law and accustomed to the more straightforward legal system of the north. Bellodi is Sciascia's model citizen, committed to democracy and power based on legality. He is soon mired in a world of subtle misinformation, ambiguity, *omertà*, false alibis, arbitrariness and constantly shifting sands. The women watching as Colasberna is killed have, as it turns out, seen and heard nothing at all. Bellodi's inquiries lead him to an informer, a former sheep thief called Parrineddù, whose terror feels like that of a 'rabid dog'. Parrineddù sends Bellodi a note with the names of the killers but is then shot dead. Bellodi meets the local Mafia boss, Don Mariano Arena, a suave and worldly figure not unlike Don Peppino Genco Russo, *capo* of Mussomeli.

In one of the most important and most quoted passages in the novel, the cynical, misanthropic Don Mariano philosophises on the need to hang on to power, never allowing oneself to become either a victim or a cuckold. Bellodi, while refusing to succumb to his charm, recognises that he has chosen to become a *mafioso* not on account of a criminal nature, but as a response to the society into which he has been born. Don Mariano tells him '*Lei è un'uomo*' – you are a man – and Bellodi replies, 'And so are you.' In another memorable passage, in words that would come back to haunt him, Sciascia divides humanity into five categories: men, half men, tiny men, know-alls and '*quaquaraqua*'– braggarts and overbearing lackeys of the Mafia.

When Bellodi arrests Don Mariano, alarm bells ring in the political circles in Rome which are in league with the Sicilian Mafia, a fact conveyed by a chilling meeting between two unnamed characters and a parliamentarian, with the goal of getting Bellodi removed. The captain's carefully constructed analysis is discredited and the blame for Colasberna's death is laid at the door of his widow and her lover – a crime of passion far less worrying for everyone.

Sciascia decided on the title *Il giorno della civetta*, The Day of the Owl, suitably mysterious and ambiguous for his purpose. He took it from Henry VI: 'And he that will not fight for such a hope, Go home to bed, and like the owl by day, if he arise, be mocked and wondered at.' It perfectly captured, he thought, the themes of corruption, the struggle for power, the contrast between reason – the light of day – and the unnatural and the surprising,

THE RELUCTANT *MAFIOLOGO*

in the shape of an owl seen by day. Bellodi, a northerner, is accustomed to clarity; in Sicily, he encounters obscurity. Blocked from further investigations, he returns to his native Parma for a holiday, though he has come to feel affection for Sicily. He soon learns that his case has been 'dissolved into the air'. Justice, which might have followed, does not.

There is no satisfactory resolution – a state of affairs that would mark almost every one of Sciascia's books – and the killer is not caught or put on trial. The investigator is defeated, not because he cannot solve the crime but because the State does not want him to – but he has not, it turns out, entirely failed. For the workings of the Mafia have been exposed, along with their links to State power. The blanket of silence and confusion that overhangs Sicilian life has been pulled back to reveal a world in which there is no objective legal framework and where the law is administered by whoever holds most power. To search for the truth is pointless, because it lies hidden behind the power of the Mafia. Sciascia concludes his novel with a prophecy. 'Perhaps,' he has Bellodi speculate, 'the whole of Italy is becoming like Sicily. The line of the palm tree is moving north, at 500 metres a time, probably every year.' Like the arrow in a thermometer, it had already passed Rome. This was literature as denunciation, and writers, as Sciascia kept repeating, have a duty to testify.

The book written, he sent it off to Calvino, now consulting editor at Einaudi, though he kept fiddling with his characters, trying to make them both anonymous yet also transparently recognisable, 'in an agony of perplexity' lest he might be sued for describing 'imbecilic policemen, Fascist (or *mafioso*) police chiefs, corrupt magistrates, frightened policemen'. He waited anxiously for Calvino's reaction and grew agitated when he heard nothing. He need not have worried. Calvino had been away and when he returned to his desk he was full of praise. Sciascia, he wrote, was doing something that no one else had ever done, producing a beautiful and sensitive 'documentary-story', full of colour, using just the right amount of facts and no more. There was some dispute about whether it would be published by Laterza or Einaudi. Sciascia had been irritated when Einaudi refused to print a second edition of *Gli zii*, saying that he would prefer that his books had full and not half days of life. Calvino won the day and it went to Einaudi. The proofs were finished by late December 1960 and *The Day of the Owl* reached the bookshops in May, with a jacket by Renato Guttuso, with whom he had become friends. Sciascia, nervously, had included a postscript. The book was very short, he explained, because he had pruned and pruned again, not feeling 'heroic enough to face charges of libel and slander'.

It was an immediate success. Then it became a play, staged in Catania at the Teatro Stabile, its first night attended by the whole Sciascia family, with Sciascia himself grumbling that the audience treated it as folklore. A few years later, Elio Petri turned it into a film starring Claudia Cardinale and Lee J. Cobb. Requests poured in for foreign rights and the book won the prestigious Premio Crotone. Sciascia, a reviewer declared, was a 'lucid moralist'. In *The New York Times*, Herbert Mitgang declared that now that Vittorini had moved to mainland Italy, Sciascia was the 'big gun' of Sicily, speaking for it as a poet, an essayist and a novelist. The writer Luigi Barzini praised Sciascia as the greatest contemporary Italian writer. Sicily, Sciascia told a friend, 'is suddenly terrifyingly fashionable'.

No one, before Sciascia, as he would repeat with some pride, had written in fiction about the Mafia, not as folklore or Pitrè's '*mafioso* feeling', but as a system with political and economic power working inside the State. No one, after they had read his book – at least in theory, since few people took his warnings seriously – would be able to say they were ignorant about it. Read as a portrait of Sicilian culture and criminal power, it provided a convincing and uncomfortable picture of corruption and illegality imbedded in the very heart of the island, with two sets of laws in place, State law and Mafia law, with the Mafia code the more important of the two.

The Day of the Owl once again raised the question dear to Sciascia's heart: what did it mean to be Sicilian? How did you reconcile honour, respectability and truth on one side with feelings of envy, revenge and violence on the other, in a world of insecurity and fear, without inhabiting a different universe, far removed from reality? In the absence of a strong, law-abiding state, what alternative did people have but to rely on a network of criminals? In Sicily, the Mafia was now normal; everything else was unreal, untrustworthy and destabilising. It was a 'tragic vision of existence'. You needed to break the pact between stupidity and violence 'which is becoming ever more present'. Sciascia had been reading Eric Hobsbawn's *Primitive Rebels*, with its distinction between bandits, mythical Robin Hoods, and *mafiosi*, who had emerged out of feudalism to become enforcers with lucrative rackets and deliverers of votes to corrupt politicians.

Sciascia had become a *'mafiologo'* – a Mafia expert – and people flocked to consult him. He hated the label, and said repeatedly that as a Sicilian, he was not himself free of the *'mafioso* feeling': 'Fighting the Mafia,' he wrote, 'means fighting against myself: it's like being split up or torn apart.' He was simply a man from the west of Sicily who tried to understand the reality that surrounded him, the 'things seen and felt, the things lived through and partly suffered'. 'I am,' he would say, 'an Italian writer who writes about Sicily.'

The Day of the Owl included a crucial proposal. Captain Bellodi, while thwarted at every turn, does manage to carry out bank checks on Don Mariano's assets and thereby proves that his high standard of living could be achieved only by illegal sources of income. To attack the Mafia you needed, Sciascia insisted, to get hold of bank statements, look at ledgers, take stock of expensive villas and cars and even mistresses, measuring salaries against signs of wealth. It would be twenty years, and many deaths, before his words were heeded.

While the many critics who read *The Day of the Owl* greeted his analysis as 'shiny and new', there were inevitably others who suggested that Sciascia had himself colluded with the Mafia by acknowledging its importance. 'Sciasciaism' came to be seen as a combination of pessimism and a 'tendency to be bewitched by the monster'. His 'so-called Mafia', said his detractors, was nothing but a chimera in the fevered imaginations of Socialists and Communists. Sciascia's outspokenness was not without risks. No one sued him for slander, but after addressing a conference of sociologists, he received an anonymous letter. 'If Sciascia is not happy in Sicily,' it read, 'we can send him somewhere he'll feel much better off.' He refused to take it seriously. Writers, he declared, were not in the Mafia's sights.

Sciascia remained calm and prophetic. He had done what he had set out to do, to identify what he saw as the current state of

Sicily, describe the network of collusion between politicians, clerics and the Mafia, the links between corrupt politicians in Rome and those in Palermo, and he had charted the move of the Mafia from the countryside to the city. It was only by understanding what was happening, he said, that one could hope to fight the Mafia.

7
Irredeemable Sicily

Sciascia was not, of course, alone in his anxiety about Sicily or in his efforts to understand it. As a figure in the public eye, he was now solicited for his opinion on every matter. One of his first brushes was with the work of Giuseppe Lampedusa, author of *The Leopard*, though Lampedusa had died shortly before its publication, missing the huge acclaim – and criticism – it attracted, and Sciascia never met him. As with Pasolini, the two men were very different: Lampedusa aristocratic, a lover of exotic travel, the owner of land and property, and Sciascia, the son of a sulphur family, reluctant to stray far from home. While Lampedusa considered James Joyce a 'great artist and noble figure', and declared that to understand *Finnegan's Wake* 'you would need to be God', Sciascia thought Joyce's language incomprehensible, his 'Catholic despair' deeply boring and *Ulysses* a shapeless, red-hot flow of 'schizophrenic lava', embarrassingly crude to the deeply modest Sciascia.

But both he and Lampedusa owned large collections of books and revered Montaigne and Stendhal, both were fascinated by quirky subjects, and both sought to write about a lost Sicily before it disappeared. No one had hated the *gabellotti* who had bought up the feudal lands at derisory prices more profoundly than these two men. As Lampedusa has his character Don Fabrizio Salina say, 'We were the Leopards and the Lions, those who will take our place will be little jackals, hyenas.' Just as Sciascia had declared that he could write about the Mafia because it was in his bones, so Lampedusa said about his feudal milieu: 'I come from the same stock, with them I must make common cause.' Like Sciascia, Lampedusa loved Sicily as much as he hated it.

When Elena Croce, a literary agent and the daughter of the

philosopher Benedetto Croce, was sent the anonymous typescript of *The Leopard* she had sat on it for almost a year, believing it to be the work of some elderly spinster. A reader at Mondadori dismissed it with the words 'as a book, it doesn't work'; Vittorini called it 'very serious and honest' but too much like an essay. It was only when it reached the desk of the writer Giorgio Bassani, who selected books for Feltrinelli, that its real value was recognised. Published in November 1958, fifteen months after Lampedusa's death, it won the Strega Prize. E. M. Forster called it a 'noble book'. By 1960 it had gone through fifty-five editions.

Few contemporary novels have attracted such controversy. Loved by the general public, the tale of the weary Don Fabrizio meditating on the twilight of the feudal class with irony, scepticism and deep melancholy was sharply attacked by the left as an apologia for a worthless class. It was not the first Sicilian novel to paint a family torn between the old and the new: in Federico De Roberto's *The Viceroys*, a novel about the wily, avid, quarrelsome Uzeda family, he has a character say: 'History repeats itself monotonously: men have been, are and always will be the same.' But that was in 1894 and Sicily in the 1960s was in a mood to change. What became the novel's most famous credo – everything must change in order for nothing to change – was interpreted as unacceptable pessimism and denial of progress.

Even as sales soared, *The Leopard*'s condemnation of Sicily as 'irredeemable', doomed to immobility by the violence of its climate and landscape, even before its chaotic history, was greeted with bafflement and outrage, not least by Sciascia. For all its fascination, he thought its Proustian memories were no more than a 'reductive' approach to reality typical of a '*gran signore*', rather forgetting that his own Don Mariano's philosophising was not unlike that of Don Fabrizio. Lampedusa, in short, did not understand history. As Sciascia told an interviewer, 'It does not allow for much optimism'; and for the moment at least, Sciascia was clinging on to his own optimism, conveyed, people speculated, by his owl appearing in daylight, a possible dawn.

Sciascia had more in common with the sociologist and writer Danilo Dolci, the lay member from the Order of Servi di Maria who arrived from Trieste in the early 1950s and settled in Trappeto, 'one of the most miserable and bloody corners of the world'.

Aldous Huxley called Dolci a 'modern Franciscan'. This was the bandit Giuliano's territory and rife with Mafia. Sociology was largely unknown in Sicily and the authorities were perplexed by this figure, intent on doing good, but who was neither priest nor lawyer, doctor nor trade unionist. Wanting to belong to local life, rather than just observe it, Dolci married a widow in the village with five children and rallied peasants and fishermen to protest against the Mafia's illegal practice of using motor trawlers with explosives in shallow waters. Then, having watched a five-month-old baby die of malnutrition, he launched a 'back-to-front strike' to draw attention to the hunger and chronic lack of work: in pouring rain, villagers gathered to mend a road made impassable by mud and potholes and abandoned by the local council. They staged a sit-down and declared a hunger strike.

Dolci was arrested and charged with 'land invasion'. But by now he was famous well beyond Italy and jurists and journalists descended on Palermo for the trial. Like Sciascia, Dolci described the Mafia not simply as a product of high unemployment and illiteracy, but as a consortium, an association, which cohabited with the State, protected by a wall of silence. The State and the Church were both guilty, he said, of allowing people to starve at a time of rising prosperity. In the witness box, Carlo Levi declared that 'we are all assassins', responsible for the utter misery of the south. Police branded Dolci a political agitator, a demagogue, an 'atheist pornographic writer'. He received an eight-month prison sentence, but the trial sparked off an immense debate on Sicily and its backwardness.

In 1960, Sciascia attended a conference put on by Dolci, at which he spoke about Lampedusa's view of an unchanging Sicily and the need for everyone, especially writers, to unite against poverty. The people who suffered and those who knew about it, like himself, had to speak out. The world needed to know about the *'furbi troppo furbi'* – the cunning and crafty people – the 'hypocrites who are too hypocritical', the illiteracy and backwardness of an island 'cut off from the great currents of human endeavour' ruled by 'so-called men of law and order'. The time had come to tell the world what Sicily was really like and 'even those whose conscience is opaque and whose sleep is deep have to wake up and take note'.

But Sciascia and Dolci were not natural friends. The more the lively, frenetic Dolci urged Sciascia to take action, the more Sciascia retreated into his characteristic posture of silence and withdrawal. Sciascia had written an article for *L'Ora* saying that he considered Dolci's non-violent methods made no sense in a country in which the immediate reaction to wrongs was not to turn the other cheek but to reach for the *lupara*. It was a mistake to think Sicily was like India, where even the lives of ants were respected. Gandhi had no place on the island and nor did 'seraphic benevolence': you needed banking knowledge and local understanding. Dolci, irritated when Sciascia refused his invitations to visit his village and see for himself how it was working, dismissed him as a *mafiologo*, a brilliant but essentially regional writer. For his part, whenever asked, Sciascia would say how much he personally admired Dolci and his writings.

Palermo's irascible, authoritarian Cardinal Ruffini, who was an outspoken opponent of John XXIII's reforms, had taken against Sciascia's depiction in *The Day of the Owl* of the Church as an accomplice to the Mafia. He launched an attack on him, as well as on Dolci and Lampedusa, accusing the three men of a conspiracy to denigrate Sicily with their dishonest portrayals of poverty and the invention of a so-called Mafia. It was a slur, he said, fermented by the Communists, and they were nothing but publicity seekers. Sicily was an earthly paradise, for tourists and citizens alike, and the so-called *mafiosi* simply patriots defending their country.

Dolci and Sciascia did not seek each other out again, but they did meet at a cultural event in Palermo not long afterwards. A somewhat cross and perplexed Dolci asked Sciascia: 'Who are you?' To which Sciascia, with characteristic irony and evasion replied: 'I am an elementary school teacher who took to writing books, perhaps because I was not a good teacher.' But they had more in common than they cared to admit. Both believed passionately in denunciation.

Calvino had become Sciascia's second reader; but Maria was his first. The Sciascias lived an intensely domestic life in Caltanissetta, both having taken their teachers' pensions. For Sciascia, tormented by his pupils' poverty and needs and bored by the endless repetition of lessons to which no one listened, it was a great relief. But there was very little money, not least because Sciascia, so frugal in many ways, could not refrain from buying books and etchings. Later, Anna Maria would describe the way the family money ran out before the end of every month. Both girls had money boxes and on the 20th Sciascia would appear in their room and ask for a loan; on the 27th, he paid it back, adding 5,000 lire. 'He called us,' she wrote, 'his little usurers.' His irony 'made every hardship light'.

Maria, influenced by the aunts, continued to make her husband the very centre of her existence: the little house in Caltanissetta revolved around his habits and his wishes. Kind but tenacious, saying little and never complaining, she spent her days reading, seeming to prefer life in the shadows. Nica continued to cook. There was never a cross word. Conscious of his own need for peace and solitude, *'una serenità familiare'* – family serenity – Sciascia felt no impulse to describe it or indeed to refer to it at all. 'The family,' he told an interviewer, 'is neither a problem nor a source of inspiration.' It was simply there.

He was, however, extremely protective of his daughters, took them everywhere with him and kept watch over their friends. When boys rang up, he said that the girls were out. As she grew up, Anna Maria went on fretting about her own inadequacy. It was a house of silence, still marked by Peppino's suicide and Pasquale's tormented end.

Since *La Noce* had neither electricity nor water, and the Sciascias had grown used to greater comfort, they were spending less time there. But a neighbour who was a builder offered to put up a new house for them alongside the two existing ones, now falling into disrepair, and a plain, white, square house went up, with a stone courtyard, wooden shutters and terracotta tiles. Neither Sciascia nor Maria showed any interest in its construction, though Sciascia asked that his study have a view over the hills. When it was ready, their long stays at *La Noce* resumed and Sciascia filled the house with his books and etchings and covered the walls with pictures of the people he needed to have around him: Voltaire, Pirandello and Stendhal. Eucalyptus, umbrella pines and almond trees surrounded the house and in the summer you could smell the tomatoes ripening in the sun and then the scent of them boiling as Nica turned them into sauces. Neither Sciascia nor Maria could drive, so friends took it in turns to drive them in and out of Racalmuto. Sciascia, who barely drank, decided to make his own wine; he called it Regalpetra. When friends came, the aunts hovered, in their dark clothes, saying nothing. The publisher Elvira Sellerio's daughter Olivia always remembered long hot Sundays at La Noce when she was growing up, with Sciascia teaching the children how to shoot with an airgun at a target and long meals around a table under the trees.

Sciascia had been slightly bitter about the reception of *The Day of the Owl*. He complained that it had been too successful as a novel and had not served any 'real social or political' purpose. Despite his and Dolci's insistence – and that of a plethora of younger commentators – Sicilians proved extremely reluctant to see anything but a peculiarly Sicilian way of doing things in the criminal workings of the Mafia. Questioned one day about the Mafia wars that had broken out in Palermo's Acquasanta fruit and vegetable market, Giuseppe Alessi, President of the Region, asked what else could be expected from a country as poor and backward as Sicily. And was it so very different from the north of Italy, where people manipulated the stock market? Reality was kept effectively at bay by the Sicilian deputies who owed their positions to votes delivered by the Mafia and who continued to tell the Parliament in Rome that the organisation was a 'literary chimera' in the minds of the Communists.

But the murders were piling up. Palermo was becoming a city at war. In 1962, in the teeth of considerable opposition from the Christian Democrats and the far right, and in part in response to repeated calls by the Socialists and the Communists for something to be done, a parliamentary commission into the Mafia had finally been set up. It was based in Rome, with fifteen senators and fifteen deputies serving as commissioners; its brief was to 'suppress the manifestations' of the Mafia and 'eliminate its causes'. As if to underscore its importance, soon after, at Ciaculli, not far from Palermo, seven policemen lost their lives when examining an abandoned car which turned out to be full of dynamite. A wave of arrests followed, bringing to the fore a woman called Rosa Messina, the first to challenge the code of silence, who had lost her husband and two sons to the Mafia, the youngest just thirteen. Rosa talked to the police; but she would not appear in court to give evidence. The time had not yet come for women to speak out. It was simply too dangerous and, alone, she was too vulnerable and exposed.

In September, the commission presented its first proposals for anti-Mafia laws to the Senate. It would battle on, against huge odds, for the next thirteen years, accumulating a vast number of documents and occasionally helping to bring *mafiosi* to trial. But very few were ever found guilty, contributing to Sciascia's increasing feeling that the State was not just powerless in the face of the Mafia, but complicit. And it was telling that when a group of experts arrived in Sicily to explore possible aid from European banks, they pronounced at length and with disbelief on the primitiveness and poverty they saw but said nothing at all about the Mafia. When a survey was carried out asking Italians what they knew about the Mafia, a third said that they had never heard of it and another third that they were familiar with the word but had no idea what it meant.

Sciascia himself was pressing on, repeating to everyone who asked him that his plan was to pin down exactly who a *mafioso* was and what he did. The phone rang constantly with newspaper editors asking for comments and articles, and since the telephone was in the girls' room he frequently dictated his stories sitting on their beds. Somewhat to his surprise, he secured an interview with Don Calò's friend, Don Peppino Genco Russo, the youthful sixty-seven-year-old boss of Mussomeli, nattily dressed and widely consulted as mediator and councillor on all matters. Don Peppino was reputed to achieve law and order 'without squeezing'.

Knowing that there would be no point in tackling the question of the Mafia head-on, Sciascia listened to Don Peppino describe what sounded rather like a mutual aid society among friends; his manner was sly and delicate, his eyes distant and gleaming with 'impenetrable malice'. Don Peppino was the perfect confirmation of Sciascia's character in *The Day of the Owl*, Don Mariano Arena, an embodiment of his times, obliged to speak and act according to his own inner logic, however warped. He told Sciascia, with some complacency, that he carried out many good works, and gave an example. There was an orphan girl, he explained, who had failed to secure the grades she needed to get her degree, and so he visited her professor, who soon saw sense.

'I do only good,' Don Peppino told him. Then he described, 'with icy determination', how he had kept Mussomeli free of banditry: 'I would have shaken the bones of anyone who dared to put a foot wrong.' For this phrase alone, and for the tone in which it was said, Sciascia was pleased with his interview; he recorded that Don Peppino had added that in the world there were the 'strong and the weak, the cunning and the suckers. To succeed you have to be ingenious.' To his embarrassment, Don Peppino asked him to sign a copy of *Gli zii di Sicilia*. Sciascia thought for a moment and wrote: 'For the *zio* of Italy, this book which is against other uncles'. Later he would remark proudly: 'I think I handled that very well.' Both accepted and furtive, occupying a shadowy zone in which things were never what they seemed to be, and pressure was both subtle and unmistakable, the ambiguities of the Mafia delighted him.

Sciascia had asked Don Peppino what he thought about the killing of a police officer called Cataldo Tandoy, shot dead while walking down the street in Agrigento with his wife, a beautiful woman known to be having an affair with a local psychiatrist. Tandoy had been the man who had arrested six *mafiosi* in connection with the murder of Miraglia, Sciascia's model for the victim in *The Day of the Owl*. 'A shocking affair,' Don Peppino said, dismissing it with a wave. Sciascia now took Tandoy's story for the second of his *gialli*. *A ciascuno il suo* – To Each his Own – is the tale of a stubborn, cerebral, innocent man who discovers too much about a local murder and is then no match for the intricate web of *omertà* which surrounds the killers, who have delivered warnings in messages made up from letters cut out of *L'Osservatore Romano*, the Vatican daily newspaper. There is no arrest, no trial and the Mafia is never mentioned. But the novel ends with the marriage between the two culprits – a coming together of *roba*, the religion of wealth in possessions. It is a perfect portrait of the collusive axis between Church, State and Mafia which was now coming to obsess Sciascia. It also introduces a concept dear to Sciascia's heart, that of the *cretino*, the idiot, the man who is unable to perceive the danger of the game being played around him.

When he received the manuscript, Calvino pronounced it superior to *The Day of the Owl* because it was fuller of irony. Sciascia, he told him, was exceptional in creating his 'comedy of characters' and setting them in a context which blended history, literature and society, even if he thought his title too 'Pirandellian'. Published in 1966, his new 'ironical disquisition' sold very well. It was, said Calvino, just like a chessboard with an infinite number of moves, each of which was both 'clever and solid'. On the contrary, Sciascia replied, he was spending his whole time writing 'about Sicily, on Sicily, for Sicily', when in fact everything about him was disintegrating into a desert. He felt bound not to follow other Sicilian writers into exile but to stay and fight. He had written *A ciascuno il suo* with passion – though 'indignation and disdain' were perhaps the better words.

The Church was also in Sciascia's sights. While he was somewhat ambivalent about his own faith, quoting Pascal but saying there was nothing that he precisely believed in, he had always felt very strongly about the hypocrisy of priests without scruples. He had long regarded the religious festivals of his childhood, with their slow, swaying hooded monks and thudding drums, more as pagan theatre than expressions of religion. Sicilian prelates liked to describe Sicily as '*cattolicissima*' but he saw it more as something essentially irreligious and materialistic, very resistant to all mystery or metaphysics. He had been introduced to a young photographer, Ferdinando Scianna, and together they travelled around the island, producing a book of photographs with captions. The Church was outraged by their depiction of a bartering, transactional faith, in which Sicilian Catholics were shown to have 'one candle for the saint and another for the serpent'.

For the twenty-year-old Scianna, Sciascia's company was mesmerising: he felt that he had found his spiritual father. You need, Sciascia told him 'always to tell stories, record the life around you'. Sciascia's taste for polemics was growing. He was on a crusade to tell the truth as he saw it and did not much care what people thought. Deep inside him ran a vein of stubbornness and a strong resistance to forgive. When attacks were made on him, he tried to shield his daughters, and simply cut the offender out of his life.

In 1967, with money coming in steadily from the continuing sales of *The Day of the Owl*, Sciascia decided that the moment had come to move again. He was, he told a friend, in an appalling state of boredom, lack of ideas or any desire to work, all of which

Sciascia and Scianna's friendship lasted until Sciascia's death

contributed to 'a persistent climate of autumn'. His daughters were ready for university. There had been talk of Catania, Messina or Milan, but in the end they moved to Palermo, to a new apartment block surrounded by green gardens some way from the city centre. The aunts were devastated; Angela, weeping constantly, said that it seemed to her treachery. As a first step, Sciascia transferred 10,000 books to his new study; the number gives some idea of his attachment to collecting.

Early in 1968, a serious earthquake struck Belice, a village in the mountains above Racalmuto, and a friend drove him and Maria up to the worst hit area where aftershocks were continuing. It was snowing and very cold. Sciascia wrote an article for *L'Ora*, describing the political shenanigans being played out. In *The New York Times*, to which he was now contributing occasional articles, he described the Italian government as unstable and incompetent, its bureaucracy virtually useless and the funding of the political parties a matter of profound corruption. 'The Italian governing class,' he wrote, must not be allowed to use the earthquake as a smokescreen behind which to hide 'its old guilt with regard to Sicily'. Something in him was becoming more troubled, more accusatory.

8
The *terribiltà* of power

Sciascia did not immediately warm to Palermo. He told Einaudi that he was not quite sure what he would gain 'in human terms' by leaving Caltanissetta, even if it was 'the capital of boredom', except perhaps in the way of work. Once the heart of the *belle époque*, Palermo was now a 'city of forgetting' in which everything was getting steadily worse. A journalist from *L'Ora*, Mauro De Mauro, who came to interview him soon after his arrival, described him as a man 'of a great many thoughts but few words', apparently little pleased either with himself or his work; and essentially timid. Sciascia told his friend Mario La Cava that he found it hard to write in the city: 'I am allergic to the climate ... and even more so to the people.' But, he went on, 'I am still trying to tell the truth, that is to say my truth.' Living in the green and leafy Viale Francesco Scaduto, in what had been the park of the seventeenth-century Villa Sperlinga, with new blocks of apartments sprouting up all around him, made him feel as if he were in a field of giant white mushrooms. When he ventured out into the old city it felt to him like a theatre set, awaiting some 'impossible play'.

Wherever he was, like a small animal marking its territory, Sciascia put his particular mark on his surroundings. He filled his study with books, his collections of the French Enlightenment authors, his Spanish poets, the early Sicilian authors he loved, and he covered his walls right up to the ceiling with his lithographs, etchings and prints. Occasionally he added a watercolour or an oil painting, but he preferred what he called the 'less mendacious' black-and-white. On his desk he placed his Olivetti 22, a bronze art deco lamp, the all-important ashtray and a selection of seals, in silver, stone or terracotta. Voltaire, in a white wig, and Stendhal, round-faced and serious, lay close to hand.

When it came to friends, Sciascia was more drawn to the company of artists than fellow writers. He liked to travel around with them, visit art galleries and antiquarian bookshops, and he happily wrote prefaces for their catalogues. As his friends and relations discovered, he was extremely generous, presenting them with works from his collection if he detected that they loved them as he did.

He had become close to the artist Renato Guttuso, though as with many of his friends, the two men were very different: the 'volcanic' exhibitionist, who lived in a sea of bright colours, always in movement, and the muted, meditative introvert. While Guttuso's world was full of allegory, of fantastical journeys and hallucinating brilliance, Sciascia inhabited lands of subterranean rancour, peopled by small, grieving men and women aware of their own troubled destinies. Guttuso sought the public eye; Sciascia shade, doubt, the small canvas, words picked with infinite care. What bound them together was their shared sense of Sicily. I am becoming 'ever more Sicilian', Guttuso wrote to Sciascia, 'ever more in need of friendship – your friendship'. He painted a portrait of his

Sciascia with Guttuso

friend, trying to capture his ironical expression and the 'piercing stare of his coal-black eyes'.

He made two other new artist friends, the sculptor Emilio Greco and the painter Bruno Caruso, recognising in their work the vast dry landscape of the island, its blinding midsummer light and a 'deep consciousness of place', a shared understanding of '*Sicilianità*', Sicilianness. The visual world had always been central to his writing, and very little that he wrote did not contain at least one reference to a specific painter or a work of art. Neither with literature nor with art did he make allowances for his readers: he simply expected them to possess the same deep culture and learning as himself.

There was no artist more important to him than Antonello da Messina, the fifteenth-century painter and portraitist whose subtly enigmatic expressions, 'pensive, ironical and mocking', seemed to capture the closed, suspicious and knowing essence of Sicilians, who 'liked to contradict themselves and be contradicted'. He loved the slyness of Antonello's subjects, their sensuality, the suggestion that they could solve every problem with their 'dry intellects'. In Antonello's *Portrait of an Unknown Mariner* in Cefalù he thought he could see not only a *mafioso*, but a right-wing as well as a left-wing politician, a peasant, a prince, a baron and a captain – and himself – all 'victims of human ferocity and destiny'. For Sciascia art, like life, like history, reflected a reality mediated by literature and words.

With Calvino and Einaudi, Sciascia said that he had learnt to love the 'elegance and refinement' of an editorial 'utopia'. But Einaudi was based in Milan, which, together with Turin, was the heart of the Italian publishing world, and a chance encounter not long after settling in Palermo opened a new chapter in Sciascia's writing life. He had been introduced to Enzo Sellerio, a much admired photographer and producer of art books, who invited him home to meet his wife Elvira. Enzo was tall, patrician, given to tailored blazers, jeans and striped shirts; Elvira, who was the daughter of a former Prefect and worked for the regional government, was ebullient, handsome, assertive and full of curiosity, quite a different sort of animal from the matrons of Racalmuto. The three of them agreed that what Sicily needed was its own publishing house, to reprint forgotten Sicilian writers, to promote new ones and to try to pin down Sciascia's perennial question of what it meant to be

Sicilian. Elvira gave up her job and put her severance pay into their new venture. They were joined by an anthropologist friend, Antonino Buttitta, and in the afternoons they gathered in the Sellerios' house to plan the launch.

Elvira Sellerio

For the first few months, the men took the floor, usually in a haze of smoke from Sciascia's cigarettes as he lit one from another; Elvira made the coffee. But it was not in her nature to be retiring and soon all decisions were shared, the talk rambling on amid much laughter so that it was hard to tell what was work and what literary gossip. As the afternoon wore on Elvira would make martini cocktails, shaking them like a barman, with contagious cheerfulness, and they sipped on into the evening. She called him Sciascia, never Leonardo. They named their publishing house

Sellerio. Its first publications were folders of art, tied with ribbon; their first actual book a story of poison, Rosario La Duca's *I veleni di Palermo*, which, as Sciascia explained in his foreword, were not the slow and subtle poisons of Palermo life, but those slipped into the Sicilian dishes, with intent to kill. Others followed, many of them part of different series, small, beautiful matching books, all of them chosen because the four editors loved and admired their authors. One of these was a then unknown Gesualdo Bufalino, whose introduction to a collection of old photographs of Sicily Elvira and Sciascia spotted. They asked him whether he did not perhaps have a novel in a drawer somewhere? He said that he hadn't but a year later sent them something that he had secretly been working on since the early 1950s and which they published as the best-selling *The Plague Spreader*, launching him as a hugely successful writer.

It was everything that Sciascia most enjoyed. He helped select the books, foraged for lost authors, sought out engravers and designers, advised on publicity and wrote most of the copy for the jackets, sitting at a desk with his Waterman fountain pen, writing very rapidly, seldom pausing to correct or change a word. This collegiate life pleased him greatly. The Sellerio office became his club, and he was driven there by friends, often pausing at art galleries or antiquarian bookshops along the way. Sometimes he stayed on to help the two Sellerio children with their homework. They found him quiet, gentle but very rigorous and never afraid to contradict their teachers.

Friendship in Sicily, Sciascia was discovering – real friendship – was its own variant of *Sicilianità*: close, intimate, faithful to the bitter end, a 'dialogue of the souls' which allowed for long silences but was subject to bitter jealousy so that at times it felt more like passion than comradeship. It was a thread that permeated everything. As he had learnt with the *zie*, belonging could be suffocating and carried with it extreme difficulty in ever extricating oneself. Letters between friends could sound surprisingly amorous: they started with '*carissimo*' and often ended with '*ti amo*'. Betrayal was unforgivable. Once such a friendship was broken, there was 'no glue strong enough' to mend it. '*Amicizie Siciliane*,' as one writer put it, 'are like love stories. When the friend feels rejected it's like the end of a love affair.' After life as a small-town schoolteacher, it all felt delightful to Sciascia. '*Quaggiù*' – down here – he told a friend, 'we have a decidedly fierce idea of friendship'.

Sicily was changing, at great speed. A new political grouping, a junta of Communists, Socialists, monarchists, members of the neo-Fascist Movimento Sociale Italiano and dissident Christian Democrats, backed by groups of powerful northern industrialists, had seen the Presidency of the Region conferred on a former Christian Democrat deputy, Silvio Milazzo, at first greeted as a popular, defiant rebel, free of any Mafia taint. Regarded as a protest against Rome's failed promises of autonomy, what became known as *Operazione Milazzo* lasted sixteen months, with three separate coalition governments, before the Christian Democrats lured the voters back. For a while, Milazzo did push through development, increase public spending and promote tourism. But the group's very composition as an alliance between left and right made it vulnerable, and the Mafia, ever on the lookout for new opportunities, did not hesitate to exploit every loophole. In theory, Sciascia should have been delighted to see the Christian Democrats defeated by what looked like popular rebellion. But he was, down to his very bones, opposed to 'accommodations' and hated everything that Milazzo represented. It was another example of everything changing in order for nothing to change. He was increasingly despondent, saying that Sicily was becoming a metaphor for the 'continuous defeat of reason, an Enlightenment without light, without hope', trapped in eternal immobility. Sicilians seemed to him depressingly capable of enduring an enormous amount of suffering.

By the early 1960s, the 'sack of Palermo' was well under way. The Mafia, as so subtly portrayed in *The Day of the Owl*, had always been attuned to the political world; what it now perceived was how readily it could be manipulated in order to produce great wealth. With the return to power of the Christian Democrats, much pushed by Rome, where the ruling party under Amintore Fanfani depended heavily on the Sicilian vote, two men in Palermo were rising fast. One was the silver-haired, nattily dressed Salvatore Lima, who became mayor; the other Vito Ciancimino, a barber's son from Corleone, who took over as assessor of public works. Lima was quickly dubbed 'the viceroy of Sicily'. Between them, building up a clientele based on the control of municipal and regional bodies, playing contractors off against each other, squirrelling away and doling out public money, enriching themselves and their friends, the two men issued 4,025 building licences; 80 per cent of them went to just five bidders. As Sciascia had warned, the Mafia had discovered the cities.

Many of the people who declared themselves to be builders were in fact shoemakers, shopkeepers, mechanics and porters, with no training in construction but able to raise funds, sometimes through protection rackets. The Christian Democrats, firmly in control of every aspect of Sicily's bureaucracy, were ruthless, while Giulio Andreotti, having already served as Minister of the Interior and of the Treasury and founder of the right-wing faction of the Christian Democrats, courted their votes, on the surface professing himself little interested in their actions, provided they delivered the numbers. Palermo was on a vast, corrupt, unregulated spending spree. Jungles of cement spread unchecked across the historic city centre, swallowing up elegant but bombed-out and decaying palazzi and monuments. Provision for public housing, landscaping, parks or services was negligible. In his report on Palermo, Danilo Dolci had identified 3,000 families living in cellars and holes in the ground. The only difference by the time the Sciascias arrived was that they had been joined by thousands of destitute people driven from the land and now seeking work in the new property boom. They lived and slept on streets unchanged from the Middle Ages, which flooded when it rained. Typhoid was rife; few of their children went to school. Two hundred yards from Palermo's immense, ornate cathedral, 498 people shared 118 rooms.

In Palermo, Cardinal Ernesto Ruffini had just retired after a twenty-year rule of 'religious magnificence', wilfully blind to the Mafia to the end. Asked by a journalist, Ruffini famously exclaimed: 'Mafia? As far as I know, it's the name of a washing powder.' He had earlier brushed off the charges of extortion against the monks at Mazzarino as a 'Socialist-Communist and Masonic plot'.

Both Guttuso and Sciascia's young photographer friend, Ferdinando Scianna, came from Bagheria, the once delightful suburb of orange and lemon groves, created by rich Palermitani in the seventeenth century and where the Prince of Palagonia had built a villa full of deformed and grotesque sculptures, described by Goethe as a 'lunatic asylum'. In Bagheria, the sackers were at work smashing fountains and villas to make way for roads and modern developments. Bagheria had become a byword for backhanders.

The Mafia had always found ways to get rich; now they planned to get richer. By warning of the dangers of Communism and calling on the Church for support, politicians and local councillors were able to justify every corrupt deal and compromise. 'The ills that you find,' wrote a reporter from *L'Unità*, 'are always worse than you expected.' The Mafia itself remained a black hole, seldom mentioned: it was far more comfortable simply to pretend that it did not exist. Even for those who lived in its midst, it remained largely invisible. As the writer Dacia Maraini said: it was '*roba per turisti*', tales with which to regale foreign visitors.

Sciascia had hated Milazzo but he hated the Christian Democrats even more. It is impossible to understand him without understanding the depth of his hatred for this overweening, dogmatic party, which seemed to him devoid of all the Christian charity it professed. As he said, and repeated, 'a writer should always be able to say that the politics in which he is involved are ethical. It would be wonderful if everyone could say the same. But at the very least, writers must say it.' Each work of Sciascia's is in some sense political. One of his strongest beliefs was that people had founding moments of consciousness and that his had come with the fall of Fascism and the birth of Italy as a democratic state. With the passing years he remained as fervently committed to the left, and as fervently opposed to party politics.

The writers, academics and sociologists who had gathered at Danilo Dolci's congress to debate the causes of Sicily's ills continued to meet and talk. The offices of *L'Ora*, on the first floor of an old palazzo in Piazzale Napoli, became a centre for them and for the many visiting journalists and left-wing politicians eager to discuss Sicily's enduring anachronisms. Nisticò, though a somewhat dour and severe Calabrian Communist, was an exceptional editor, mentoring young reporters and inviting people he respected to write for him, whatever their politics, though what all shared was a visceral dislike of the ruling Christian Democrats and a desire to understand why Sicilians remained so sceptical, so self-destructive, so incapable of promoting an alternative to the Mafia. Among its supporters, the paper was known for its crusades against injustice, its celebration of men who stood up for truth and justice. The late 1960s was its golden age.

Now that he was settled in Palermo, Nisticò asked Sciascia to work for the paper in any way he chose. Knowing him to be short of money now that he had given up teaching, he suggested that he join the staff, but Sciascia was reluctant to embark on the apprenticeship and exams that the profession of journalist in Italy demanded. Though he took no formal part in the daily production of the paper and refused a desk of his own, he went to its crammed and untidy offices most late afternoons to join its meetings. It became his other club, like the Sellerio offices an oasis of culture and sanity in a city of frenzied expansion. Punctual, reticent, hesitant, ready to take part in any debate or provide an article or opinion if one were needed, he would arrive silently, a bit hunched up, as if wanting to remain invisible, 'small, fragile with his high forehead and pale face permanently enveloped in smoke from his cigarettes'.

Sometimes he said nothing but when he returned next day he would be carrying a sheet of paper, neatly folded in four, and murmuring, 'I hope this might work.' When *L'Ora* published a number of comic spoofs, Sciascia contributed a review of a new edition of Diderot's *Encyclopédie*, in 144 volumes. Even as Lima and Ciancimino hacked away at the very fabric of the old city, *L'Ora* promoted art festivals and theatre, books and music. Sciascia, Guttuso and Caruso lent their names willingly to new projects. As Michele Perreira, another contributor to the paper, observed, Sciascia was among those who 'hunted down cultural values as an obsession'. He had not softened his views on James Joyce, claiming in a review that *Ulysses* lacked the 'grace of God and the grace of poetry', and that Joyce's language was indecipherable, addressed only to himself and to the mutterings of Babel. Ireland, he said, was a 'peripheral' island, unlike Sicily, and he declared that he was not much interested in Yeats or Beckett either. As with Pasolini's forays into the culture of violence, he found Joyce's linguistic outpouring excessive, even embarrassing. Such things were best kept to oneself.

One of *L'Ora*'s best, most alert, investigative journalists was Mauro De Mauro, who had interviewed Sciascia on his arrival in Palermo, describing him as introverted and modest, and so punctual and precise as to be almost 'Teutonic'. De Mauro was a strange figure, prickly and irascible when he felt overlooked but generous and loved by his friends. He was dark, tall, his nose slightly disfigured by a mysterious accident. A former Fascist who had served with the infamous Decima Mas brigade in the war, he had put Fascism behind him and in 1947 settled in Palermo where his brother Tullio, a gifted linguistician, lived. The Sciascias and the De Mauros were friends. De Mauro was helping Francesco Rosi put together a film about Enrico Mattei, the founder and head of the largest state industry ENI, who had died some years before when a bomb had been put on his plane, apparently by the Mafia, at the airport in Catania. De Mauro had informers everywhere, but kept them to himself. His friends called him a '*cronista di nero*' – a reporter of the dark. He loved scoops.

One day De Mauro went to call on Sciascia. He was in an excitable mood, but there were other people present and Sciascia barely took heed when De Mauro told him that he was on to a story that would certainly win him many prizes. A few days later, De Mauro disappeared.

He had been on his way home that evening, having bought a bottle of whisky, coffee and cigarettes at a nearby shop, and his daughter and her fiancé had seen him get out of his BMW. After he failed to appear in the house, she went out into the street to look for him and heard a voice say 'Let's go' before his BMW drove off. In the fading light, she thought she saw the shadows of two or three other men with her father in the car. When he did not return, journalists from *L'Ora* joined the police to search for him. The headline in the paper, in very large type, was 'Help us'. The BMW turned up in a street not far away. Of De Mauro himself there was no trace. One of the results of the Mafia wars was that Sicilians had become extremely nervous about finding themselves in any way drawn into unexplained events. Though De Mauro's colleagues continued to follow up every possible lead, former friends kept their distance, avoiding all contact and going to some lengths to demonstrate that they knew nothing. De Mauro's brother Tullio would always remember that, in the days that followed the kidnapping, Sciascia went out of his way to be especially friendly.

One of the most dogged, determined investigators was a policeman called Boris Giuliano, a man very much in the same mode as

Sciascia's Captain Bellodi. He was making a name for himself for the zeal with which he was pursuing the Mafia, and a colleague overheard him, 'somewhere between rage and depression', swearing that he would never give up on the search for De Mauro. One of the many leads he was following up was the link between the Mafia and Nino and Ignazio Salvo, two cousins who were deep in Palermo local politics; another was the rumour that a right-wing coup was being planned in Rome. Sciascia met and liked Giuliano, who helped him decipher a mysterious case that he was thinking of writing about. He was at work on a new version of a nineteenth-century play by Giuseppe Rizzotto set in a prison full of *mafiosi*, a perfect vehicle for his apprehensions about the current state of Palermo.

De Mauro's disappearance, which most people put down to his possible revelations about Mattei, shocked and unnerved his colleagues, all of them now conscious of the Mafia all about them. He was the first journalist to vanish and it seemed to them, as it did to Sciascia, to mark a new step in boldness and indifference to public reaction; they feared his kidnapping would not be the last. It did not stop them – nor did it stop Sciascia – in their determination to keep digging and documenting Palermo's politicians and their links to the Mafia; but it made them understandably wary.

At the heart of everything that Sciascia ever wrote lay the idea of justice. He had wanted it for his pupils and his incorruptible Captain Bellodi believed in the law and a 'just justice' but had no faith in the State or the judiciary to deliver it. 'Everything,' Sciascia declared, 'is linked, for me, to the question of justice, in which the problems of liberty, human dignity and respect of man are tied up.' It drew him close to Manzoni, whom he considered the Italian writer nearest to the French Enlightenment and whose stories of persecution, false accusations and execution seemed to him models of what injustice meant. Sciascia's characters are hungry for justice, but very rarely get it. And, as he grew older, so the idea of justice and injustice came to consume him.

The Day of the Owl, *Le parrocchie di Regalpetra* and the *Fables* were all underpinned by this conviction that while the true and natural sense of justice must find expression in respect for the laws 'used with precision', the actual law as wielded by the weak Italian State was something arbitrary, a show of strength, violence and cruelty. *'Garantismo'* – the rights of the accused – a word often used pejoratively as a blinkered response to criminals, was for Sciascia unreservedly necessary and good, 'a respect of the rules, of the law and of the constitution'. One of the most quoted passages in *The Day of the Owl* comes when Bellodi finds himself reflecting that the methods used by the Prefect Mori in the 1920s against the Mafia – the suspension of constitutional guarantees – might indeed lead to the capture of the culprits; but then concludes that no one, in any circumstances, must put himself above the law. 'For the greater good' can never be used to justify illegality by the State, for it will only encourage illegality in its citizens.

Not surprising, then, that what Sciascia called the *'terribiltà'* of power coincided with the *'terribiltà'* of justice, or that he was repelled and horrified by torture and the death penalty. In a new preface he wrote for Manzoni's *La Storia della colonna infame*, his appendix to *The Betrothed*, he repeated that it was an illusion to think that torture and Fascism were things of the past. 'Torture is still with us, and Fascism is always there.' As a boy, hearing of the execution of Michele Schirru for his plan to assassinate Mussolini, he had been disgusted by the idea of 'death handed out by a sentence'. He likened Manzoni's 'honest' judges who sent falsely accused plague spreaders to their deaths to the Nazi 'bureaucrats of evil', who lived family lives by day and tortured by night.

In a world as equivocal as Sicily, in which Mafia and family were perceived as legal arbiters above the State, in which corruption had contaminated the very fabric of authority, no one, and especially no writer, could be allowed to waver. Sciascia became, as he admitted, obsessed, and his obsession became a crusade. He worried ceaselessly about how judges judge, about the dignity of the accused, about evidence and sentencing, the presumption of innocence, the crucial responsibility of magistrates and the fact that justice in Italy had been allowed to degenerate. It would lead him in painful, and often lonely, directions.

Storytelling, he had come to feel, was not an end in itself: it was justice. It also had to be an assertion of intellectual commitment – an *'impegno'* – towards society. In his quest for justice, a writer needed to abandon the traditional role of reporter and engage in an exchange of ideas. He had to dig down to find the truth, offer alternative explanations, ask uncomfortable questions, try to remedy the Sicilian acceptance that there was one law for the poor and another for the rich and that the law itself was infinitely malleable. Literature was there to 'deliver justice', especially in the case of historical events too quickly archived. He called himself an 'impure' narrator, wanting to 'intervene directly in the events I describe'. Literature was a 'breviary' for a lay religion offering a different and more human justice. But it had to be good literature, readable, well written, gripping.

'History, for me,' Sciascia once told an interviewer, 'is a kind of detective thriller.' He now had a historical novel in mind, one that would combine his feelings about justice and torture while taking him deep into Sicily's overlapping pasts.

Before settling in Palermo, Sciascia had come up with the story of a Maltese chaplain, Don Giuseppe del Vella, who, in an eighteenth-century Sicily still under the rule of the Bourbons, had embarked on a 'great deception'. He had forged an Arab Codex, inadvertently brought from the Escorial to Palermo and purporting to show a new picture of the Muslims in Sicily. With immense patience and skill, using coloured inks and pastes, gold leaf and papers of different weights, and dipping in and out of real history, Don Vella manages to fool not only his clerical superiors, but also the Viceroy, Domenico Caracciolo. His forgery takes place against the backdrop of a Jacobin plot involving a lawyer, Di Blasi, who is eventually identified, tortured and executed. Led to his torture, Di Blasi thinks: 'This should not happen to a man.'

Il Consiglio d'Egitto – *The Council of Egypt* – a remarkable portrait of Palermo under the Bourbons, with its feuds and cabals and battles between the Curia in Rome and the Kingdom of Sicily, was Sciascia's first and very pleasurable foray into the archives. With nods to Montesquieu and Diderot, he foraged in works on Malta, on the clothes and costumes and food of the eighteenth century, on the lives of the Spanish viceroys and envoys. Since the only possible conclusion in Sicily is one of failure, and all heroes are ultimately defeated, Di Blasi goes to the stake and Caracciolo, an enlightened viceroy who abolished the Inquisition in Sicily, is recalled, knowing that all his reforms diminishing the power of the barons will be overturned immediately. Sciascia's moral endings are seldom ambiguous. Here, history is nothing but a 'perverse game played by powerful people in a setting of immutable social structures', torture is endemic to Sicilian life, as is ignorance, bad faith, resignation and the tendency to be duped. There are battles that are never won: 'the past, its errors, its ills, never go away: we have continually to live them and judge them in the present'. Caracciolo, like Sciascia himself, muses: 'What is it to be Sicilian?' On reading the manuscript, Vittorini wrote to Sciascia that his book was filled with 'Goya-like colours'. Many readers thought it his most important book.

Soon after the publication of *Il Consiglio d'Egitto* in 1963, Calvino wrote to Sciascia to urge him to dig deeper into the 'tragic-baroque-grotesque' perversions of Sicily's history. Sciascia had been reading the Argentinian Jorge Luis Borges's *Inquisiciones*, short, erudite meditations, and was beginning to think of a new kind of writing, the *'inchiesta'* or short investigation into a historical event that had never been properly understood.

He intended to use it to throw light on the present, what Borges called 'stories without fiction, fiction without stories'. Sciascia planned to begin with investigations into episodes of injustice in Sicily's past, in which the truth had been obscured by the manipulation of witnesses, the inaccuracy of documents, reliance on contradictory evidence and lawyers swayed by self-interest.

Straddling history, fiction and essay, Sciascia's *inchieste* were to be adventures of the mind, with himself as narrator-investigator, digging, sifting, deciphering, conscious always that there was no such thing as definitive truth. These *inchieste* – none longer than sixty or seventy pages – would invite readers to join him in a labyrinth in which everything is deceptive, fleeting and multifaceted and where the investigator has no choice but to press on, through the dense web of secrecy and mendacity, evaluating every clue afresh. Sciascia's task, as he saw it, was to bring his curiosity to bear on the dark corners, and to persist, even if at the end there was no answer, no new truth, but simply an enigma, reframed. Doubt was to be his guide.

Sciascia, wrote one critic, was becoming a sulphur miner himself, digging into the subsoil of history in order to get at 'the hidden minerals' of Sicily's soul, which had crystallised over the years into the island's collective consciousness. If the roots of modern Sicily's sclerotic, Mafia-ridden, infinitely troubled present were anchored in its history, then, so Sciascia's thinking went, a forensic excavation of miscarriages of justice, abuse of power and distortion of facts might help free Sicilians to face a more realistic and honest future. Literature would provide the memory of falsehood. Manzoni had chosen to paint on large canvases. Sciascia would take small ones, minute, long-forgotten incidents, and by presenting alternative narratives, restore justice to the persecuted.

Drawn instinctively to rebels, to the defeated and to heretics, Sciascia turned to the Inquisition for his first *inchiesta*: *Morte dell'Inquisitore*.

The Aragonese had brought the Inquisition to Sicily, where it ran from 1487 to 1782, during which time the Jews were expelled and 234 people handed over to the secular authorities and burnt at the stake. One of these was Fra Diego La Matina from Racalmuto, where the Holy Office employed eight investigators; Fra Diego was the second local man to fall into its clutches, accused of heresy, and he had spent some time hidden in a cave on the edge of the village. Sciascia gained entry into the now abandoned Palazzo Steri in Palermo, the former prison and headquarters of the Holy Office, where supposed heretics were interrogated. It was in the Steri that Fra Diego, anticipating further torture, had used his handcuffs to break the skull of his tormentor, the Inquisitor Don Juan Lopez de Cisneros, early in April 1657. Sentenced to be burnt alive, he was taken by cart, pelted with mud by people lining the roads, to the square by the Palazzo Steri where Palermo's Inquisitors were seated on a high dais. Trumpets sounded. 'In this atmosphere of *festa*,' wrote Sciascia, 'are organised the most sumptuous ceremonies of cruelty.'

Fra Diego, staunch, brave, was the perfect subject for Sciascia. His story involved fanaticism, an Inquisitor who personified cruelty, an enigmatic victim and a great deal of delving. In 1906 the historian Pitrè had visited the Steri and, using a knife and chisel, uncovered what he called a 'palimpsest' of graffiti on the walls of the cells occupied by the condemned men. He found prayers, laments, verses, protestations of innocence, written in Sicilian dialect, Italian, Latin, English and even Hebrew and Arabic, and these were now seen and examined by Sciascia. In the archives he also unearthed wills, testimonies, memoirs and letters. Fra Diego's tale was a clear example of the *terribiltà* of power and oppression, and it gave Sciascia the chance to speculate and invent, explore ethical dilemmas and use morality and critical reasoning as weapons with which to judge and condemn fanaticism. It was, he said, not just a perfect example of the fundamental irreligiosity of the Sicilians, but of the realpolitik of the Bourbons, and their use of informers and spies.

Just what Fra Diego's heresy had been was never explained. *Morte dell'Inquisitore* became Sciascia's favourite book: all the others, once finished, he put aside and forgot. The very incompleteness of this *inchiesta* kept it alive in his mind and all his life he would keep hoping to find fresh clues. Fra Diego had been a 'martyr saint' who upheld 'the dignity of man'. Sciascia dedicated the book to the Racalmutesi, dead and alive, who, like Fra Diego, were inflexible, dignified and able to tolerate suffering and sacrifice. And he had found a new concept, that of the man of *'tenace concetto'*, tenacious and unyielding, who held to his beliefs against every attack, the kind of man, in short, he most admired.

Sciascia was now in his early fifties, but he looked older; his face was lined and he walked with a slight stoop. When writing, he spent the mornings at his desk in the study that acted as sitting room when visitors came to call in the afternoons. He liked to complete two pages each day, set them aside, return to them next morning, reconsider them and write two more. He smoked steadily as he worked. Above the window behind him was an engraving of the Inquisition, a long procession of people accompanying a heretic to the stake. Over his head hung an art deco chandelier, with lights shaped like flowers.

His collections were growing all the time. There was a bookcase almost completely filled with Stendhal and new acquisitions of Graham Greene, whom he considered one of the finest writers of his time, and illustrated books by Arthur Rackham. Books occupied every available space, and when that ran out they were put into cupboards and sideboards. Pictures by his friends Caruso and Guttuso vied for space on the packed walls with a Goya etching and some drawings Picasso had done of Vuillard. The post that poured in every day lived briefly on the desk; when the pile grew too high, it moved to the sofa; then, much of it unopened, to behind the books.

Angela, the aunt who had introduced him to the evils of Fascism and the murder of Matteotti, had recently died, but Nica and Maria Concetta lived on in the house in Racalmuto. Sciascia continued to thrive on domesticity. 'The fact is,' he told an interviewer, 'I like things not changing. I want habit, tranquillity, restful things.' Though he would later join the campaign for divorce in Italy, marriage was what he believed in. As a writer, he said, it gave him an essential 'sense of serenity'. Maria, ever present, ever in the background, his first reader, was exactly the person he needed.

Nica with Genoveffa

And his fame was growing. When Primo Levi was looking for signatures to a letter he wanted to send to President Johnson about Vietnam, a war that 'contaminates the entire human species', turning the US into a 'land of jailors', he asked Sciascia for his support. Sciascia replied that he had an 'invincible' repugnance about addressing anything at all to Johnson; it would be as if, he wrote, he were asking the head of the Mafia for help in defeating the Mafia itself. In *Le Monde* a whole page had been devoted to an admiring profile of his work and the French sales of his books were climbing rapidly. Though he was taking longer to win readers in the Anglo-Saxon world, the *TLS*, reviewing his short stories, described their author, an 'elegant and witty writer', as making 'erudite raids on Sicilian history' with tantalising moral implications. *To Each his Own* was praised for its spiciness, perfect for 'gourmets with jaded taste buds'. Sciascia had acquired one devoted critic in Herbert Mitgang in *The New York Times*, who called one of his books 'gemlike' and he would soon find another in Gore Vidal, who said that Sciascia was the 'perfect Virgil' to lead American writers along the path to Sicilian literature. Requests for translations began to pour in.

An interviewer asked Sciascia why he wrote. 'Because I could not do without it,' he answered. 'It's the way I live.' Writing was for him a privilege, a vocation, a joy, as for Montaigne, and a 'state of grace', and he liked to quote Stendhal's words: 'I write, I console myself, I feel happy.' His best books, Sciascia thought, were those he wrote most happily, sitting at his desk at *La Noce*.

He was not at his best at images, but he was an exceptional writer of words, of dialogue, digressions and allusions, and he had a strong authorial voice. He was never a humorous writer, saying of himself that he was not *'spiritoso'* – witty – but he was a superb master of irony, for which he had to thank the Sicilians, who had it in their bones. Irony was his way of portraying reality and of unmasking impostors and hypocrites. And his prose was exceptionally incisive, as if, people said, it had been sculpted out of a hard rock. Since nothing was ever quite what it seemed to be, only thoughts in their most perfectly limpid form could hope to establish the true state of the world. 'I prefer to lose readers,' he said, 'than to fool them.' He wanted them to be certain, always, that they would get from him 'the truth, the bitter truth'. Both extremely beautiful and also terrifying, truth could in the end be delivered only by literature. Writers had to 'speak for mankind' and deliver it. If his first duty to the world was as a teller of truth, his second was to do it well. 'A thing is true,' he wrote, 'only if it is said well.' Books had to entertain, and to do so they had to be 'constructed', much as houses were: they needed to be inhabitable, and entice readers in. Books that had no readers had not been properly built.

Sciascia was now regularly being described as a pessimist. Brancati

A SICILIAN MAN

had spoken of Sicily as a place of 'suffering, nostalgia, boredom, courage, fear of death', which, however you chose to look at it, was inevitably what you were forced to come back to. Sciascia agreed with this and it was true that with time his mood was growing darker. He had come to think that what allowed Sicilians to survive at all was that life was like an iceberg, most of it submerged and unknown; and that where reality is so ambiguous and elusive, where crimes are conspiracies, priests rapacious and ungodly, and investigators themselves turn out to be victims or murderers, there is little consolation. But he believed passionately in fighting, in not giving up. 'I believe,' he said, 'that the very act of writing is essentially an optimistic one.'

He liked to quote Flannery O'Connor when he said that it was not enough to simply say no: 'You have to act no.' His goal now, as he saw it, was to expose facile credence, shed light on immoral actions and unjust justice and he would do so unflinchingly, wherever it led him. Pirandello had made him see reality in the refraction of mirrors; Montaigne had introduced him to benign scepticism, and Voltaire to the light of reason. But it was Manzoni who had made him see writing as a moral act. Sciascia described it as *'fermezza civile'*, resolve, never evading your civic duty. Like the Enlightenment philosophers, he planned to use his inexhaustible curiosity to call 'monstrous power' to account, painting on a small canvas, selecting small events to illuminate the larger world, drawing simplicity out of complexity. When people called him a prophet, warning of things that would soon come to pass, he shied away. He was, he said, simply a man who chose to look, while others turned their backs.

9
Tweaking the tiger's tail

On 12 December 1969 a bomb exploded in a bank in Milan's Piazza Fontana. Sixteen people died and eighty-eight were wounded. That same day, a similar bomb went off in Rome, but there were no casualties. Members of far-left and anarchist groups were rounded up and one, an anarchist train driver called Giuseppe Pinelli, fell to his death from the windows of a police headquarters. In the investigations that followed, it emerged that the culprits were not anarchists but neo-Fascists, with links to the Italian secret services. One of the legacies of Italy's eighteen months of civil war between Fascists and partisans during 1944 and 1945 was a plethora of rivalrous far-right nationalists and former Fascists, brought together by a fear of Communism, and closely in touch with the United States. The openly neo-Fascist MSI, Movimento Sociale Italiano, formed in 1948, had never abandoned its explicit goal of a return to the past and its moral, civil, religious and military values. Now, in the wake of the bombings, it was discovered that a 'strategy of terror' had been planned, on the model of Greece, which had brought the colonels to power in 1967.

A year later, in December 1970, an attempted coup by Prince Giulio Valerio Borghese, veteran leader of a Fascist squad, was foiled but not before the plotters had occupied the Ministry of the Interior in Rome for several hours. Borghese was the former commander of the Decima Flottiglia Motoscafi Armati Siluranti – usually known as Decima Mas – a naval flotilla, a close supporter of Mussolini and had fought against the partisans alongside the Germans. Saved from execution at the end of the war, he had been spirited out of Milan by the Americans, in a US military uniform. Dreaming of an alternative to a constitutional republic, organised along military lines, and vowing to defeat the 'Bolshevik' menace, as well as immorality and drug addiction, he had gathered around him other ardent former Fascists. The plotters, calling for a new 'aristocratic and heroic' concept of life, had planned to kidnap the President, Giuseppe Saragat. De Mauro had been on the right track. Borghese managed to flee to Spain. The decade of terror, when Italy seemed at war with itself, was now in full swing. No other Western democracy would see the same degree of violence, the same pervasive sense of subversion against accepted authority, or the same number of bombings, the right and the left blaming each other and everyone suspicious of everyone else.

On the far right, the violence took the form of attacks on opposition party headquarters, trade union offices and public buildings; Molotov cocktails were thrown and bombs exploded on trains and in crowded streets. Groups formed, fell apart, formed again, plotting and arguing, talking of a new Europe free of the Bolsheviks. With the strongest Communist Party in the West, Italy had become a political arena in which secrecy, links and deals proliferated and where, 'for reasons of State', the far right regarded every means as justified.

On the far left, the student movement took shape in Pisa when, in February 1967, students occupied the law faculty in the Palazzo della Sapienza. Unlike France, with its May 1968 uprising which lasted seven weeks, student protest in Italy spread and continued, feeding on the Vietnam War and the dire need for educational reform, promised, but never delivered. The extra-parliamentary left, uniting workers and students, formed small Marxist–Leninist groups, some of them financed by Moscow, preaching revolution and demanding better conditions for workers – also promised and never delivered – and the 'liberation of the proletariat'. One of these was Lotta Continua, which campaigned for better pay and better conditions; but it lay at the moderate end. Others were not so restrained.

In August 1970, Renato Curcio and his wife Margherita Cagol founded what they called the *Brigate Rosse*, the Red Brigades, to challenge the 'violence of power'. They had met as Marxist students of sociology and philosophy at the University of Trento, one of almost half of all Italian universities where students were clamouring for reform. Their first 'action' was to throw a Molotov cocktail into the garage of an industrialist called Giuseppe Leoni. Street fights and occupations followed. Two years later, seeing how little they were achieving, they decided to carry out their first kidnapping, capturing the director of Siemens, Idalgo Macchiarini, and threatening him with a revolver, but then deciding that releasing him served their cause better. When they discovered that his gold watch had fallen off in their van, they posted it to a press agency, saying that it was not their policy to steal what belonged to others. But these were early days, and the seeds of armed rebellion were only just being sown.

The 'economic miracle', the golden age in Italy for international trade and mass production, had seen much of the textile industry replaced by factories turning out motor cars and dishwashers. Agricultural workers left their farms in Southern Italy and emigrated north to the industrial triangle of Milan, Turin and Genoa, where some joined in the protests. In Sicily, factory workers had become isolated in the huge new petrochemical and steel plants along the eastern coast around Augusta; they took part in the turmoil, but in a more muted way.

In Rome, the ruling Christian Democrats, one government succeeding another, had offered an opening to the left, an '*apertura a sinistra*', or coalition. The master tactician Prime Minister Aldo Moro, it was said, was never happier than when mediating between conflicting interests in a way that resulted in immobility. 'It is not always right to throw light on hidden things,' Moro had once said. 'Sometimes it is better, on the contrary, to keep them shrouded.' Sciascia's loathing of the Christian Democrats had increased and he feared any compromise with the left, warning that it would only lead to the silencing of all proper political opposition. Watching with dismay Rome's apparent drift towards ineffectual coalitions, ever vigilant whenever he perceived a decline in morality and ideology, he talked about a 'monstrous power' engulfing everything about him. Literature was his 'sword thrust'. He would write another *giallo*, for, as he had discovered, *gialli*, with their vast sales, were an excellent vehicle for his exposés of abuses of power. This time his target was to be nothing less than the Italian State itself.

Captain Bellodi had been an essentially good man, honest, scrupulous, averse to violence. As Sciascia grew older and more disenchanted, his good men became more ambiguous, less willing to sit by and watch evil triumph. In *Il contesto*, *Equal Danger*, a police detective called Rogas is told to investigate the unexplained death of a judge. While he does so, a second judge is murdered and then another and another. People in the government and the magistrature grow agitated. Rogas identifies the killer as a chemist called Cres, who believes himself to be the victim of judicial error. His superiors, however, find it more convenient to lay the blame at the feet of a shadowy group of left-wing dissidents, the Partito Rivoluzionario Italiano. Finding himself ensnared in a confusing vortex in which government and opposition have become indistinguishable, Rogas allows Cres to kill his last victim, and is then executed himself by the police.

This new book, Sciascia explained, was set in an imaginary country, one in which principles were routinely ignored, ideology was reduced to party games and only 'power for the sake of power' counted. This unnamed place, like Hamlet's Denmark, is rotten to its core, a state held captive by those who represent it. But one could, of course, 'think of Italy, or even Sicily'. As his friend Guttuso put it, 'even when what I am painting is an apple, there is Sicily in it'. His story was, Sciascia said, an apologia for an ever more 'degraded and impenetrable power', which might loosely be called '*mafioso*'. Rogas has principles 'in a country where almost no one else had'. As Sciascia has his fictitious Minister for the Interior say about his own party: it had 'misgoverned for thirty years' and would now 'misgovern better', with the revolutionary party.

Uncharacteristically, Sciascia had some trouble writing his book. He complained that he could not find the 'lightness' of tone he needed for the troubled political times, and he feared that readers would fail to see that it was a parody fashioned with irony. He started and stopped, grew bored, dallied, became interested in other things, then took time off to write another *inchiesta*, about an eight-year stand-off between the Bishop of Lipari and the Spanish Viceroy at the beginning of the eighteenth century. When the manuscript of his *giallo* was finally ready, he suggested to Einaudi that it might perhaps be better not to publish it at all. 'I started to write it with enjoyment,' he told an interviewer, 'but by the end I was no longer enjoying myself.' It was a terrible position for a man wedded to Montaigne's dictum of doing nothing without joy.

Calvino's reaction – that the novel was entertaining and fascinating – somewhat reassured him. He trusted Calvino and had come to enjoy what he called his '*piccoli bocconi amari*', his tart little mouthfuls of observations. But he knew that a storm lay ahead. His book could be read in many ways, but there was no escaping its condemnation of collusion between government and opposition and its attacks on the judiciary. Where creeping madness infiltrates the State, Sciascia spelt out, there the distinction between reason and delirium become fatally blurred. Described as a 'political-thriller pamphlet', it was published in November 1971. He chose its title with care. *Il contesto* meant literally 'the context', but as he explained, it also meant a weaving of power, in which all ideology is absent, and a suggestion of cunning.

Sciascia had been right to foresee trouble; but perhaps not the fury that accompanied the publication of *Il contesto*. Though many of the young defended him, *L'Unità*, the Communist daily paper, devoted pages to attacks by the old guard, men he had known all his life. His old friend Napoleone Colajanni said that Sciascia's scepticism was a distortion of reality and claimed that he was only lending support to those wishing to discredit and weaken the left, while his description of mysterious power at the heart of government was banal. Its author was obviously suffering from some kind of crisis and should stop indulging in moralistic abstractions. In the pages of *Avanti!*, Walter Pedulla accused Sciascia of being reactionary. The novel, he said, was filled with linguistic and ideological infelicities, and it amounted to no more than superficial chatter disguising Sciascia's own feeling of moral superiority. Others called the book 'dull', full of 'useless visions and digressions', lacking in proper analysis, mentally lazy and 'ideologically aggressive'. Sciascia had become 'a sad man', resigned, exhausted, reduced to 'bitter irony'. Before long, the personal attacks had spiralled out to become a debate about personal and collective responsibility and the right to say what one wanted – even in the febrile, touchy world of Italian politics.

One of Sciascia's few defenders was Renato Guttuso who, though a lifelong member of the Communist Party, insisted that Sciascia was never a 'banal' writer, and that his friends on the left would have done better to perceive and address his obvious crisis of faith.

Sciascia's reply to his critics was defiant. Having started out with the story of a man wrongly accused of trying to poison his wife, he had ended up writing about the death of idealism and morality that he believed was now taking hold of Italy. You did not have to be a prophet – a label now widely pinned on him – to see that the play of power between the Christian Democrats and the Communists was deeply unhealthy, or to be terrified of a regime in which dissent was regarded as a heinous crime. As for the vehemence of the attacks, well, they were simply a sign that he had hit his mark. And when they became ridiculous, he enjoyed them very much, 'because imbecility entertains me'. Privately, he told Mario La Cava that all the bad faith disgusted him.

Cushioned from the worst of the public opprobrium by Maria, his comfortable home life and his close circle of friends, Sciascia was becoming if possible clearer about his duty as a writer. Laura married a university lecturer called Salvatore Fodale in 1971 and Anna Maria an engineer, Antonino Catalano, a couple of years later, both marriages conducted in the church above the *zie*'s house in Racalmuto. Sciascia considered himself, he would say, a 'normal' husband and father, neither overly demanding nor overly possessive, respectful of people's independence. Loving, certainly, but also highly protective. As he admitted, he would not have enjoyed 'rebellious, uncontrollable children'. He felt lucky to have found himself a father 'at a time when rules were respected'. Mild at home, he was rapidly moving into a public world in which rules and mildness were of very little account and where he was expected to have views, at all times and in all places. He had become pricklier, more defiant, very vigilant about *cretini*. He saw them everywhere, both on the right and on the left, 'numerous and inexhaustible and, which is serious, very healthy'.

'The countryside this year is filled with monsters,' wrote Sciascia in the diary that he began in 1969. He was referring to an outbreak of sightings of the mythical figures dear to Sicilians, such as the *biddina*, the fat snake that was as fast on land as it was in the water. Sciascia's own monsters were more prosaic. He had not quite finished with the Christian Democrats, the Mafia or the judiciary, but now he returned once more to the Catholic Church, in his eyes another potent centre of unscrupulous power. *Feste Siciliane*, his illustrated book on the pagan aspects of Sicilian worship, had not brought him friends in ecclesiastical circles; what he wrote next was considerably more confrontational. A new polemic was in the making.

In the summer of 1971, Sciascia had taken Maria and the girls on a holiday to Zafferana Etnea. Their hotel in the woods above Catania doubled as a summer retreat for a group of senior Christian Democrats and in the evenings Sciascia watched them as they walked around the courtyard, saying their rosaries. It reminded him of Dante's circle for thieves.

Todo modo – *One Way or Another*, from St Ignatius of Loyola's approach to Catholicism through meditation and penitence – became Sciascia's most metaphysical thriller. He wrote it, unusually, in the first person, taking as his narrator a successful but not altogether likeable painter who, while driving around the countryside, stumbles on a monastery which is also a hotel. Here he finds a number of Christian Democrat luminaries who have gathered for spiritual exercises under the auspices of the crafty, entrepreneurial Don Gaetano, who wears a sinister pince-nez and is full of chilly paternal benevolence. The religious retreat, intimate and secretive, is the perfect setting for the senators, industrialists and bankers to plot, make deals, broker alliances. Like Sciascia, Don Gaetano enjoys 'contemplating imbecility'.

There are several murders. Against a background of continual theological debate, in which Voltaire and Pascal are often quoted, Don Gaetano, who believes not in a just God but in a world riven by destruction, is himself murdered. His killer is almost certainly the painter, but in true Sciascia style nothing is quite nailed down. The agitated representatives of corrupt wealth and power, 'very intelligent and terrible men', disperse, to further their own nefarious ends. 'I have attempted', Sciascia told interviewers, 'to come to terms with the Catholic Church' as a centre of 'misused power' and with the 'way of governing, or rather not governing, of the Catholics'. His portrayal is almost unremittingly grim: the Church is seen to behave like a capitalist company exploiting its guileless followers while acting as an accomplice to a *mafioso*-business-political network. Don Gaetano is its *capomafia* in the mould of

Don Mariano, with all the characteristics that Sciascia considered most perverse and negative about Catholicism.

Pasolini told Sciascia that he thought *Todo modo* the best metaphor he had ever read for thirty years of Christian Democrat rule and *mafioso* power, which had seen 'a true genocide of good feeling and true men'. Calvino, initially put off by the religious content, said that he quickly became gripped by this 'infernal' vision of State power. He suggested that Sciascia remove at least some of the more obscure and recondite literary and historical allusions that fill *Todo modo*'s pages. Sciascia paid no attention. Apart from anything, he was enjoying himself. He had spent, he said, the past twenty years joking. He had joked about the Communists, the Catholics, the Mafia, the Risorgimento and family life, in ways that most Italians disapproved of. But with his own particular take on joking, which for him carried clear overtones of morality and ethics. 'You have to joke,' he wrote, 'about things that you fear and hate and love.' Like Voltaire, he saw it as a way of freeing oneself to confront real emotions. When dealing with important subjects, you needed a 'sphere of lightness'. *Todo modo* had been his 'confession', his account with the Church; and he would not change even a comma.

The clerical world was predictably outraged. The milder Catholic reviewers called Sciascia 'intemperate'. As ever, sales were excellent.

As if the Christian Democrats and the Catholic Church were not enough, Sciascia next took aim at an unexpected new target: science. Iconoclasm seemed to have entered his soul.

Soon after the war, Camus had written that the twentieth century was one of fear, and that scientific theories were 'threatening the whole world with destruction'. Human beings, incapable of controlling violence and indifferent to injustice, might be heading towards collective suicide rather than the intelligent use of scientific discoveries. 'Everything,' he declared in *The Myth of Sisyphus*, 'is ordered in such a way as to bring into being that poisoned peace produced by thoughtlessness, lack of heart, or fatal renunciation.' Sciascia had been thinking about his words when one day he received a parcel of papers and letters, discovered in a chest in Catania, relating to a young physicist, Ettore Majorana, who had worked with Enrico Fermi on nuclear power in the Institute of Physics in Rome in the early 1930s. Busy with other things, Sciascia had put them to one side, but at the back of his mind was what Brancati had also said: that the only response to destructive scientific power was death. Then he was invited to take part in a Swiss television programme on the thirtieth anniversary of the Second World War, together with Alberto Moravia and the physicist Emilio Segre. What struck Sciascia was the way that Segre, while they sat watching footage on Hiroshima, looked so 'serene', even satisfied; and then he remembered how anguished Majorana had seemed in his letters.

Majorana, an odd, unhappy figure with black hair and cadaverous cheeks, had been a brilliant scientist but a perpetual outsider, the kind of *uomo solo* – man alone – dear to Sciascia's heart. Part of his appeal was that he too read Pirandello. How far Majorana actually understood the implications of his work was not clear, but Sciascia came to believe that he had seen where nuclear science was heading and been appalled. In 1938, while travelling from Naples to Palermo, the thirty-one-year-old Majorana had written what appeared to be two suicide notes, one to the head of his department in Naples, where he was now Professor of Theoretical Physics, and another to his family, saying 'remember me, if you can, in your hearts and forgive me'. He followed these up immediately with a telegram, indicating that the notes had been a mistake. However, after a brief stay in Palermo he boarded the boat back to Naples, and disappeared. Every effort was made to trace him; Mussolini wrote a note to police all over Italy, saying, 'I want him found.' There were many apparent sightings, all followed up, but the young scientist was never discovered.

The sighting that intrigued Sciascia most came from his friend Nisticò at *L'Ora*. Overhearing Sciascia say one day that he was having trouble finding an ending to his new book, Nisticò recalled how, in 1945, he had been taken to a Carthusian monastery in Calabria where he had heard tell that among the monks were two lay visitors. One was an American pilot who had flown the B-29 at Hiroshima and was spending the rest of his life expiating his sin; and the other was a 'famous scientist'. Nisticò and Sciascia decided to pay a visit to the monastery together. There they found an elderly monk who said that he had no memory of either man;

and the cemetery did not have their graves. The ending was, in best *inchiesta* style, left open.

Had Majorana really foreseen the atom bomb? Sciascia decided that he had. In his *inchiesta* he was hard on the scientists working on the Manhattan Project, who as 'slaves' chose to deliver the bomb, and he was admiring of Heisenberg and his German colleagues, who kept theirs from Hitler. Majorana, he wrote, was a man of courage who had foreseen the catastrophe and chosen to disappear rather than contribute to a science that 'had so arrogantly split away from humanism, humanity, the moral life . . . and the negation of culture'. Of all Sciascia's books, *The Mystery of Majorana* is his most analytical, full of probings into neuroses and the unconscious and following up a strange tale of a burnt baby that had apparently obsessed the scientist as a young man.

The *inchiesta* appeared first in seven instalments in *La Stampa*, then as a book, seventy-eight pages long, with eight pages of notes. Predictably, it caused a furore in the scientific world. Teachers, philosophers, theologians all weighed in. Scientists protested that Sciascia's various claims were mistaken, that to blame the Manhattan scientists when Germany looked set to win the war was monstrous; and that in any case many of them had petitioned Truman not to drop the bomb unless Japan refused to surrender. His book, they said, was nothing but an 'anti-scientific ideological cocktail'. Sciascia himself was, as ever, both defiant and provocative, and broadened his attacks to include scientists in general, heedless inventors of things hostile to humanity. Men, he declared, were now enduring 'dogs' lives' in factories, afraid and angry, often precisely as a result of scientific discoveries. In any case, those who 'deal in death' were 'on the side of death', much in the same way as the Fascists, the Mafia and the Spanish Inquisitors had been: 'There exists just one culture, and it is the one that loves man.'

Scientists, he repeated, be they biologists, physicists or doctors, have the same moral responsibility as everyone else for their actions. He told a friend, 'They frighten me.' As a 'free man', Majorana had chosen moral responsibility over collaboration with death. Angry scientists called Sciascia 'profoundly reactionary', full of bile, and claimed that he was taking himself too seriously.

There was almost nothing that Sciascia now wrote that did not invite controversy. Some of it pained him, but there was also something in him that really enjoyed needling the establishment, especially one that seemed so often profoundly wrong-headed. But the next controversy was not entirely of his making.

Feminism came late to Sicily. In 1953, a first Congress of Sicilian Women had brought 1,500 delegates from all over the island to Palermo, described by one reporter as a 'spring time of women on the roads'. The gathering proved exciting and even explosive; but then the impetus for change stalled. Sicilian families remained great constructs of mutual protection and obedience, in which women were enslaved to domesticity, young girls were sometimes referred to as '*toppe*' – useless things – and widows eked out their lonely lives enveloped in perpetual black.

The first currents of female freedom that swept through the rest of Italy in the 1960s took some time to make their way south, but as inflation took its toll and men emigrated, so women found it hard to balance their budgets and thus became involved in battles for better housing, higher wages and changes to family law. Influenced in part by feminists in the United States, middle-class Sicilian women denounced violence and inequality. Many rallied around the referendum on divorce, called in the spring of 1974 by the very Catholic Christian Democrats, who hoped to repeal a law passed three years earlier. As the current secretary of the party, campaigning against divorce, put it to an audience in Caltanissetta, if divorce went through, homosexuality would surely follow. Would they like to see 'their wives run off with the maid'? Sciascia was a firm supporter of divorce, saying that while for him personally a single marriage was what he wanted, he believed that it was right that couples should have a choice.

Sciascia's novels, as his readers have noted, have almost no female characters. Women such as his aunts, shrewd, loving but controlling, have no voice. Where they do appear, women are depicted as frivolous, faithless, mendacious accomplices, as in *To Each his Own*, or as nebulous widows, as in *The Day of the Owl*'s witness, about whom we know nothing beyond her chestnut-brown hair, black eyes and fleeting, malicious smile. Perhaps the most explicit, and also the bleakest, is a wife in a collection of short stories, *Il mare colore di vino* (*The Wine Dark Sea*), who, having married for love and finding that her husband is both worthless and a cheat, gets her own back by acquiring *roba*. 'We adore material things,' she declares. 'We have put them in the place of God in our universe of love . . . Built-in wardrobes and fitted kitchens contain our world.' She has abandoned traditional values in favour of 'dysfunctional and narcissistic capitalism'.

While Italy was readying itself for the divorce referendum, and most prudent men were keeping their heads down, Sciascia gave an injudicious interview to Franca Leosini in *L'Espresso*. The heading was '*Le zie*' – 'The Aunts' – '*di Sicilia*'. Why, she asked him, were his women so marginal? Did women not make good characters? Was he afraid of psychological insights? Cushioned by his family of affectionate women, all of whom looked to him for guidance, it was as if, unusually for Sciascia, this was something that he had not thought through.

Sciascia was never a man to equivocate. Indeed, he told Leosini, he did not write much about women, but that was because he was more interested in Sicilian power and politics, in which they played little part. For all the obvious contradictions, he might, just, have got away with this. But then he went on: 'Sicily', he declared, was a '*matriarcato*' – a matriarchy – and he felt deeply hostile towards a society so steeped in it, because 'I have seen the way that women have always been in command, annihilating men'. The reality was that 'women rule here in oblique and negative ways'. In their 'deceitful and cunning dictatorship', Sicilian women counselled cowardice, caution, self-interest and opportunism, 'and men have always obeyed'. Furthermore, while men contemplated death with respect, 'women administer, arrange, manage death as if they were immune to it'. In short, while in the less absolute and hidebound north, there was real progress for women, in Sicily mothers and mothers-in-law, ruthless and tenacious, were continuing to transmit Mafia values to their servile sons, thereby perpetuating a Mafia mentality. It did not stop him, he went on, apparently oblivious of his audience, feeling in some way complicit, just as he felt over the Mafia. 'In the way that I write about Sicilian women,' he continued, 'there is also condemnation of myself . . . I feel responsible for her condition.' What was so interesting was that in the mid 1970s in Sicily there was still very little talk about the role of women in the Mafia, the general assumption being that they were powerless and subservient. Sciascia may indeed have been deaf to

Italy's dawning women's movement, but his antennae were sharp when it came to the criminal underworld. As with his prescient definition of the Mafia in *The Day of the Owl*, he was touching on something others preferred not to see.

Leonisi was not quite done. Did Sciascia think that a 'feminist movement' existed in Sicily? No, he replied, digging the hole below him even deeper: it was a sign that there was no need for one. Did he like women? Indeed he did, and especially Sicilian ones, which 'means I am a bit narcissistic'. He regarded himself as a *'femminista convinto'*, a persuaded feminist; in fact, even a bit of a libertine.

After a brief, stunned silence, furious women rushed into print. How could such an intelligent and thoughtful striver after truth be so ignorant? Did he not realise that Sicilian women were being kept subjugated by men and were looked at askance if they went out on their own? That contraception was regarded as the work of the devil? How could a writer so profoundly aware of coercion and degrading poverty be so obtuse? In *Il Giorno*, Carla Ravaioli accused Sciascia of mental confusion. Others spoke of his vulgarity, his grotesque ideas, of his being driven by a misogyny so deeply buried that a psychoanalyst would have trouble finding the key to it. Many were particularly outraged by his assertion that it was better for women not to work but to 'conserve the family' just at the very moment when they were struggling for economic independence. Sciascia, they pronounced, was nothing but a *'uomo privilegiato'*, interested only in preserving his own position.

Sciascia, who prided himself on his total independence of thought, his refusal to accept anything as given, did not take the attacks lying down. In any case, he was developing a taste for these polemics, in a country where public arguments were invariably heated and provocative. His reply, in the weekly magazine *Panorama*, was headed: 'Antifeminist? Me?' He professed astonishment. He had never regarded women as inferior, and he despised the men who did. But he was a writer wedded to the idea of describing what he saw as an extremely complex society. Among his most vivid childhood memories, he said, were ones of women who had been terrible advocates for avarice and cowardice, wielding 'senseless and capricious' dominion over their sons and grandsons. It was not his fault if what he remembered was brutalisation and madness; such things should not be forgotten. These remarks were clearly not intended to portray the *zie*, though what they, or indeed Maria and his daughters, thought about them is not recorded. But they were a measure of how much, even as a boy, Sciascia had noted and observed, how deeply he had thought, even when he did not speak or write about things.

The attacks took some time to simmer down. It was a measure of Sciascia's immense popularity that most critics were soon agreeing that there were two Sciascias: one the intelligent observer of Sicilian power, the other an ignorant and unfortunate product of his times, inhabited by 'childish ghosts' and terrified of occult, omnipotent female power, though nowhere near as bad as Tolstoy or Thomas Mann. As the writer Dacia Maraini put it, he was a man who had 'never applied his intelligence to the question of women'. Courageous and outspoken when he wrote about injustice, he was 'timorous and blind' over women. But, many admitted, Sciascia was personally a good friend to women, generous and eager to engage in conversation with them.

Sciascia, repeating that he would not take back a single word he had said, emerged unbowed, though it was noticeable that in the years to come, his female characters became somewhat more lively, if never intimate, as if to delve too deeply were somehow in bad taste. And in May, the referendum passed with a satisfactory majority, 59.9 per cent to 40.9 per cent, in favour of keeping divorce on the Italian statute books.

Three very public controversies in as many years; and there were more to come. As they built up, they seemed to be turning into indictments of modern Italy itself.

For many years now, Sciascia and Pasolini had regarded themselves as fighting side by side against what they saw as the ruinous forces at play in Italy: the distortions of the Christian Democrats, the demonic destruction of Palermo, the spread of corruption and Mafia power. Regarded as two of Italy's most outspoken dissidents and heretics, they were described everywhere as public intellectuals, though Sciascia hated the term while Pasolini embraced it. There was something schoolmasterly about them both, scourges constantly asking questions, and friends described Pasolini as the 'fireman' of Italy, trying to put out its devastating fires. Together, they continued to mourn the lost dialects and peasant world of their youth and rail against the 'culture of conformity' into which Italy had fallen. Both men were intrigued, sometimes almost obsessively, by the idea of death, Pasolini speculating on the means and place of his own and Sciascia trying to understand it as an experience. Their writings sometimes came across as matching allegories about a perverse, enigmatic power, a country without truth, which in the end can be countered only by literature and art. Everything that needed writing, they agreed, had already been written; they were simply 'ruminants'.

Pasolini was, by far, the more outspoken, more given to wild provocation, pouring out day after day his rage, his fantasies and his political diatribes. He attacked the Church, was charged with the corruption of minors, protested against what he called a 'culture of conformity and neurosis', denounced the student movement and claimed that there was little to tell between Fascism and anti-Fascism. For the sheer volume of his work – 3,500 pages of novels and short stories, 15,000 of poems, journalism and scripts and many films – only D'Annunzio could compare.

Like Sciascia, Pasolini courted polemics; unlike him, he also courted scandal. Sciascia kept faith with him, cautiously, choosing to ignore the seamier aspects of Pasolini's life. 'Perhaps my vision of things,' he told an interviewer, 'is less radical than his ... but my deeper fear lies very close to his.' Pasolini might indeed make mistakes and contradict himself, but he knew 'how to think with the freedom few others today possess'.

The two men, Pasolini so vibrant and profane, Sciascia so dry and sibylline, had grown somewhat apart, but they remained friends. Reviewing *Todo modo*, Pasolini wrote that Sciascia, for all his immense success, 'had always kept himself very pure' and that his authority was that of a *'uomo solo'*. As he grew older, Pasolini's looks became more saturnine, the lines in his face deeper. He could be very hard on friends, nasty, unfair, but he was not arrogant or ungenerous. His films shocked, but they were admired and, even when banned on grounds of obscenity, they won prizes. There was a rumour that Callas had been in love with him.

In Stockholm, at the end of October 1975, he railed against consumerism, saying that it was causing Italians to lose their identity in a 'chaotic equilibrium'. He had just finished reading Sciascia's book on Majorana, declaring, *'E bello! E bello!'*

A few days later, on 2 November, Pasolini's body was found on the beach at Ostia, not far from Rome, beaten to death then run over by a car. Within hours, seventeen-year-old Pino Pelosi was caught driving Pasolini's Alfa Romeo and charged with his murder. It was said that Pasolini had been working on the story of the unsolved Mattei murder, which had already seen De Mauro kidnapped, and he had often denounced the Christian Democrats in the pages of the *Corriere della Sera*, saying that he knew where the bodies were buried.

Photographs of his battered body sparked off a 'gigantic psychodrama'. The Communist Party, which had once rejected him, reclaimed him as a 'master of life'. Pino Pelosi pleaded self-defence but the reasons for the killing remained murky; he went to prison, but over the years repeatedly changed his story. There were many fresh trials, but each folded without resolution.

Soon after Pasolini's death, Sciascia was invited to a screening of his last film, *Salò e le 120 giornate di Sodoma*, an allegory about a pervasive, enigmatic and evil power, showing a group of Fascists subjecting adolescent boys to sexual and mental torture. Younger writers in the room observed Sciascia sitting in one corner, with his cigarette in his mouth, reading an Agatha Christie. Seeing them stare at him, Sciascia looked up 'with an expression that seemed to come from the most remote and silent depths of the world'. He appeared agitated, shifting in his seat, occasionally covering his eyes. When the lights went up he was visibly overcome, muttering, 'It's terrible, terrible ... One should never make such despairing films.' Later, he would write that, watching the film, he had kept trying to conjure up images of love, and that all he could think of was, 'God, why have you forsaken us?'

Later, too, he would write about the 'shadow' that had seemed to come between himself and Pasolini. It had been caused, he thought, by Pasolini's suspicion that Sciascia disapproved of his homosexuality. Indeed, perhaps he had. So fundamentally wedded to morality, he had chosen to close his mind to Pasolini's other life with its sexual adventures with young boys. But never to the extent that he would have allowed his disapproval to prevent him from standing up for his friend against the 'hypocritical and corrupt cretins' who attacked him. What saddened Sciascia was that he had never told him so. They had thought the same things, suffered and paid for the same things; in some profound sense they were brothers. After Pasolini's death, Sciascia said, he felt his world grow smaller, as if it was now up to him alone to fight the battles they had once fought side by side. 'Now he is no longer there, I realise that I have to speak louder.'

10
'Clean, always clean'

Before Vittorio Nisticò stepped down from his post as editor of *L'Ora*, he invited Sciascia to a dinner with Enrico Berlinguer, secretary-general of the Italian Communist Party (PCI) since 1972. Local and regional elections had been set for June 1975 and there were hopes that Sciascia might be induced to run on the PCI ticket. The two men, both dour in public, said very little. Sciascia excused himself and left early. 'How do you think it went?' Nisticò, somewhat dismayed, asked Berlinguer. 'Excellently,' he replied.

His instinct was right. Sciascia did agree to run, a decision some considered surprising in a man so wedded to intellectual independence, so averse to following party lines, so prone to tell anyone who asked him that just as he was a Christian without a church, so he was a socialist without a party. But as he said himself, by consistently refusing the label of *'intellettuale impegnato'*, a committed intellectual, a phrase much beloved by the left to describe its paid-up supporters, he felt like Voltaire's flying fish, attacked by birds when out of the water, devoured by larger fish when below. Of his lifelong intense commitment to the left, there was never any doubt. Called a 'liberal Jacobin' by Calvino, Sciascia would say that he felt himself at all times to be a rebel, not as a man of action but as a thinker, in the libertarian intellectual tradition of Simone Weil, Camus, Orwell and his friend Pasolini.

Where Berlinguer was wrong was in believing that Sciascia was capable of the compromises that he would soon be called upon to make. Sciascia was a man who disagreed profoundly with the notion that it was better to err in company than be right on your own: you had to follow your conscience, wherever it led you, even to solitude. There was something of the Protestant in this attachment to the idea of an inner guiding light, and it would make him an awkward, uncomfortable politician, particularly in a Roman world so riven by subterfuge, obfuscation and deals. But for the moment, lulled by the PCI's backing of the divorce referendum and Berlinguer's apparent successes in modernising the party and softening Togliatti's heavy-handed obedience to the USSR, he ventured out into the public arena, like a tortoise, from his normal shell of reticence. It helped that Guttuso, too, had put his name forward, and that Achille Occhetto, the newly arrived party secretary, had brought with him a pronounced distaste for illegality. Sciascia was careful to stress that he would be running as an independent, though his name was on the PCI ticket, an arrangement made possible by Italy's system of proportional representation.

In 1975, Palermo was an unhappy city, decrepit and crumbling, its streets filthy, the wind carrying swirling currents of dirt and dust. Promises from Rome about prosperity and justice had amounted to very little, public money was drying up, the parliamentary commission on the Mafia was mired in documents and inaction, and Ciancimino and Lima continued to preside over a city administration choked by inertia and chicanery. Sicily's votes were crucial to factions within the ruling Christian Democrat Party and they were being willingly delivered by the vast army of workers and entrepreneurs who owed these factions their fortunes and enjoyed being friends with the powerful.

And, as Sciascia had warned, the Mafia had not stayed still, though he had not foreseen just where it would go. Palermo had become a major producer of heroin; five refineries had been built by the Mafia just outside the city, exporting some five to six tons every year to the United States. An air of violence had settled over the streets. '*Narcolire*' – the profits from drugs – were being laundered and invested in the property boom. Palermo, wrote the playwright and theatre director Michele Perreira, had, like an ageing star of the silent cinema, become 'ugly as a witch' and even the famous irony and wit of its inhabitants had fallen silent.

The elections in June, which brought significant gains to the left all over Italy, carried both Sciascia and Guttuso into City Hall. They wanted, they said, 'good government' for Palermo. As Sciascia said to Guttuso, the city was 'sullied with malfeasance'. Asked why he had agreed to stand, Sciascia was characteristically terse and ironical. Despite the fact that men like himself were traditionally regarded as 'fragile and precious *imbecilli*', his presence should serve to signal that the PCI itself was changing, becoming a true and responsible party of opposition. Confrontation, vigorous opposition, was something he believed in deeply, and he was loud in denouncing the PCI's clear drift towards accommodation with the Christian Democrats. In Palermo people greeted his move into politics with approval. In the pages of *L'Ora*, a young woman reporter wrote that Sciascia was of 'the highest stature, clean, always clean'. As Perreira put it, the difference between Ciancimino's crassness and Sciascia's moral rigour was 'vast'.

Sciascia's life, in the mid 1970s, took on a rhythm that it would maintain until he died. In Palermo he had created his own map of the city as he wished to inhabit it, the triangle formed by the Villa Sperlinga, the offices of Sellerio and *L'Ora* and an art gallery called Arte al Borgo. He moved between them, he said, 'as on tiptoes', in a tunnel of his thoughts, walking but not seeing. He looked older, moved and sat like an older man, always with a cigarette in his mouth. The area around the Villa Sperlinga had become an oasis for the '*diversi*' – the rebels – surrounded by grass and flowers, full of prams and dogs and small children. Living here was a way of keeping the violent, noisy and crumbling city at bay, of avoiding what Sciascia described as the effective mulch out of which the Mafia grew, the efficient, entwined alternative government of the 'other power'.

He had been rethinking his opinion of *The Leopard*. Having initially criticised Lampedusa for being 'sublimely indifferent' to the reality of Sicily, too bound up in his own Proustian memories, he had since come to believe that he had really understood and described the fundamental contradiction inherent in Sicilian life: '*ne tecum, ne sine te, vivere possum*' – neither with you, nor without you, can I live. Lampedusa had achieved what he himself had tried to do with his *Parrocchie*, which was to convey through the most painful moments of the island's history its 'way of life, the reality, the idiosyncrasies, the impediments, the travails, the culture, the values'. With the word 'irredeemable' Lampedusa had effectively described all that was best and worst in what it was to be Sicilian, unaltered and inalienable. It was the Sicily of Guttuso and Guccione's paintings, a land of noise, bright colours and picturesqueness, but also of stillness, emptiness, the earth brown and burnt, the sea vast and empty, the land naked and primordial.

In Palermo, in his perfectly arranged study, surrounded by the books and images of the philosophers and writers he depended on, much as the ancient Romans had displayed portraits of the scholars they revered in their libraries, Sciascia spent his mornings writing. Then it was time for friends, journalists, fellow members of the Palermo city council, foreign visitors. For all his reticence, Sciascia had a real gift for friendship, and he gathered around him a remarkable group of writers and painters, rooted in the history and politics of Sicily, but also instinctively European. Like him, these men and women – but mostly men – were full of curiosity, ironical, sceptical, attached to civil rights and all of them trying to understand and interpret the world about them and work out how best to live in it. With the Christian Democrats still firmly in power, there was little they could do beyond paint and write, arrange music festivals and theatrical events, defying Benedetto Gentile's dictum that Sicily's culture had gone down with the sunset. In contrast, in the evenings on the city council, Sciascia struggled with a sense of his own irrelevance, sitting in profound silence through interminable sessions in which nothing was ever concluded.

One of the gravest failings of Italians and especially Sicilians, Sciascia maintained, was that they lacked memory; perhaps on account of the painful and thorny things that were there to be remembered. At Sellerio, he, Elvira and Enzo had come up with a new idea for a series they called *La Memoria*, to bring back forgotten Sicilian writers or reprint what they considered lost jewels, capricious items, 'plots and ecstasies', designed to help them remember the past. The books had enticing dark-blue covers and lettering in different colours and sold well; soon readers collected each new one as it came out. Sciascia said that he sometimes felt that they were like conversations he was having with the readers.

But where Sciascia really liked to be, where he dreamt of being, was at *La Noce*. Here he continued to spend long hot summers, arriving as the poppies turned the fields into a sea of red, writing the books he had spent the cold winters researching. This digging and delving into the archives could be exhausting, full of agitation and uncertainty, but the summers were like a holiday when an 'interior order' took over, bringing with it 'the alchemy of writing'. The routine was much the same as in Palermo: he wrote in the morning for three or four hours, his shutters closed against the brilliant light and intense heat, then went into Racalmuto, came home and read and devoted the evenings to friends.

The conditions for a writer, he said, were ideal: it was pleasure, not work in the sense of teaching or being a sulphur miner. As the dusk brought cool, and the landscape seemed to hover in the air, as if suspended in time, he would set out between the almond trees and vines, arm in arm with Maria, to pay calls, a cigarette in his mouth. A public telephone had been installed in the hut of an old farmhouse not far away and as Sciascia grew increasingly famous so newspaper editors, journalists and publishers tried to reach him, only to have their calls taken by any small boy who might be playing near by. Messages would be noted down carefully in a lesson book to be picked up later by Sciascia on his evening strolls. Then the word went out: *'C'è il professore in cabina'*. Sometimes he stayed on the phone for hours dictating an article. He had agreed to give television a trial: but sent the set back after twenty-four hours. No newspapers were delivered.

La Noce was a place of happiness. Sitting in the moonlight in a circle of friends outside his house, with the occasional sound of distant voices across the valley, Sciascia said that it was where everything made sense to him, even the idea of death. Maria hovered, ever attentive, in the background. Between the long silences he thrived on, which disconcerted acquaintances and delighted his friends, the assembled companions engaged in the kind of talk he most enjoyed, debates about where the world was going. Often, the talk turned to the spreading vulgarity in Sicily and *'mafiosità'*, the threats to cut back the plantations of olives, which seemed to them all to represent what was best in the landscape, the degradation of their island. Late into the hot nights, they laughed, talked, smoked, moving from one anecdote to the next, one shared memory to another, telling each other that literature was the last bastion of a ruined world. *Amicizia* – friendship – Sciascia would remind the others, comes before *amore*, not only in the alphabet, but in the list of moral imperatives.

Sciascia's tastes remained simple. He said that he liked to model himself on Voltaire and Montaigne, who kept their houses open to all who wanted to come. His wife Maria continued to cook the food that Sciascia loved – stews of veal head, grilled pigs' livers, fish soup – and his aunt Nica to complain whenever he returned from the city with new things, such as smoked salmon and mascarpone. But Sciascia himself liked to cook, picking the wild asparagus that grew in the fields and adding them to omelettes and sauces. Though he seldom drank his own wine himself, he liked to see friends enjoying it.

Occasionally strangers could be seen standing in the road below the house, on a pilgrimage to see the writer whose name was now becoming known throughout Italy and beyond. As the years passed, Sciascia had become a mentor for younger writers and artists, and the photographer Ferdinando Scianna was not alone in thinking that Sciascia had taught him what friendship really meant, and that being a man of *'tenace concetto'* – never weakening – was something that really mattered. Another younger friend, Nicolo d'Alessandro, spoke of the way that Sciascia gave them faith in themselves. His generosity was always discrete: presents of art, the paying of school fees. The friends no longer went out with their guns, but the countryside around *La Noce* was full of quail, pheasants and rabbits, and the warbling birds dear to Italian hunters. Sciascia himself once told an interviewer that he was a 'bit *mafioso*' when it came to friendship: not in the sense of wanting to impose his own views, since he was always filled with doubt and scepticism, but in the way that he desired to be, always, in complete harmony with those he loved. It was his way of practising *Sicilianità*, being Sicilian, in its most benign form, and *Sicilianità*, he told an interviewer, is the 'very flesh of my books'.

1976 was Sciascia's year of films. He was often consulted by filmmakers, asked to write scripts, and he wrote extensively on the cinema. One day Sergio Leone had taken him to lunch in Palermo with a view of getting him to collaborate on a western. The encounter did not go well. Leone was exuberant and boastful; Sciascia felt patronised. He left before lunch was over, saying later that he disliked stars and celebrities. Over time, he had become increasingly wary of the films being made of his own books, telling directors who bought the rights that they should go their own way, make their own films, without involving him. 'The truth of literature', he declared, 'and the fiction of the cinema', worked on 'two untranslatable planes'. They were two different animals.

Todo modo, Cadaveri eccellenti (from *Il contesto*) and *Una vita venduta* (from the novella *Antimonio*) were all released in 1976, the first two sparking considerable hostility. *Todo modo*, directed by Elio Petri, was accused of being 'uselessly apocalyptical and narratively deranged'; it was withdrawn after a month and Petri was sued for 'slandering the institutions'.

Of all of them, Sciascia liked Francesco Rosi's *Cadaveri eccellenti* the best, saying that it penetrated deep into the 'agitated labyrinth of our daily existence' and seemed to him to keep faith with his own view about venal leaders and discredited institutions. The film starts with one of the most arresting scenes in modern cinema: a man in a dark suit is walking slowly through the catacombs of the Capuchin friars in Palermo glancing at a long line of grimacing skeletons on hooks. It touched a nerve with the Italian public, too, currently being shaken by a wave of terrorist attacks taking place across Italy from both right and left.

In keeping with the kind of Sicilian he felt himself to be, Sciascia did not care to stray far from the shore. He never set foot in Britain or the US, though after Luigi Barzini called him the greatest contemporary Italian writer he acquired something of a cult following on both sides of the Atlantic. Like all Sicilians, he carried the idea of emigration in his heart and one of his finest short stories, 'The Long Journey', follows a group of men who sell everything they have to pay a smuggler to get them to the US with its 'big warm houses and cars as big as houses'. They plan to return home rich, with 'well-fed pale faces', but then, after eleven nights at sea, find themselves deposited back on the beach in Sicily they had embarked from.

Paris, however, was part of his restricted map and he had taken to going there several times a year, always by train, almost always with Maria, most often staying in the Hotel Vernet off the Champs-Elysées. Occasionally he even talked of settling there, but would then decide that he was too lazy, another way perhaps of saying that he needed Sicily. He said that Paris was his 'book-city, writing-city, printing-city' and it made him feel as if he were living in a 'dream of a library', in the pages of Diderot's *Encyclopédie*, or in Proust or in the novels of Victor Hugo or Guy de Maupassant. The city itself provided him with a labyrinth of memories, as if offering him a constant rediscovery of known and loved images. Paris was the city of thinkers, of the just, who had freed themselves from ordinary terrors and discovered hidden truths. Walking in the streets once walked in by the *Encyclopédistes* took him back to his boyhood in Racalmuto and Caltanissetta, when he dreamt of exploring the unknown in order to 'document it with a good technique'. He sat in the Café Lipp 'eating and drinking according to literature'.

Every day, he wandered, often on his own, enjoying the feeling that Paris was built for those who wanted to stroll as if they had nothing else to do. Sometimes he took a small Zeiss camera with him, to help fix things in his mind. Often, his prowling took him to the Rue de Seine and its antiquarian bookshops, to add to his collection of books and the prints of the writers he loved. Yet, even in familiar Paris, Sciascia could feel deeply lost. One day, when he was there alone, a friend rang to ask how he was. 'I am here,' Sciascia replied in a low and mournful voice. 'I have flu. I am in bed.' He made it sound as if he were a man who had been abandoned, far from the friendly shore of his roots.

It was in Paris, in 1974, that Sciascia began to think about a book with as hero a *cretino*, one of his guileless, innocent men, indifferent to wealth and possessions, adrift in a world of opportunists with vested interests and out of sync with the morality of his times. He would call it *Candido*, in homage to Voltaire. After finishing *Majorana*, in which he had grappled with a man of great intelligence, it would come as a 'rest, a holiday'. At *La Noce*, in the summer of 1977, he sat down to write.

Italian politics had reached a new low, terrorism was rife, he was still at odds with the scientists over *Majorana*, and he had just written another of his *inchieste* into injustice. *I Pugnalatori* is ostensibly about an event that took place in 1862 when thirteen random people in Palermo were stabbed at precisely the same time in different parts of the city. The princely *'mandante'* – the man who ordered the killings to sow panic against the Bourbons – goes free while three hired assassins pay with their lives. But Sciascia's message was really about the feeling of fear to which Italians had been reduced. The mainspring of a good historical tale, he told an interviewer, is one based on truth, and this had been so always, the past illuminating the present.

He had resigned from his seat on the Palermo Council, saying that the sittings were 'spectacularly absurd', that he understood virtually nothing of what was said, and that people droned on for hours and were never stopped. He had found the whole experience 'detestable'. 'In there,' he told a reporter, 'I am totally useless.' The new wave of conformity meant that everyone was too frightened to do anything, and fear in the end was a terrible councillor. He had joined because he had believed that the PCI intended to present a brave and decisive opposition to nearly everything that the Christian Democrats stood for, but discovered that they were not interested in addressing the real issues in the city, such as the water or the drains. Under the pretence of new faces, there was nothing new: it was another case of *The Leopard*'s 'everything changing so that nothing changes'.

But when it came to writing *Candido*, he had seldom enjoyed himself so much. Some days he completed an entire chapter.

Born in a cave during the night the Americans landed in Sicily in July 1943, Candido Munafò is believed by his father to be the son of an American officer, an impossibility which serves to introduce an element of absurdity. Candido grows up different from other Sicilians: he is afflicted with the un-Sicilian need to tell the truth at all times and in all places. He forms his own opinions, is not swayed by others, remains uncompromising and never flatters. His mother considers him a monster; he drives his father to suicide. When he reports misdeeds carried out by the Catholic Church and the Communist Party they both reject him. At every turn, this candour and innocence are shown to be regarded as suspicious and ultimately weak. But *Candido*, Sciascia's most autobiographical book, also contains something rare in his work: a real relationship between a man and a woman.

Candido was a book of breaks, not just with the PCI but with Einaudi, with whom he had been on bad terms since they put him in for a prize after he had specifically asked them not to. He did not mind small prizes, he told Giulio Einaudi, but 'clamorous ones' were not to his taste. The draft of the book was ready in early October and was published by his French editor, Maurice Nadeau, before appearing in Italy. He would have made it longer, Sciascia told friends, perhaps even as long as the *Three Musketeers*, except that he now had a self-imposed limit of 150 pages, though he grumbled about how much harder it was to write short books than long ones. He told a reporter from *L'Epoca* that he had set out to invent a 'formula for happiness', which lay not so much in cultivating your garden as in cultivating your mind, by minding less what others think of you – not that he had ever allowed himself to brood over the bad opinion of others – and never trying to revive things that are over and dead. He hoped it would serve to remind the Communists to reject myths and return to thinking creatively. Complication, he said, is the modern form of stupidity, and imbeciles complicated everything that was simple. For its jacket, he chose a picture by Picasso of a circus.

Candido, which ends not in death but in hope, is the only one of Sciascia's books to have a happy ending. He told his readers that he had tried to be light-hearted. 'But the times are heavy, very heavy.' Critics were more than usually full of bile. One called him 'a little neo-Enlightenment professor ... a jackal on all things Sicilian'; another claimed that, petty minded and dogmatic, he no longer understood Sicily and had taken to repeating himself. After *Candido*, Sciascia would write no more fiction for ten years.

Happy writing *Candido*, Sciascia was at the same time at war once again with the Italian State.

The mid 1970s had seen the merger of several far-left revolutionary groups under the banner of the Red Brigades. Their tactics had become more effective and more lethal, and a series of kidnappings of prominent people had led to the setting up of a Special Anti-Terrorist section of carabinieri under General Dalla Chiesa. On 18 April 1974 – the anniversary of the 1948 elections which brought the Christian Democrats to power – a magistrate called Mario Sossi had been kidnapped in Genoa. The Red Brigades demanded the release of a number of their colleagues in Italian prisons and their safe conduct to Cuba. Squabbles broke out between police, government and judiciary, Sossi remained in captivity and his wife declared that the State was signing her husband's death warrant. Sciascia weighed in, perhaps intemperately. It was the role of the revolutionary movement, he wrote in *L'Espresso*, to 'expose the internal contradictions in a society ... to exacerbate and make them explode'. In the event, Sossi was released without a deal being made. It was a huge propaganda coup for the Red Brigades and they made the most of it, particularly after Sossi emerged from captivity to describe the group as well organised and efficient.

It was about now that Sciascia began to use the word *cretino* more insistently for what he saw as spreading idiocy everywhere. Aggression was the daughter of stupidity and the Red Brigades had displayed 'murderous imbecility'. He had harsh words too for Salvatore Pappalardo, the new Archbishop of Palermo, who opened an exhibition of art in the Papal Palace and announced that it was impossible to 'reconcile a Christian vision of life with the ... ideologies of Marxism'. Sciascia fired off an irritated open letter to *L'Unità* suggesting that the Archbishop would do better to exhort his flock to safeguard dignity, justice and liberty than to attack artists, since many of them were in fact Marxists. And why, come to that, did he not see fit to condemn the daily alliance between the Mafia and those who held public power – for there indeed was to be found an offence against mankind? 'When I lived in Caltanissetta,' he wrote crossly, 'in order to encounter one intelligent person I had to put up with seven *cretini*. In Palermo there are still seven *cretini*, but to them you have to add twelve thieves.'

The violence in the streets across Italy continued. The police deployed armoured vehicles and there was talk of civil war. Arrests were made and a first trial of terrorist suspects was fixed to take place in Turin. When the pool of jurors came to be sworn in, however, one after another produced medical certificates explaining that since they were suffering from a 'depressive syndrome' they were in no condition to serve. Commentators took to the airwaves to condemn them for cowardice. Sciascia, joining forces with the Nobel Prize-winning poet Eugenio Montale, declared in *La Stampa* that he too would have refused to serve, not because he was afraid, but because the Italian State, riven by corruption and discord and injustice, was not something that could or should be defended. To oblige jurors to serve was to make them complicit with the iniquities of the government. The trial was nothing but a dance, conducted by the Red Brigades, and the law had been made to seem impotent. With Pasolini dead, Sciascia had indeed stepped into his scourge's shoes.

There was, predictably, outrage. Loudest to speak out was a prominent figure in the Communist Party, Giorgio Amendola, who chose the pages of *L'Espresso* in which to condemn both Montale and Sciascia for defeatism and lacking in 'civic courage', something, he said, typical of many intellectuals of their kind. Then Alberto Moravia declared that he had come to feel a stranger in the country in which he was born. The ill-tempered exchanges spread. Sciascia fought back, saying that his critics were exercising a 'kind of terrorism by typewriter', and that it flowed 'directly from Fascism'. What made the attacks so absurd was that they were, in fact, based on a misunderstanding. He was thought to have said that he was neither with *the* State nor with the Red Brigades: in fact, he had chosen his words with great care, saying that he was not with *this* State and he had no intention of supporting a State so unjust. As he put it to an interviewer from *El Pais*, 'Just where is *this* State?' But his stance had lost him good friends, most particularly Calvino. 'The State is decomposing,' Sciascia declared. Not so, Calvino replied, 'The State is us.' It was an unhappy estrangement. Not long before, Calvino had declared that Sciascia was the 'last truly local author, rooted, who had made the universal out of these very roots'. Sciascia himself had said that of all contemporary writers, Calvino was the one he loved the best.

In the early autumn, militants from all over Europe attended a conference in Bologna on State repression, producing a manifesto inviting people to condemn police tactics in Italy. From France, Jean-Paul Sartre and Roland Barthes both added their names. Sciascia's contribution was to point out that what was happening was not new: there always had been repression in Italy, from the first days of the post-war Republic. The question was not of Italy 'remaining' a state in which the law was upheld, but of becoming one. He would take back nothing of what he had said, neither the accusations he had launched against the Church and the government with *Il contesto* and *Todo modo* nor his defence of the revolutionaries, though he did not believe in the redemptive power of revolution. Furthermore, terrorism was a 'phenomenon of desperation'. He wanted no part in what he called a 'class of power that does not change and will not change other than by committing suicide'. Increasingly, people were speaking about Sciascia's uncanny prescience and his growing status as Sicily's most acerbic and thoughtful writer.

The breach with Amendola was never mended. And all this was just a dry run for what was about to follow.

11
A death sentence

Just before nine on the morning of 16 March 1978, Aldo Moro, President of the Christian Democrats, five times Prime Minister, was kidnapped. He was taken on the Via Fani, in central Rome, on his way to Parliament. His driver and four bodyguards were shot dead and Moro himself was forced into the back of a car which disappeared into the traffic. His kidnappers were the Red Brigades.

That afternoon, special editions of the newspapers and all the television channels put out a first 'communiqué' from his captors, along with a photograph of a resigned, weary but unharmed Moro in his 'people's prison'. Moro, it said, would be put on trial. The *Corriere della Sera* described him as showing neither fear nor

Aldo Moro photographed by the Red Brigades

defiance, only composure. Other papers spoke of him as lucid, solitary, Christian, serene, sad, cautious, retiring, pessimistic, patient and tolerant. Virtually every reference included the phrase 'a great statesman'.

Sciascia was on a train to Paris when he heard the news. He had never felt any sympathy for Moro, with his 'contorted, impenetrable language', regarding him as synonymous with all that was worst about Italian politics. The Christian Democrats, he repeated, had spent the last thirty years colluding with the Mafia and wasting public money in 'rivulets' of unpunished and illicit deals. He knew that he was expected to make a comment, but at first, uncharacteristically, he said nothing; and commentators were quick to berate him for his silence. But, as he explained later, he had been confused, and he was exhausted and disgusted by the way that every time he spoke out he was 'misrepresented by intolerant and imbecilic people'. In *Todo modo* and *Il contesto* he had effectively been writing precisely about this kind of situation and he was unnerved by 'having seen the things I imagined come true'. Yet again he was appearing as prophetic. He began to be frightened of his own imagination.

The Red Brigades had planned the kidnapping with great precision. They had been preparing for such an event for the past four years and had five 'columns' ready to act. They had already assassinated more than a dozen people, among them magistrates and policemen, and wounded many more. The time had come to terrorise the ruling elite and stop the State from functioning. The defining moment of a decade of destabilisation had arrived.

The timing, too, was chosen with care. Moro had been on his way to watch the very Catholic, arch-conservative Andreotti be sworn in as head of state and present his new government, the first to have the support of the Communist Party. After the PCI had gained a historic 34 per cent of the vote at the 1976 elections, Moro, the 'master weaver' of the Christian Democrats, had argued passionately for widening the base of the government to include the far left. As he saw it, the Christian Democrats would form the centre of the coalition, until new elections would return his party to full supremacy. Berlinguer, as leader of the PCI, who had broken with the Soviets and formed, with the French and the Spanish, a new Eurocommunism, saw it differently. Coalition would give him the opportunity to push through social and welfare reforms. But both men believed that this *'compromesso storico'* – this historic marriage between right and left – given cultural and intellectual legitimacy by Moro, was worth trying.

For Sciascia, this was all that he hated most. Had he not written in *Il contesto* that the Christian Democrats, having misgoverned alone for thirty years, had now decided that they would do better to misgovern together with the 'International Revolutionary Party'? As he told a friend, he believed that 'priests should be priests, trade unionists trade unionists and Communists Communists' and that the *compromesso storico* would in fact simply turn the Communists into Christian Democrats, introducing into Christian Democrat corruption the 'vigour' of the left. There would be no effective opposition, so crucial in governance, no PCI *'di combattimento'*, no militant opponent. While the Christian Democrats represented 'monstrous, deformed' power, the Communists, whatever their faults, were the party of morality, committed to improving the lives of the poor. How could the PCI, ostensibly so opposed to secrecy and subterfuge, choose to accept co-existence with such profoundly dishonest people? What alarmed him when he thought about his recent books was that they had so accurately described the scheming of influential people and their desperate attempts to hold on to power. Think carefully, he warned the PCI, before you enter the government 'through the door of repression'.

Moro's kidnapping stunned Italy. The new government was quickly voted in: 545 in favour, 30 against. People had grown used to attacks and murders, but this assault on the very pinnacle of power was something new. The trade unions called a general strike. Pope Paul VI, a close friend of Moro's, offered to take his place. Some sixteen million Italians gathered in public demonstrations. Increased funds had been allocated to the anti-terrorist forces, but since the different brigades were deeply rivalrous with each other and reluctant to pool information, it had been slow in showing results. In a scramble to respond, 12,000 policemen and carabinieri were now deployed to carry out house-to-house searches and follow leads as they came in.

By nightfall, the government had put out an announcement. There would be no deal, no negotiations. Sciascia said to a friend: 'This is Moro's death sentence.'

From his soundproof cell in a cavity between the studio and

sitting room of a flat somewhere in Rome, with a chemical lavatory, an air conditioner and a camp bed, Moro was able to talk to his captors through a microphone. His cell was so small he could take just two steps, an agony for a man accustomed to walk two kilometres a day and known to suffer from hypochondria and claustrophobia. He saw no one, apart from two silent hooded men who delivered his food. With no radio and no newspapers, but given paper with which to write, Moro began to communicate with the world.

His first letter arrived with communiqué number 3. It was addressed to the Minister of the Interior, Francesco Cossiga. Moro's tone was reasonable, measured, if sibylline. 'The sacrifice of innocent people in the name of an abstract principle is,' he wrote, 'inadmissible.' He pointed out that there had been prisoner exchanges before and they had served their purpose. However, a veiled threat followed. Since he was totally under the control of the Red Brigades, it was possible that he might be coerced to 'speak in such a way as to say unwanted and dangerous things'. And, as the Christian Democrats knew all too well, there was much that he could, if he chose to, reveal. Not long before the kidnapping, three of their ministers had been accused of taking bribes from Lockheed, the aircraft manufacturers, in exchange for securing orders for planes. There were also rumours that the United States wanted Moro to be prevented from revealing the secrets of the Atlantic alliance.

Any suggestion that anything would or could be kept secret was quickly dispelled by the Red Brigades. Secrecy, they announced, was precisely what the State, the 'democratic mafia', was all about, and for themselves they wanted transparency and clarity. Nothing was to be kept from 'the people'. Moro wrote his letters, the Red Brigades delivered them to the press, and most of them were promptly published. Moro addressed them to friends in the government, to senators, to journalists and a great many very loving ones to his wife Eleonora. They were, given his appalling handwriting and convoluted sentences, lucid, a mixture of anguish, bitterness, reasoned argument and spirituality, a day-by-day reflection on thirty years of Christian Democrat rule and on the need for change and reform. All bore signs of his faith in the Christian Church. But none, so far, contained embarrassing revelations.

A DEATH SENTENCE

The hunt for Moro intensified. By the end of the first fortnight, 35,000 houses had been searched and 6.7 million people questioned. Just under four million cars had been stopped. Groups of experts of all kinds – policemen, university professors, secret servicemen – had been set up to pool their knowledge and come up with ideas. A 'political-technical' group was formed. Clairvoyants sent in suggestions. The *Corriere della Sera* dispatched a respected journalist called Ugo Stille to interview the guru of mass media, Marshall McLuhan, to discuss press strategy. McLuhan was clear: the only thing to do was to starve the Red Brigades of the publicity they craved. But it was too good a story. All calls for responsible, non-inflammatory reporting went unheeded. Newspaper editors insisted piously that it was their duty to keep the public informed; most, indeed, increased the number of their pages, pouring out 'an intoxicating saga of rhetoric', each pursuing its own line, leading to ever greater mystification.

Meanwhile, the Red Brigades remained in control – of initiatives, surprises and timing. Even no news was made to seem like news. Italy appeared to freeze into paralysis while a picture of impotence and incompetence by the forces of law and order settled over the country. When the suggestion was made that the Red Brigades already in captivity should be tortured to obtain information, General Dalla Chiesa, recently appointed coordinator of all forces in the war against terrorism, was quick to declare: 'Italy is a democratic country that can allow itself the luxury of losing Moro, but not the luxury of introducing torture.' There were, however, offers of a reduction in sentences for imprisoned terrorists if Moro was released.

Though the political parties kept jostling for position, each trying to prove itself the toughest and yet at the same time the most humane, the decision remained unaltered. There would be no deal. On this, Andreotti and Berlinguer were as one. The only main political parties to disagree were the Radicals and the Socialists under Benedetto Craxi, though this was thought to be more about the fact that they wanted to break up the DC–PCI alliance than out of any feelings of humanitarian concern. Apart from isolated politicians and intellectuals, one of the few lone voices in favour of a deal was that of the President of Italy, Giovanni Leone. As Sciascia observed, it was interesting to see how the Communist

Party, so adept at weaving and ducking, had suddenly discovered within itself a rock-like commitment to a strong State. Moro had undoubtedly been a great politician, Sciascia acknowledged, but he had as undoubtedly never been a great statesman, not least because there was no strong State in Italy; in fact, there was no State at all. That was the problem. Nor, he passionately believed, could one possibly be fashioned out of a marriage between two such diametrically opposed political parties.

Moro's letters kept coming, long, meditative analyses of post-war Italian politics, reflections on his own life, the choices he had made, his mistakes. As if to paraphrase Lampedusa, he wrote that 'the truth is that we speak of renewal and then renew nothing... For something to change, we too must change.' It was as if, providing he kept writing, his life would be spared. More and more openly, the letters contained – so Sciascia and others believed – carefully coded messages about where he thought he was being held. The master craftsman of words knew how to conceal clues. The authorities paid no attention. The days passed. But the government was becoming worried by the prospect that embarrassing revelations might soon follow.

On 20 April, after Moro had been a prisoner for just over a month, communiqué number 7 brought an offer: the Red Brigades planned to put Moro on trial, but once that was over they would spare his life if thirteen of their comrades, awaiting their own trials, were released. It came with a photograph of Moro, looking somewhat crumpled, his expression sad and a bit puzzled, his hair tousled and freshly but not very carefully shaved. It also brought a letter with a somewhat sharper tone. With 'great bitterness' and surprise, wrote Moro, he thought he detected an 'attitude of rigid intransigence' in the government. Did they really believe that his death would solve Italy's ills? Behaving with humanity, with the 'piety of Christianity', would, on the other hand, bring honour to his party. The Italian constitution, he reminded them, had done away with the death penalty; to let him die would be to reintroduce it. Since not one of the several million house searches had revealed anything, he had stopped trusting in the police to rescue him; he was now counting on a prisoner release.

Moro had been right to detect a hardening in the government position. The Red Brigades had recently carried out a number of

A DEATH SENTENCE

kneecappings of industrialists, and the cumulative effect of Moro's letters, splashed across every newspaper and picked up all over the world, was to portray a party of cover-ups and intrigues, little interested in the welfare of its people, with completely ineffectual police forces. Fearing what might come, the Christian Democrats acted.

Fifty long-standing 'friends' signed an open letter saying that the Moro of the letters, the man who was begging for his life, was no longer the Moro they knew, whose spirituality and political vision they had shared. It was clear that he had been drugged or coerced, 'Stockholmised' and gone over to the Red Brigades, or had simply been altered beyond recognition by his long captivity. He had metamorphosed into someone else. Moro was no longer Moro. Among the signatories was a cardinal; others were men he had known all his political life. The *Corriere della Sera* obligingly reported that Moro's personality had obviously been distorted by 'isolation, drugs, sleeplessness'. What Moro had written about some of his colleagues was so 'vulgar and childish' that it could not possibly have come from the man he had been. A graphologist was consulted and declared that the letters showed not just exhaustion, agitation and depression but 'real internal anguish'. When Sciascia read the letter he remarked that he now felt himself to be a better Christian than the cardinal. An American terrorist expert, sent to help, left again saying that his presence was pointless since the government had clearly decided what to do.

The open letter from his friends was a cruel blow. Moro now understood all too well what was happening. His own letters became profoundly sad. He had never, he said in his reply, been drugged and no pressure was ever put on him. He had not changed: he was still the same man. Patiently, despairingly, he rehearsed the same arguments, but the letters now carried the chilling ring of an Old Testament prophet. His friends had betrayed him, those 'friends of happier hours, the macabre obscene happy hours of power', and he was 'immensely glad' to have lost them. If you do not intervene, he wrote to Benigno Zaccagnini, one of the founding members of the Christian Democrats and its national secretary, 'my blood will fall on you, on the party ...Think hard, dear friends.' And again, 'Do not think that the Christian Democrats' problems will end with Moro's execution. I will always be there as an irreducible presence to protest and question.' Then came a chilling sentence: 'I ask that neither the State nor members of my party attend my funeral. I ask that only those who really loved me are there, those who are worthy to accompany me with their prayers and their hearts.' He no longer wished to be any part of 'those in power'. For Sciascia, hearing the word 'power' used in such a way for the first time was extremely significant, a rejection of the kind of power that Moro had enjoyed all his adult life.

The letters did not stop; but it was clear that Moro knew that he would die. There was a horrible precedent: the previous year, the Baader-Meinhof gang had kidnapped Hanns-Martin Schleyer, president of the German Confederation of Industry, then killed him after the government refused to negotiate. Even in faraway Paris, where Sciascia was staying, Moro's fate dominated the news. There was no avoiding the almost hourly spectacle of a man who realised he has been forsaken. There were appeals to the Red Brigades: from Kurt Waldheim, Secretary-General of the UN, from Amnesty International, from Moro's family. Panama offered to take the thirteen Red Brigades revolutionaries in prison. The Pope sent Monsignor Casaroli to Andreotti to discuss possible negotiations. But Andreotti and Berlinguer did not budge. There would be no deal. 'I will die,' wrote Moro, 'if this is what my party decides.' But the State should not fool itself: 'the bath of blood' would affect them all. The letters lost their energy; they became less combative, the language poorer, the sense of hope ebbing away. 'I will forgive no one,' he wrote. 'I will absolve no one.'

The fifth of May brought communiqué number 9. Moro's trial had been concluded. He had been found guilty. The verdict was death. On 8 May came a last poignant letter to Eleonora. 'Be strong, my sweetest love, in this absurd and incomprehensible trial . . . I have tried everything and now God's will be done. Kiss [the children] for me, one by one, their eyes, their faces, their hair . . . We will see each other again, meet again, love again.' He had harsh words for the Pope, who had done 'little . . . Perhaps he will have scruples.'

On 9 May a Moro family friend received a call. Moro's body was to be found in a red Renault 4 parked in the Via Caetani, symbolically halfway between the Christian Democrat and the Communist Party headquarters. There in the boot, crumpled up under a blanket, shot ten times in the back of the head, was Moro's body. The autopsy showed that he had been healthy; he was thin and ill-shaven but his nails were neatly cut. Sciascia heard of the execution on a ferry crossing the Straits of Messina. He told an interviewer who asked his opinion that he had nothing to say: he needed to think.

The Pope conducted a burial mass in the great basilica of San Giovanni in Laterano, attended by the very 'men of power' who had turned their backs on Moro. 'Oh Lord,' he prayed, 'you did not listen to our supplications.' The family was not present and there was no coffin. As Sciascia said, its absence expressed the absurdity of a man killed not because of the resolve of a state but because of the 'tormented and schizophrenic fragility of our Republic'. With his death, he told a reporter from *L'Epoca*, Moro had shed his Christian Democrat 'tunic', just as Pirandello, by asking to be buried naked so as to avoid being dressed in a Fascist uniform, had shed that unfortunate period of his life. His corpse did not belong to anyone, 'but his death makes us all guilty'. Eleonora and the children buried Moro in silence.

Even if nothing substantial had been revealed, the Red Brigades had achieved a considerable publicity coup. Day after day for fifty-five days, Moro, speaking much but saying little, had painted a vivid portrait of a chaotic, grubby, venal party, riven by secrets, though there was little that was not already known. The government did not fall, but people speculated that Moro's death would bring about the end of the *compromesso storico*. After a vast outpouring of horror, revulsion and disquiet, with the 'great statesman' turned into a 'martyr', it was clear that many questions remained, not least: why was Moro not saved? Every life has a price – but what was Moro's? It was Sciascia who decided to address these questions.

Sciascia did not initially plan to write a book about Moro. But as his thoughts turned to the man who had spent fifty-five days alone fighting for his life, he began to want to decipher what had lain behind that exhausted, disillusioned face. Without any religion himself, he felt an almost 'religious' duty to rescue the dead politician from the taint of cowardice that had been forced upon him. In captivity, Moro had become an *uomo solo*, a tragic figure buried in a sea of rhetoric and mystification. Like Zola with *J'accuse*, Sciascia decided to call the government to account. Only by knowing precisely what had happened, he said, could Italy face up to its failures.

Taking a phrase used by Pasolini not long before his death, he agreed that Moro had probably been the 'least implicated' in the gallery of Christian Democrat rogues. He saw the story as like that of Hamlet, determined not to go along with what was expected of him in order simply to make others feel better. Summer was coming. He gathered up Moro's parliamentary speeches, the many press reports, the police investigations and above all the thirty-six letters Moro was known to have written in his people's prison, and set off for *La Noce*. He had written *Candido* in the first person, in order to include his own reactions and touch on the many 'Pirandellian' aspects of the tragedy. Literature would again be used to establish truth, and he would unpick the letters, sentence by sentence, for the clues that he believed might have saved Moro's life. It would be another version of a *giallo*; and he would think of it as a 'long conversation with Pasolini'. And, as in a *giallo*, he would systematically follow up clues and decode messages, abandon the imaginary for 'naked enquiry'.

What became *L'affaire Moro* opens slowly, elegiacally. On his evening walk at *La Noce*, Sciascia sees what he thinks is a sparkling shard of glass wedged in a crack in the wall. It turns out to be a firefly, something he has not seen since his childhood, when shepherds cupped these 'flakes of emerald phosphorescence' in their fists. It makes him feel very happy and it also reminds him of Pasolini who, not long before, had compared the Christian Democrats' 'ideology of destruction', their predatory ways and degraded values, to the disappearance of the fireflies. Was this not just what happened to Moro, 'saying but not saying', trying to make himself heard in a vacuum of people who would not listen?

One letter at a time, Sciascia reconstructed Moro's life as a prisoner, tracing his growing desperation, his sense of abandonment, his frustration that none of the clues he had planted as to his whereabouts – references to the Holy See, the sounds in the apartment – were being picked up. Moro had written, 'I am under full and uncontrolled "*dominio*"' – did that not suggest a '*condominio*' – a block of flats – busy and not checked by the police?

Most importantly, however, Sciascia insisted that far from ceasing to be himself in captivity, Moro had in fact become more lucid, and that his pitiless references to the 'men of power', in all their 'true, profound and putrid reality', had been accurate portrayals of Christian Democrat rule. Moro had always been, and he had remained, a great political operator. Under the shadow of death this 'vigilant, alert, calculating, apparently flexible but actually immovable' man had given a very clear vision of the strengths and weaknesses that ran like faultlines through post-war Italian life. Moro, in short, had been telling the truth and the fact that it was a truth that none of his former colleagues wished to hear had effectively condemned him to death. Moro, he concluded, could have been saved; but he had been allowed to die by a State, which, unable to protect him, had no moral right to be so intransigent. The Red Brigades had been his killers; but they were no guiltier than those who refused to negotiate for his life. As the two great political forces, the Christian Democrats and the Communists, had grown closer, so Moro, the figure in the middle, had been 'slowly and inexorably squashed'. Pliant and tenacious, spineless and resolute, the great politician had remained faithful to his party to the end. Sciascia called his book 'a hard and naked enquiry into the hard and naked truth', an expression of 'piety'.

Some way into the book, Sciascia asked himself whether Moro had been afraid of death. Perhaps, he concluded. But he had also been afraid of life. Like all southerners – Moro came from Maglie, in the far south – his ingrained pessimism meant that every idea, every illusion came within the framework of consciousness of death. Like the sirocco, in the countries where the hot wind from the Sahara blew, the idea of death permeated everything.

As he wrote, Sciascia became almost fond of Moro, 'alone, denied, betrayed', and, though he continued to regard him as deeply scheming, he wanted to provide him with the dignity that his colleagues had denied him. Even his captors had referred to him respectfully as *'il Presidente'*. A strong State would have saved him: it was a measure of the weakness of the Christian Democrats that they did not even try to buy the time in which to find him. His friends had wanted him to die heroically; they had been disappointed that he failed to go quietly. That was Moro's tragedy and his greatness: he had died like a man. He had faced his end with considerable dignity, in sharp contrast to the lack of dignity of his former colleagues, scrambling over themselves to reject him.

In mid August, Sciascia told a reporter that he was dreaming about Moro every night. Usually so happy writing, this book was making him uneasy and obsessive; at night, unable to sleep, he felt as if he were hallucinating, walking in dense fog through a valley full of ruins. He felt permanently exhausted. 'One can't, one mustn't write books that are so grey, so suffocating.' His much-loved aunt Nica was dying and in Caltanissetta his eighty-year-old mother fell and broke her femur. Sciascia himself slipped climbing the stairs, broke his right hand, and was forced to finish the book typing with one finger. On 24 August it was complete; he spent four days going over it. It ran to his usual 150 pages and was intended to be not just about Moro but about the hypocrisy of the government and the inhumanity of the times. Serialised first in *L'Espresso*, it was published in Italy by Sellerio, rapidly selling 100,000 copies and helping to establish the publishers on a better financial footing. Of all Sciascia's books, *L'affaire Moro* is the one most filled with literary references and allusions: Borges, Pascal, Tolstoy, Manzoni and many others make fleeting appearances.

Even before it was published, reactions to the book were predictably harsh. As Sciascia pointed out, many of them came from people who could not possibly yet have read what he had written. They were led by Eugenio Scalfari, founder of *La Repubblica*, who declared that Sciascia had only used Moro to write about himself and that the book should more properly be called *L'affaire Sciascia*. One critic called it an 'operetta'; another said it was petty, contorted and not up to Sciascia's usual moral thrust. The editor of *Paese Sera* accused it of being 'corrosive, merciless, inappropriate and reductive'. Mondanelli, often his most ferocious critic, while admitting that he admired its 'penetrating insights' and its dry ironical tone, said that Sciascia had ended up falling in love with his subject but should not have tried to make his readers follow his example. There was a nasty undertone suggesting that Sciascia had become an accomplice of the terrorists. The Christian Democrats said little. The book sold magnificently.

L'affaire Moro was already in print when, on 1 October, Dalla

A DEATH SENTENCE

Chiesa and his group of anti-terrorist carabinieri broke into a flat in Milan and discovered nine members of the Red Brigades engaged in copying out more of Moro's writings. Four hundred and twenty pages were discovered, along with a memorandum. Though there was nothing in any of them not already known to his colleagues, if not to the general public, it did hint at the existence of a secret European agreement called Gladio, a right-wing state within a state, to be deployed in the case of Soviet invasion. And there were some hitherto unpublished descriptions of Moro's supposed friends. Andreotti, in particular, was described as cold and impenetrable, with the ability to do much ill, 'as he has done all his life to us and to his country', which perfectly reflected Sciascia's own view. The '*Memoriale*' painted a vivid picture of a tawdry political party; it also showed, thought Sciascia, a surprisingly reflective, even poetic man.

Assailed on all sides, Sciascia found time while at a conference in Paris to write a humorous description of all the travails that could befall an intellectual. The list included being an object of envy to colleagues and a victim of intrigues, both perfectly bearable, being judged by imbeciles and 'fanatical cretins' and becoming the subject of vendettas, which was to be feared. He was, he pointed out, accustomed to insults, having been called a hyena, a deserter, an apologist for the Mafia and many other things beside. This 'little Italy,' Sciascia wrote to a friend, had turned into a country of policemen, 'who have arrested, tried, persecuted, tormented and lynched me for almost two decades.' Seeing worms under stones had become a 'risky and dangerous' business. All one could do was return to satire, a 'frontier post, a watch tower between literature, civil society, politics'. It was a measure of the extent to which liberty had been shrunk that seeing the ridiculous side to things had become essential. It was a measure of Sciascia's extraordinary fame by the late 1970s, across the whole of Italy, that so many people wanted his opinion. So exceptionally private in his family life, he seemed to accept public fame almost as his due.

Moro's kidnapping marked an extraordinary moment in Italy's history. Seized on by journalists, writers, filmmakers and political commentators, it became the subject of countless films and pages of analysis. Dalla Chiesa's discovery of the flat in Milan eventually led to many arrests, five trials and thirty-three life sentences. But, as people were forced to conclude, there had been no sinister foreign hand at play. Moro had indeed been taken by a small number of Red Brigades terrorists, most of them children of the middle classes and either students or teachers, inhabiting a vast world of *'ultraclandestini'*, living in the shadows, convinced that only violence could save the Italians from the slavery imposed by capitalism. Mario Moretti, the man who fired the shots that killed Moro, explained in court that they had believed what they were witnessing in Italy was the total defeat of humanity. In the wake of the kidnapping came a concerted battle against extremists of both the left and the right. But the Christian Democrats and the Communists had effectively shown themselves to be incapable of governing; as Moro himself said, Italy was now *'un paese scombinato'* – a messed-up place.

Sciascia's verdict was concise. In spite of the new material, in spite of the slew of attacks, he would once again change nothing of what he had written, though had he been able to read more of Moro's letters to his family he would have got a stronger sense of his anguish and the strength of his Catholic faith. Moro's description of a rotten and ridiculous establishment shot through with terrifying power had, he believed, been perfectly accurate. With rather bitter resignation, Sciascia told a reporter from *Le Monde* that 'twenty years ago, I believed that the world could change: now I no longer do'. Lampedusa had been right. If terrorism failed, it was only because it 'was steered by little men'. However, he would never again allow himself to imagine things; he would only recount those things that had already taken place. 'I have become afraid,' he said, 'of saying things that then come to pass.' If, ten years earlier, anyone had told him that Moro and this book would alter his life, he would have laughed. But it had. Whatever he wrote or said 'always becomes a scandal'.

As his friend Bufalino put it, Sciascia had become the 'spokesman for the collective conscience of Italy'. Sciascia himself remarked only: 'I feel very isolated.' But then he added that being criticised by both left and right was a sign that he served neither, and that this, sometimes, gave him a feeling of *'allegria'* – cheerfulness. The Moro book, he said, indeed changed his life. In some way it stood for everything he had ever written, or might write.

A DEATH SENTENCE

The image of Moro's crumpled body in the boot of a small red car brought the 1970s to a close.

Aldo Moro's body

12

A thin and porous line

In 1975, while reviewing *Todo modo*, Pasolini had remarked that for all his growing success, Sciascia 'always kept himself very pure, like an adolescent', and that his considerable authority was linked to 'that something of weak and fragile that makes *un uomo solo*, a man alone'. The words pleased Sciascia. Defiant and a little bruised by the furore over *L'affaire Moro*, he continued to cling, like the detectives in his *gialli*, to the idea that reason and the intellect could be used to counter life in a profoundly corrupt state. Torn between this belief in the rational and his own experience of being Sicilian, and very conscious that the line of palm trees was indeed moving steadily north, turning all Italy into Sicily, he refused to give up asking questions, prodding, commenting, delving. As his friends remarked, Sciascia had his own particular ethical vision of the world and his own way of navigating life as a sceptic, with touches of Christian thought, Montaigne tinged with Pascal.

In Rome, the political fallout over Moro's kidnapping had seen increasingly desperate attempts to form new governments. As President Saragat observed, 'side by side with the corpse of Aldo Moro lies that of the First Republic'. It was quickly apparent that the links between the Communists and the Christian Democrats were too fragile to survive. Berlinguer, sick of being lulled and deflected by the wilier Andreotti, called an end to the *compromesso storico*. It was too late for Sciascia, disgusted by the PCI's lack of humanity and greed for power. Hitherto he had thought of them as 'vital' and a force for life; in abandoning Moro they had 'taken the side of death'. In any case, there was no going back to them after Amendola had dismissed him as 'the little elementary school teacher from Racalmuto'. Sciascia now told his friends that Italians should avoid politicians and politics altogether and instead invent some other system. His experience on Palermo's city council had left him with a sense of 'vertiginous impotence'. His friends agreed that, whatever else happened, Sciascia would never again be lured into active politics.

They were wrong. Just as nothing he ever wrote or thought was not in some way political, even now he could not quite give up the thought that he had a personal duty to confront the 'compromises, games, schemes, *omertà* and Mafia behaviour' in which all Italy seemed mired. For all Dalla Chiesa's successes, the Red Brigades killings continued. Berlinguer's promises of 'profound changes' in the social services had come to nothing; in the health services the profits of the chemical companies soared unchecked; the public sector debt remained crippling, fuelled by inefficiency and waste. Nowhere was this state of collapse truer than in Sicily and the south, where a fifth of the population lived below the poverty line and villages, emptied by emigration, were kept alive on pensions and subsidies. Water, everywhere, was in short supply. Much of the best of Sicily's magnificent coastline was a building site.

On 27 April 1979 Marco Pannella, the flamboyant, crusading leader of the Radical Party, flew to Palermo to meet Sciascia. He knew that his party stood for many things the Sicilian writer believed in, such as divorce and women's rights, and the Radicals had, after all, argued for Moro to be saved. He was hoping to persuade Sciascia to stand as a Radical both for Parliament and for the European Union. Few believed that he would succeed.

When Pannella broached the subject, there was a very long silence, the kind of silence for which Sciascia was now famous. Pannella was a big bullish man; Sciascia small and folded in on himself. He said later that he had been thinking about life and death, and that a writer interested in such things ought to go to Parliament in order to talk about them. Then, paraphrasing the Apostles, Sciascia spoke. 'You knocked,' he said, 'because you knew that the door was already open.' At the elections of 3–4 June, in which the Communists lost heavily, he was elected both for a European seat and for the Italian Parliament. He chose the Chamber of Deputies and Rome. Leaving Maria in Palermo, where his daughter Anna Maria had just had her second son, Vito, his fourth grandchild, he took a train to the capital and moved into the Hotel Nazionale, just by

Palazzo Montecitorio, the seat of the lower house. Asked what he hoped to achieve, he said: 'I am going to look, with great diffidence and great scepticism. One must see for oneself.' He had chosen the Radicals because they were least like a party, more in fact like a group of dissidents, and because their ethics were his own. 'Radicalism, when all is said and done, does not age.' And Sciascia, at heart, was an old Radical. He felt at home.

Worried about his health, Laura and Anna Maria tried hard to persuade him not to go. A recent fall had left him with a cracked vertebra. He was now fifty-nine and found travelling exhausting. At times, sitting down to rest in the shade, he dropped off.

Not all his friends forgave this move. Guttuso, whose attachment to the Communist Party remained almost fanatical, wrote an open letter to Sciascia in *La Repubblica*. Open letters were a standard forum for feuds of this kind. Sciascia's decision, he said, 'has made me reflect on the depth and quality of my friendship with you'. Sciascia's reply was terse. 'Dearest Friend and Inquisitor. You want to save my soul and I don't want to save yours. You are guided by certainty as I am by doubt.' They should agree to disagree. Friendship, for Sicilians, was always tricky. As Sciascia remarked, when he first joined the PCI on the city council in Palermo, his friends on the left had called him '*un grande scrittore*' – a great writer. After he published his attack on the party in *Il contesto*, they called him a coward. Now, they spoke of him as a traitor.

Sciascia's dislike for the Italian State was well known. But as he frequently said, he believed strongly in the constitution and above all in legality. He had a duty, he decided, towards himself as towards others, to challenge the general flouting of all rules; and the Radicals, he hoped, might break the eternal Italian pact 'between stupidity and violence'. As he told Elvira Sellerio, what was important was never to betray oneself in order to provide favours for people with whom you have nothing in common. As he saw it now, his job was to keep a wary eye on everything. Bufalino had been right; there was now something unmistakable about Sciascia as the conscience of the nation.

A large part of Sciascia's decision to accept Pannella's invitation stemmed from his desire to sit on the commission being set up to look into the whole Moro affair. Though the Christian Democrats protested strongly against his inclusion, saying that Sciascia was biased, he was nonetheless given a place on it. He wanted to be certain that he had missed nothing when doing his research. On 10 October, as if to lay down a marker of his interests, he delivered an excoriating attack on the new government. The elections, he said, had been fought on the question of the ungovernable nature of Italy. This had been to see it wrongly. The Italians were in fact the most governable people in the world. They were adaptable and patient; their acceptance of things was inexhaustible. It was those who governed who were inefficient and out of control, and everything that appeared ungovernable – principally subversion and criminality – came from the way the country was run and the failure of its leaders to understand what moral governance actually meant. As for the Mafia, it was a 'pathology' and should be treated as such. Asked what he would do were it up to him to govern, Sciascia replied: get rid of Andreotti. His 'Machiavellian paranoia' was turning Rome into the rule of the Borgias.

Sciascia was not a good speaker. But in a parliament in which interventions were known for their loquaciousness and impenetrability, he stood out for his brevity and the clarity of his words. He spoke very slowly, in a flat, anxious, hoarse voice, reading from scraps of paper, so softly that the other parliamentarians fell silent as they strained to hear. Someone observed that his words seemed 'almost sculpted in stone'. They were not accustomed to such concision. Emma Bonino, a fellow Radical, found him reserved and closed, 'more like a Piedmontese than a Sicilian'; she thought of him as a man who perfectly understood vice and malfeasance but was never overly judgemental. On the rare occasions when something moved him deeply, however, his sense of passion was unmistakable. When the Red Brigades kidnapped a judge called Giovanni d'Urso and threatened to kill him, Sciascia was vehement in his demands for a ransom to be paid. (It was and the judge was released.) Asked about his first impression of the Chamber of Deputies, Sciascia replied: 'The amount of words that are wasted here.'

His friends greatly enjoyed an anecdote that was soon doing the rounds. Sciascia had a young Roman secretary, gregarious and outspoken. Soon after his arrival in Rome, Sciascia received a visit from his friend and fellow Sicilian novelist Vincenzo Consolo. The young woman showed him in and was astonished when no word seemed to pass between the two men. A few days later, Consolo returned. Again, no word was spoken. At last, she could stand it no longer. Why, she asked Sciascia, do you not talk? Because, he replied, 'we already know everything about each other'. Gesualdo Bufolino told his own version. Waiting for Sciascia to reply, he said, was to listen to a series of 'little moans, gurgles, mutters, gentle sighs and fleeting mumbled breaths', and that, often, was all that you got.

Sciascia was invariably pleasant and courteous with his colleagues but made few friends in Parliament. Soon after arriving in Rome, he was asked to attend one of the regular reunions organised by the Radical Party in the Alban Hills. He came, 'sniffed the air' and wandered off, saying he wanted to visit the neighbourhood. He never attended another reunion and was as singularly uninterested in party schisms and disagreements as he was in all parliamentary obstructivism. He was, on the other hand, assiduous in sitting in on every hearing of the Moro Commission. Becoming increasingly heated, he was dogged, terrier-like, pressing witnesses on and on in his slow flat voice, asking why certain things had not been done, why clues had been overlooked. One day, four different carabinieri gave four different versions of the same event. Hesitant but also acute, Sciascia was always ready with '*un ultima domanda*' – a last question – irritating Dalla Chiesa and the other police witnesses by his endless 'what ifs'.

Sciascia was not without good friends in Rome, a city still weighed down by the memory of Moro. He was introduced to Fellini, who took him to the film studios at Cinecittà and introduced him to Ingrid Bergman, who, he said, reminded him of a Swiss governess. Bruno Caruso, the painter, had a studio close to the Piazza di Spagna, which had become a gathering place for Sicilians. In his breaks from Parliament, Sciascia joined them, arriving with little trays of Sicilian pastries, cheerful, quizzical, silent, conveying his thoughts by almost imperceptible movements of his head and a slight rise of his eyebrows, charming those present with his ironical smile. He was invariably perfectly turned out in a white shirt and tie and a well-tailored grey suit. In the afternoons, he and Caruso set out for the antiquarian bookshops and art galleries for Sciascia to acquire additions to his collection of portraits of writers. Caruso had painted one of D'Annunzio for him and one day they came across a walking stick with the head of Voltaire as its pummel. Pirandello had paced the streets of Rome during the 1930s and the two friends followed in his footsteps with 'Sicilian melancholy'. In Caruso's studio, a Venetian friend made the rigatoni with *melanzane* that all Sicilians love for their lunch.

Sometimes their route took them to the Caffè Greco in the Via Condotti, where Alberto Moravia and Elsa Morante held court. Sciascia kept saying that writers often treated him with reserve and even resentment. One visitor to Caruso's studio was Judge Cesare Terranova, for many years a highly principled prosecutor against the Mafia in Palermo and shortly to take up a senior job in Palermo's Ministry of Justice after nine years in Rome on the anti-Mafia Commission. Terranova was known for his doggedness in bringing the Corleonesi Mafia to trial, including Luciano Leggio, and for the stoicism and fury with which he was forced to accept their acquittals before a court in Bari. Another was a childhood friend of Sciascia's, the now successful tenor Luigi Infantino, tall, bulky, exuberant and gossipy, who talked loudly over the others in a long stream of reminiscences about Racalmuto and towered over the slight, sometimes taciturn Sciascia. Guttuso, now a Communist senator, was conducting an affair with a married Roman woman and came to implore Sciascia and Caruso to help him escape his jealous wife by keeping watch on street corners. At a dinner, Guttuso raised his glass to Sciascia: 'He has taught us Sicilians to love Sicily.'

Whenever he found time, Sciascia kept writing. He had recently published a collection of articles written over the past decade, mordant and incisive comments on literature, art, people, ideas and memory, testament to the extraordinary range of his interests. He called the book *Nero su nero*, as a parody of the pessimism he was so often accused of, 'the black writing on the black pages of reality', and he used the metaphor of a comb that gets rid of knots, the comb being the State, the knots all the violations and malfeasances, saying that unfortunately Italy currently had no comb. He was also working on three volumes of an anthology of literature for secondary schools, impressing his co-editors with his prodigious memory and erudition, insisting on including pieces that spoke of 'respect, tolerance, pity, discretion, humility and love of justice', and railing against any suggestion that culture was simply an ornament detached from real life. Though he often repeated that 'either one writes or one teaches' and that for him there was no contest, he also said that he remained a teacher at heart. And he found time to put together an *inchiesta* about a bold and intransigent cleric who had been persecuted by his superiors for failing to ensure that his parishioners voted for the Christian Democrats in the 1946 elections. He called it *Dalle parti degli infedeli* and was delighted, having written so often about bad priests, to have finally found a good one. This *inchiesta* provided him with what he called a delicious 'holiday' from the tedium of Parliament.

In the autumn of 1976 Sciascia had written an article for the *Corriere della Sera* saying how much he approved of the PCI leader, Berlinguer, and though his stance over the *compromesso storico* and Moro's abduction had alienated him, he went on considering Berlinguer a good man. Soon after Sciascia joined the Moro Commission, Andreotti came to give evidence. In the course of the questioning, Sciascia mentioned how, at a meeting he had had with Berlinguer in 1977, the Communist leader had said that he believed it possible that the Red Brigades had received help from Czechoslovakia, and for that reason the Italian government had thought to expel two Czech diplomats. Andreotti, with his customary slipperiness, said that he knew nothing about it.

The conversation in 1977 had been private and Guttuso had been present. When Sciascia brought it up in the Moro Commission, it was picked up by the newspapers and exploded as a scandalous story. Berlinguer denied that it had ever taken place, called on the President, Francesco Cossiga, to back him up and threatened to sue Sciascia for defamation. Sciascia turned to Guttuso to support him. Guttuso, flustered, announced during a television interview that he and Sciascia were indeed old friends, but that by asking him to lie for him he was behaving like a *mafioso*. 'It's something I would never do to a friend.' The political obedience imposed by Togliatti on artists, writers and scientists still held many Communists in its grip.

Sciascia's furious rejoinder came quickly. It was a perfectly simple choice between lying and telling the truth. He did not feel himself to be in any sense *mafioso*, and he had believed that his friendship with Guttuso included a code about truth, and not one about *omertà* and false testimony. Pressed further, Guttuso sided with Berlinguer. Sciascia counter-sued for calumny. The case was then dropped, but the feeling among many parliamentarians was that Sciascia was in the wrong. Berlinguer, said Sciascia, had behaved 'like a child stamping his feet', and he was angry that he had not had a chance to put his case across in court. 'I only know,' he said, 'that lies are never justifiable, neither when they involve people, nor before the law, nor out of ideology.' It was, he said, a question of the sanctity of truth; to deny it was to 'despise humanity'.

There is a saying in Sicily that when enemies fall out, they make it up. But that when friends fall out there is no going back. The break with Guttuso was unmendable. Their long, close, mutually admiring and affectionate friendship was over and they never spoke again, though from time to time Guttuso made overtures in Sciascia's direction. When a publisher not long after asked Sciascia about some pictures that Guttuso had been meant to deliver, Sciascia replied: 'My relations with Guttuso are not terrible: they no long exist.' The incident was, for him, not just another example of the profound incompatibility between power and truth in Italy. It was an unforgivable exercise in non-friendship. And Sciascia, stubborn, unwilling to reconsider or show a gentler side, was not always a forgiving man.

Moro's kidnapping had appalled and stunned Italy; but it did not change it. The absence of 'a sense of State', as lamented by Sciascia, continued, with the vein of endemic cronyism running through the Christian Democrat Party, the '*razza padrona*' – the race of bosses – which did not see itself bound by the law. While the State became an abstract concept, the political parties colonised the banks, industry, the trade unions and the press, making fortunes from every kind of financial chicanery. No one was held accountable. The lawbreakers identified by brave magistrates and reporters were rapidly freed for lack of evidence.

Quick on the heels of the Moro case came a further, enormous, scandal.

The Banco Ambrosiano had been founded in 1896 by a group of devout Catholics in Milan wanting to provide a counterpart to the lay banks they deemed to be hotbeds of Freemasonry. Its current chairman was a dapper, unprincipled, secretive man who looked on the world as a place full of predators. Roberto Calvi was also deep in a great web of shadowy financial deals. One of the directors of Ambrosiano Overseas was Archbishop Paul Marcinkus, President of the Vatican Bank, the 6 foot, 3 inch prelate who liked to play tennis and golf. Another banker, also deeply mired in shady operations, was Michele Sindona, the son of a florist from Messina, a tax lawyer who did business on behalf of Italian and American financiers and owned the Franklin Bank in the US, said to be a deposit for Mafia money. Sindona had trafficked illegally in grain in Sicily at the end of the war, with the tacit acceptance of the Allied Military Authority. By the end of the 1970s, he had put in place a tapestry of shell companies, using tax havens for large sums of money spirited out of Italy, helped by the liquid state of international capital markets. Calvi and Sindona, along with their friends and clients, prospered greatly. They were rumoured to be laundering heroin money in Switzerland. But then their fortunes changed. Debts mounted. Cornered, they turned to ever wilder and more illicit schemes. Their speculations floundered.

A suspicious Bank of Italy decided to send a lawyer, Giorgio Ambrosoli, to explore suspect transactions involving the far right and the Mafia. Ambrosoli was diligent and courageous. By 1979 he had unearthed a slew of fraudulent deals involving Calvi and Sindona. He said to his wife: 'Whatever happens, I'll pay a high price for this.' At midnight on 11 July, returning home from dinner in Milan, he was shot dead. Coming at a time when the Red Brigades were still at large, the shooting caused little surprise.

Before his death, however, Ambrosoli had given vital evidence to the US authorities about Sindona, already wanted on charges of fraud and falsifying balance sheets and now holed up in the Hotel Pierre in New York, complaining that he was the subject of a witch hunt. The Franklin Bank went bankrupt, the biggest bank crash in history. Arranging to have himself 'kidnapped', Sindona disappeared. Bearing a passport in the name of Joseph Bonamico and disguised by a beard and moustache, he managed with the help of the Mafia to get himself back to Italy, where he hoped to drum up support.

One of his ports of call was Palermo, where, having met some of the Mafia bosses, he got the brother of a mutual friend from

Racalmuto to visit Sciascia, show him documents ostensibly proving his innocence and ask for his intervention. Sciascia, the friend said, had prestige. Sciascia took the documents but wisely did nothing, saying later that Sindona epitomised the world that was most crooked in Italy, its politics, banking and the increasingly terrifying reach of the Mafia. It was yet more proof that corruption was now to be found in all places and at all levels of Italian society. Sindona was eventually sentenced to twenty-five years on ninety-nine counts of perjury, misappropriation of funds and fraud, with thirty extra months for false kidnapping; he was said to have cost Italy $4 billion.

The whole murky business was only just beginning. Enough had emerged to make the Italian authorities act. They dispatched the Guardia della Finanza, the financial police, to the villa and offices of Licio Gelli, Venerable Grand Master of the P2 Masonic lodge of which Sindona had been the financial brains and Calvi an active member. To his friends, Gelli described himself as 'part Garibaldi, part Cagliostro', a reference to the flamboyant eighteenth-century adventurer. There, in his clothing factory near Arezzo, they discovered a wall safe and in it a list of 962 names, including two cabinet ministers, fifty generals and admirals, sixteen newspaper editors and thirty-eight members of parliament. It looked suspiciously like a parallel Italian State, though the P2 network extended far beyond Italy, to Brazil, Argentina and Uruguay. Many of the names on it were Sicilian.

The documents found in the safe provided ample proof that Gelli had been trying to put together a vast anti-Communist network, effectively a whole other State. Arrest warrants were issued and investigations launched. Many individuals on the list were put on 'leave' from their jobs in the army, the police, the secret services and the civil service; others sat at home, trembling. Gelli, accused of spying and posing a danger to the State, managed to escape abroad. There were rumours that Andreotti had had links with P2, had tried to protect Sindona, and that he had had a hand in the murder of a journalist called Mino Pecorelli, who had written but not yet published an incriminating article. But, fighting off the accusations, he refused to step down and, though bruised, remained in place, at the heart of the political establishment. As a Milanese prosecutor called Giuliano Furone put it, what the whole

Sindona affair had made clear was that the line in Italy between the legal and the illegal, the respectable and the criminal, was now 'very thin and very porous'. It was not simply, as Sciascia had infuriated people by writing in *Todo modo*, a question of Mafia infiltration, but of a whole society rotten to its core, on which the Mafia had skilfully found lucrative ways to feed.

The police now had enough to arrest Calvi, whose Banco Ambrosiano, where shareholders included orphanages and old people's homes, was revealed to be sunk beneath $1,300 million in unrecoverable loans. Half had been used to buy shares; as for the rest, it could not be traced. Cut lose by the Vatican and his former friends, Calvi, out on bail, disappeared. Obsessed with his own safety, he had reinforced his office with bullet-proof windows and a double-locking lift and he travelled everywhere with eight bodyguards. No one ever established precisely what path took him to London. But there, on 18 June 1981, his body was found hanging from scaffolding under Blackfriars Bridge. In his pocket was £7,400 in cash. There were also heavy lumps of stone weighing down his trousers. Five weeks later, a coroner ruled death by suicide. The Ambrosiano bank was declared insolvent and 39,000 investors lost everything. As with the Moro kidnapping, speculation filled the newspapers day after day, suggesting that it was far more likely that the banker had been murdered, whether at the hands of the Freemasons, the Vatican, neo-Fascist extremists, the Mafia or Opus Dei. The choice of Blackfriars Bridge, with its connotations with the Dominicans, was thought significant.

Sciascia, talking it over with various friends, among them Moravia, was more inclined to think that Calvi had decided to take his own life, driven to a kind of schizophrenia by the prospect of imminent arrest. He feared being charged with the murder of Ambrosoli, and he was terrified of the idea of prison. In his luggage was found a large quantity of barbiturates. Calvi had arranged, Sciascia thought, his suicide to look like murder, so as to be remembered as the victim of a complicated, obscure intrigue involving secret powers. Calvi, Sciascia concluded, with characteristic terseness, was one of Italy's many men of 'absolute mediocrity'.

Calvi, Gelli and Sindona: they alone were proof of the degree to which, by the early 1980s, the Italian State, along with the army, the political parties and the Church, had fallen into aberrant ways. It was all uncannily as Sciascia had foreseen. The collapse of the Ambrosiano was a clear example of what could go wrong when financial structures went unchecked, political parties craved power and money, the State indulged in flagrant corruption and allowed its relations with the Vatican to become murky. Nor was terrorism quite spent. The last decade had seen over 12,000 violent deaths, 650 of them in 1979 alone, the worst attack carried out in August 1980 when a bomb went off in Bologna station killing eighty-five people and wounding two hundred. In no other Western democracy had assassination become such an instrument of political warfare; nor had mysterious crashes, unexplained deaths and attempted coups become the pattern of daily life, with everyone suspicious of everyone else.

For Sciascia, there was a somewhat ambiguous rider. Late one night in Palermo he was summoned to appear before the magistrate soon to occupy centre stage in the unfolding drama of the Mafia. Giovanni Falcone was investigating Sindona's Sicilian contacts. Having got wind of the approach to Sciascia made by the Racalmuto contact, he wished to know more, but, tactfully, chose a time late in the evening when Sciascia would not be seen. But Sciascia had nothing to say, repeating only that he had no memory of the occasion. And he was indignant about the summons, feeling himself to be above suspicion in these matters. Falcone later remarked that he could have indicted Sciascia (he could not, for Sciascia still had parliamentary immunity) but had not done so out of respect for the writer whom he considered had first put the Mafia accurately into fiction. But for Sciascia, the incident left a slightly bad taste. He was at a low ebb, telling Mario La Cava that everything in his life seemed distant and useless and that he had lost all wish to write and, what was worse, to read.

Sindona was not the only man who attempted to court Sciascia for his stamp of approval, but he was becoming adept at avoiding petitions. One day Ciancimino, the building assessor and sacker of Palermo and briefly its mayor, spotting Sciascia in the Hotel Plaza in Rome, hovered and then accosted him to ask for a favour. Sciascia was cornered and felt obliged to say that he would read anything that was sent to him. In the event, to his great relief, nothing came. He was wilier when Salvatore Lima, described by the Anti-Mafia Commission as one of the pillars of the Mafia in Palermo, was announced to be arriving at a gathering which he was attending, slipping away before he could be approached. Fame was bringing encounters he did not care for. As he said, the links of Sicilian friendship were very long and you could never be certain which of them were *mafiosi*.

And it was hard, in Sicily, to keep yourself untouched by the Mafia, especially if, like Sciascia, your instinct was to befriend underdogs and people you suspected of being unjustly treated. Some years earlier, he had received a letter from a man called Sirchio, serving a long sentence in a prison on the island of Linosa for Mafia crimes. That he turned to Sciascia was both a measure of his fame and a reflection on the grey area inhabited by Sicilians who saw in him a champion of all victims of injustice, whoever they were. Sirchio wrote that he had heard about *The Day of the Owl* and longed to read it, but without money he was a 'poor devil who longs to escape this inferno' in books and was unable to buy any. Sciascia sent him a parcel of books and the two men continued to correspond. Always on the lookout for the names of politicians and senior figures in business and the judiciary connected to the Mafia, Sciascia pressed him for information. Sirchio was evasive, saying that in his world *omertà* had to be respected. He told Sciascia that he was longing for the day of his release when he would take his family to some country far from Sicily. When that day came, he was shot dead, together with his wife, as he left the prison.

While politics remained extremely fragile in Rome, they had become critical in Palermo. 1979 had seen the true beginnings of the *cadaveri eccellenti*, the policemen, magistrates, judges and reformers gunned down, one after the other, by the vengeful Mafia. One of the first to go was Boris Giuliano, the jovial policeman with the flowing moustache who had helped Sciascia investigate a mysterious case and who had continued, terrier-like, to search for clues for the disappearance of Mauro De Mauro. Giuliano looked and was a good man. He was shot as he sat drinking a cappuccino in a bar in Palermo. He had just discovered a suitcase at the airport, containing hundreds of thousands of dollars, clearly linked to the explosive new profits coming from the Sicilian Mafia's graduation from cigarettes into drugs. After receiving a death threat, he sent his family off to a town in the interior, saying that he would soon join them. He never made it. The Mafia, traditionally, had steered clear of killing state employees or policemen: Giuliano's death was a message that things were changing.

As Sciascia had repeatedly warned, the Mafia was on the move, striking far beyond Sicily. By the end of the 1970s, the Sicilian Mafia, having built on the capital accumulated from building contracts and the black market, was dispatching over $1billion worth of refined heroin to the United States via Switzerland, Lichtenstein, Britain and elsewhere, having imported it, unrefined, from the golden triangle of Burma, Thailand and Laos. The *mafiosi* were no longer fixers but entrepreneurs and they were busy creating a spiralling number of drug addicts. This, Sciascia had not foreseen. When consulted now as a *mafiologo*, a term he had come to hate more and more, he would say that he no longer understood the modern Mafia, as he had in his days in Racalmuto, when he knew them in his bones, watching the local *mafiosi* doing business. He mourned Giuliano, saying that he had admired him greatly and that he had died because, uniquely, he was a man trying to do his duty.

Next to be picked off was another friend, Cesare Terranova, the heavy, bald, round-faced senior magistrate with whom Sciascia had visited art galleries in Rome, enjoying his obvious delight in the good things in life. Terranova, he said, had innate candour, the 'eyes and look of a child', along with being extremely shrewd. On a Sunday in September 1979 Terranova had arrived back in Palermo to take up his new post; by the Tuesday he was dead. He had been investigating the vast drug profits and planned to challenge the impunity of the men protecting the Mafia. Not until you get rid of compromise and corruption, he told journalists, will you make the public trust the State and its institutions. Terranova was known to his friends as a fanatical worker and he had compared the situation in Sicily to an earthquake with shifting tectonic plates. Shortly before his return, a journalist had asked him whether he was frightened for his life? No, he replied, 'the worst they can do is kill me'. With him died his long-term carabiniere bodyguard and friend Lenin Mancuso. As they left for work that Tuesday morning, Terranova's wife had heard what she thought was a lorry dropping a load of bricks. Then came the unmistakable sound of shots. She knew. Terranova had told her that the Mafia never killed judges. But times had changed.

After the death of Emanuele Basile, a carabiniere captain who had taken over Giuliano's investigations, shot while watching a Feast Day procession with his four-year-old daughter in his arms, it was the turn of Piersanti Mattarella, the President of the Sicilian Region. Mattarella had recently announced that he intended to make all building contracts transparent and that he would explore all cases of complicity between politicians and the Mafia. Six months later, another friend of Sciascia's, the Chief Prosecutor Gaetano Costa, died while browsing a stall of books in the Via Cavour, in the very heart of Palermo. His killers were two men on a motorcycle. Just two days earlier, Costa had signed arrest warrants for fifty-five *mafiosi*, doing so alone after his colleagues refused to add their names, a fact that was leaked to the newspapers. He and Sciascia had known each other since their schooldays in Caltanissetta. Questioned about these deaths, Sciascia sounded weary and more terse than usual. The truth was, he said, that the State had no real desire to confront anything.

In *La Stampa*, Sciascia again urged the authorities to follow the money: both Giuliano and Costa had seen that this was the way ahead and it was because of this, he insisted, that they had died. Asked how he was protecting himself, given that he was so outspoken, he said that he was doing so by isolating himself, closing himself away, seldom going out and frequenting only good friends. Did he feel threatened? 'No, the Mafia doesn't read books ... And if you have to ask yourself if you are afraid, then you cease to live.' Then, paraphrasing Lampedusa, he went on: 'In Italy you can say and write anything you like and everything remains the same.' The journalist who asked him the question was the round-faced, genial Walter Tobagi of the *Corriere della Sera*. A few days later, Tobagi was assassinated. Sciascia wept.

The Anti-Mafia Commission, which had endured through three separate legislatives, had been wound up after thirteen years with almost no results, beyond a vast documentation – which could have been extremely valuable – buried in the vaults of the State archives. Sciascia felt despair. It was as if, he said, the commission had never existed, and 'we are doomed to perpetual lies'.

In Palermo, the funerals of the murdered men, with their bodyguards and police escorts, had become familiar spectacles, the coffins carried through the streets to the cathedral, shrouded in the robes they had worn as magistrates and judges, people staring out silently from their half-shuttered windows.

13

Pensioning off the dead

There had been a brief moment, after the setting up of the Anti-Mafia Commission and the first Mafia wars of the early seventies over turf and territory, when the Mafia itself had seemed to falter. But that had been an illusion. Those arrested and sent to the *'confino'* – forced residence in distant outposts – had taken the Mafia with them, and as the drug market grew, so, as Sciascia had warned, the palm tree had indeed gone north, to Rome, Milan and on across Europe, creating an epidemic of drug addicts. In Sicily, the Cupola – the governing body which presided over the many clans – had used the years when the authorities were distracted by terrorism well, establishing a stranglehold on businesses and enterprises, few of which were able to function without them. It had become not just easier to work with the Mafia: it was the only way. As the magistrate Falcone would say, in words very like those used by Sciascia, the Mafia had become not so much a cancer growing on a healthy body as an octopus existing in symbiosis with collaborators, informants and protectors, its tentacles reaching high into the political parties, the Church and the Masonic lodges. But when Sciascia had said it, back in 1961, no one had listened.

Palermo itself, at the beginning of the 1980s, was still in the grip of the venal Salvo Lima, Andreotti's 'plenipotentiary' in Sicily, along with Vito Ciancimino, who had his finger in every lucrative pie. Between them they had handed out credit to entrepreneurs, administrators of banks and building consortia, and many of their cronies had grown rich. Few were richer than the Salvo cousins, the gregarious Nino and the taciturn Ignazio, small, sharp and *'signorile'* – gentlemanly – who had been allowed as private citizens – under an ancient Bourbonic law to set themselves up as tax collectors, taking 10 per cent of taxes the two of them brought in. Out of their gains, the cousins had built an empire in hotels and vineyards, feeding on EU grants. They drove Mercedes and Range Rovers. In Palermo harbour, their yacht *Alicia* was said to be hung with paintings by Matisse and Van Gogh. For the wedding of Nino's daughter Angela, Andreotti, Prime Minister at the time, had sent a large silver tray. This was the first generation of politicians and civil servants who enjoyed hunting parties attended by the '*fior fiore* of the Italian Mafia'.

The early Mafia bosses, such as Don Peppino Genco Russo and Don Calò, men known personally to Sciascia, had been grandees, enjoying the subtle exercise of power and preferring the shadows, even while indulging in brutality and exploitation. The bosses who came after them were of a more blatantly vicious breed. Having risen through the building spree and control of the vegetable, meat and cigarette markets, they seemed inured to violence. With the vast profits from drugs, the Mafia had become an international syndicate, far more dangerous than the terrorists, though it still suited many people not to think so. The clans operating in and immediately around Palermo were dominated by two Palermo bosses, Stefano Bontate and Gaetano Badalamenti, and their friend Salvatore Inzerillo; but in nearby Corleone were others who wanted control.

One of these was Toto Riina, '*La Belva*' – the beast – who passed himself off as naive but who was in fact shrewd, greedy and deeply ambitious. Riina's massacres were referred to as '*mattanza*', after the name given to the yearly spring slaughter of tuna as they swam past Sicily. Another was Bernardo Provenzano, known as 'the tractor' for his machine-like capacity for slaughter. The Corleonesi included Michele Greco, a man who looked like a country squire and was nicknamed '*il Papa*' – the Pope – for his stately demeanour. Behind these men was Luciano Leggio, the ugly hitman and cattle rustler, with his great fleshy lips and back disfigured by a spinal condition. Leggio had arrived in Palermo not long after Don Calò's sumptuous funeral in Villalba, sleek but malevolent, preceded by a reputation as a gifted killer, smoking his fat cigars and roaming the streets with his army of informers 'held together with the spittle of gold and blood'. Leggio was well in with the Christian Democrats. Though finally arrested and imprisoned for the murder of Dr Navarra the hospital director who had injected air into the veins of the eleven-year-old witness to his crimes, Leggio had been able for many years to roam Europe, helping to build up the Mafia across Italy. Penned up, he was no less active.

On 2 April, 1981, as he was leaving a party in Palermo given for his forty-third birthday, Bontate's Porsche was ambushed. No one but his family attended his funeral, but his coffin was followed by five trucks carrying wreaths, none of which bore a name. A month later, Inzerillo was shot dead through the bullet-proof windows of his Alfa Romeo. What became known as the Second Mafia Wars exploded. Young men strode about the streets of Sicily with guns; headless corpses turned up in gutters. Windows were shot out. The killings multiplied, sometimes at the rate of one or two a day, as slowly, victory went to the Corleonesi. The map of Mafia power was gradually rewritten by the silver-haired country gentleman, Michele Greco, and the physically gross Luciano Leggio. Those in Palermo who survived often chose to switch sides. Between 1980 and 1982, some thousand people were strangled, shot or poisoned and then dismembered. Twenty-one members of the Inzerillo family were wiped out, including one fifteen-year-old boy. These were the bloodiest years in Palermo's often bloody history.

But the brave men, the lawyers and journalists and judges who had been trying to foil the Mafia, were not forgotten. Terranova, Giuliano and Costa had been dealt with, but more *cadaveri eccellenti* continued to pile up. On 30 April 1982, it was the turn of Pio La Torre, a member of parliament and the regional secretary of the Communist Party, who had spent his life supporting agricultural workers against the Mafia. La Torre had drafted new laws aimed at organised crime. With him died his driver, Rosario Di Salvo. At his funeral, 200,000 Palermitani gathered to mourn and rail against the authorities. Sciascia, appalled, would have preferred to say nothing, but was as ever canvassed for his views. He said that La Torre's killing should serve as a warning, not to back off, but to multiply attacks on the Mafia.

In June 1982, while Sciascia was in Rome, a writer called Colette Rosselli, who was an old friend of President Pertini, took him with her to lunch at the Quirinale. It promised to be an agreeable occasion. Pertini, a renowned former partisan and outspoken in his advocacy for democratic reform, was a genial, intelligent man.

As they sat down, Pertini brought up a recent but not particularly acerbic exchange that the two men had had in the newspapers. Sciascia said nothing. He sat, wrote Rosselli later, 'impenetrable as a stone'. Pertini pressed on, in a light, teasing tone. Sciascia remained silent. Finally, exasperated, Pertini burst out: 'For goodness' sake, speak!' Very slowly, Sciascia rumbled into speech. '*Signor Presidente*—' Pertini stopped him. 'What do you mean, Signor Presidente? Do you consider me an enemy?' Sciascia started again, using *Lei*, the formal form of address. Pertini interrupted again. The famous Sciascia silence followed. At last, Sciascia said what he had planned to say: that the only way to remove the Mafia in Sicily was to introduce stringent bank controls, and that Pertini, as President, was the only man who could insist on it. Pertini listened but was clearly irritated. He promised to speak to the 'proper authorities'. The lunch was, as Rosselli wrote later, ruined. No one was happy: Sciascia because he felt that he had wasted a good opportunity; the President because he had failed to seduce Sciascia. 'And me, because I hadn't enjoyed myself.' As Matteo Collura would write in his biography of Sciascia, he was a man who excelled at 'fortifying himself in silence'.

The authorities, however, did react. They sent General Carlo Alberto Dalla Chiesa, the man who had scored notable successes against the Red Brigades, many of whose members were in prison or awaiting trial, to Sicily. He was now named Prefect of Palermo in the hopes that he might do as well against the Mafia. He had been studying its workings, he said, like a chessboard. He was a solid, heavy, fatherly figure, with deep pouches under his eyes and a sad and pensive look; he had a small moustache and wore glasses. La Torre had been a good friend and they had been putting together a dossier on the sources of wealth of some 3,192 Sicilian individuals. Dalla Chiesa flew to Palermo early in order to attend La Torre's funeral. Before leaving Rome he had been to see Andreotti to tell him of his intentions of investigating the political connections of the Mafia in Sicily. Andreotti, he noted in his diary, 'went white'. Soon after, an article appeared asking why Italy's foremost police officer needed to be posted to Sicily.

Dalla Chiesa knew Sicily well. In the late 1960s and early 1970s he had been in charge of the carabinieri in Palermo, where he had been active in the battles against the bandits, and he had recently been giving evidence to the Anti-Mafia Commission about the corrupt practices of Ciancimino and Lima. Since his new appointment had been made public there had been a concerted campaign against him, with the new Mayor of Palermo, Nello Martellucci, said to be head of the *'truppe Andreottiane'* – Andreotti's followers – in Sicily, arguing that any investigation into the assets and wealth of prominent Sicilians would only stifle the free market economy. Dalla Chiesa, he said, was an 'outsider', sent to destroy Sicily's riches. For his part, Dalla Chiesa declared the Andreotti faction to be the 'most compromised political party of Palermo'.

None of this prevented his appointment, but it did translate into a lack of official backing: though he repeatedly asked not for 'exceptional powers' but proper support, it was not forthcoming. In a diary he kept in the form of a letter to his first wife, who had died some years before, Dalla Chiesa wrote that he was being catapulted 'into a treacherous place . . . with no one to help me, no friendly face'. It was not like the fight against the terrorists, where he had the carabinieri and the army behind him. He was neither panic stricken nor even frightened, but, he admitted, it would be suicide not to have extra escorts and staff as well as a bit of *'fantasia'* – a bit of imagination. Miracles were expected of him, but the forces against him were formidable. He told a friend, 'I feel an immense emptiness inside me.'

Dalla Chiesa arrived to find Palermo full of dread. The streets were eerily empty. The extra powers he had repeatedly asked for – permission to explore bank records and tap phones – had been met with obfuscation. He decided to speak directly to the Sicilians, visiting schools and community groups. He told them that in Sicily there was now 'danger in the air' but that he planned to reduce this fear and bring 'serenity and peace' back to the city. He laid out a different model for the island, freed from Mafia hegemony. 'Let us grow in number and be less afraid,' he told them. The 'piranhas of the Mafia' had to be deprived of water. It was a declaration of war. As he told a reporter from *L'Unità*, he felt that he was operating in the 'forward trenches of Italian democracy'.

Dalla Chiesa took a few steps to make himself more secure. He moved his desk so that he could not be shot through the window and sacked two cleaners he discovered had Mafia connections. He resolved never to drink a cup of coffee on his own, poison being a tried Mafia method. He built up a team of trusted men. But he did not increase his escort, saying that it would only draw attention to himself.

On 12 August he was back in Rome, outlining the circuits of Mafia power to the Minister of the Interior and explaining how Catania had become its second epicentre. He told a journalist that he had four goals: to fight the Mafia, whatever it took; to extend his inquiries to Catania and beyond; to shake people out of their inertia and complacency; and to challenge the whole panoply of public administration in Palermo, weighed down as it was by Mafia interests. He knew, he added, that the most dangerous moment for figures like himself came with a particular combination of peril and isolation. It would be a 'titanic battle'. The article caused a stir.

The Dalla Chiesa family was close; that summer they met at their country villa at Prata in Tuscany to which the general talked of retiring. He seemed preoccupied. The rumbling crises in the government in Rome were creating an atmosphere of uncertainty throughout Italy. When his son Nando asked him who he felt his major enemies were, he replied: 'The *Andreottini*, who are up to their necks in everything.' But he was not without friends. The Archbishop of Palermo, Salvatore Pappalardo, was one of them, and there were many on the left who wished him well. 'I cannot betray them,' he told Nando.

After several years as a widower, Dalla Chiesa had met Emanuela Setti Carraro, a young Milanese woman working for the Red Cross. They married that summer in a castle in Trentino and she insisted on travelling to Palermo with him. What the Mafia was calling 'Operation Carlo Alberto' meant bodies left on the steps of carabinieri barracks. An anonymous caller told the newspapers: 'The operation is almost concluded. I repeat *almost concluded.*' Pictures of dartboards were being circulated with Dalla Chiesa's face in the middle.

On the evening of 3 September, Dalla Chiesa booked a table at a restaurant, though he planned to spend the evening at home. Earlier that day he had secretly met with the US consul in Palermo to see whether any support might be forthcoming from the Americans. As dusk fell, Emanuela collected him from his office in her car. His escort, with his long-term driver Domenico Russo, followed behind. They were ambushed on the Via Carini by eight men, four on motorcycles, the rest in a car. Dalla Chiesa tried to protect his young wife, and Russo, rushing to their side, tried to shelter them both from the bullets. Though Dalla Chiesa was already dead, the killers shot him again in the face, perhaps, so it was later said, because when you destroy a man's face you destroy his soul. He had been in Sicily for 127 days. Emanuela died at once; Russo of his injuries later. On hearing the news, the *mafiosi* in jails all over the island rejoiced 'as if the end of the world had come'.

Sciascia was at *La Noce* and it was not until the following morning that he learnt of the assassination from journalists who descended on him to ask his views. His immediate reply was that he could no longer decipher the workings of the Mafia as he once had: it was now a 'Mafia gone mad'. He seemed to the reporters hesitant and pained.

In both Sicily and the rest of Italy, however, something fundamental had happened. It was as if Dalla Chiesa's death was finally a step too far. The major newspapers all used the same headline: 'A National Problem'. The public, apparently apathetic and resigned to the recent murders, now burst out into loud expressions of fury, outrage and profound grief. The whole of Italy seemed galvanised. Politicians came from Rome for the funerals, for which the Sicilians lined the streets of Palermo, many of them in tears. Archbishop Pappalardo gave the eulogy, which was bold and accusatory and earned him the name 'anti-Mafia Cardinal'. But as the ministers and Christian Democrat politicians left the cathedral they were pelted with bottles, spat at and kicked. Coins were thrown, to suggest that they had been 'bought'. Dalla Chiesa's body was flown to Milan, then buried in the family vault in Parma. Everywhere, vast crowds followed the hearse. At the site of the attack in Palermo, a large placard was put with the words: 'Here lies the hopes of honest Palermitani'.

Thirteen days after his death, Parliament, which had been dragging its heels, finally passed La Torre's proposed laws. Extraordinarily, the word 'Mafia' had still, by 1982, not been introduced into law. For the first time, belonging to the Mafia was made punishable by long prison sentences; bank confidentiality for suspects was abolished and any assets acquired through violence were to be confiscated. The Guardia della Finanza was set to work its way

PENSIONING OFF THE DEAD

Falcone at Chiesa's funeral

through a labyrinth of accounts. A new high commissioner for the fight against the Mafia was appointed, with the powers that Dalla Chiesa had asked for and been denied. Consulted again, Sciascia said that to destroy the Mafia, more, much more, action was needed and far fewer words, but that they were, at last, on the right track.

But nothing in Sicily was ever quite straightforward. A furious controversy broke out, a war of bitter words that soon drew in Sciascia. Had the general been killed because he knew too much about the Moro kidnapping? Was Andreotti involved? Why had Dalla Chiesa's name appeared on the list of members of P2? Was it true that he had explained his membership by saying that he wanted to investigate what it was all about? Dalla Chiesa's son Nando lashed out at the Christian Democrats, saying that they had abandoned his father, and was accused in turn of not being in good faith because he was a Communist. Martellucci, the Mayor of Palermo, took to telling friends that Dalla Chiesa had been so lax he had effectively committed suicide. Andreotti, drawn into the fray and asked about Lima and his cronies, declared: 'They are all *galantuomini*' – righteous men. As for the constant funerals now taking place in Sicily, well, personally he preferred christenings. Andreotti's name was increasingly being mentioned, though it would be some years before his complicity became clearer. For Sciascia, however, there was very little doubt. Andreotti, many times Prime Minister and skilful courter of cardinals and politicians, was the 'quintessence of the Italy I do not love'. He was shrewd and he had an 'inner hardness'.

Andreotti and Lima

Then Sciascia joined in the furore, certainly intemperately. This might, with hindsight, have been a rare occasion when he would have done better to remain silent and sit out the reproaches. Writing in the *Corriere della Sera*, he suggested that Dalla Chiesa, not being Sicilian, had not really understood how profoundly murderous the Mafia had become, nor how much it had changed since his earlier posting. Asked whether Dalla Chiesa had been his model for Bellodi in *The Day of the Owl*, a question often put to him, he explained again that he was not, and that his model had been his friend Candida, the carabiniere captain whose book he had helped to get published. An acid exchange with Dalla Chiesa's son Nando swirled on, conducted as was usual in the pages of the daily newspapers, insults and accusations traded back and forth. Nando declared that Italian intellectuals had become cynical; Sciascia replied that he did not see himself as belonging to such a category: 'if someone behind me shouts out "intellectual", I don't even turn round.' What powers should Dalla Chiesa have been given: curfews? Mass deportations? There were, said Sciascia, too many powers already against terrorism. Once again, his overriding concern with the law and legality made him sound curiously absolute and unbending.

The tit for tat was only beginning. Sciascia had welcomed Dalla Chiesa's appointment as a man 'who had understood many things', and he had been saddened by his death. But it was important not to turn him into a myth and 'drown in despair'. There was still hope. Sciascia's intervention, Nando replied, was a 'concentrated dose of arsenic and old lace': he was clearly more interested in attacking his father than fighting the Mafia. He was 'playing the Mafia's game'. And what was more, Sciascia was known to have 'given a bit of advice' to Sindona. Sciascia threatened legal action for defamation. Not content to stay silent, in this new controversy playing out week after week in the magazines and daily papers, Sciascia accused Nando of 'furious braying' in a world of 'delirium and mania' which had long since given up analysing facts. Nando was a 'little rascal' who had come to believe that his father was, like Garibaldi, a figure about whom no ill could be said, when in fact his death belonged to the sad 'chronicle of these years' and it was perfectly legitimate to express an opinion. As for braying back, he was completely incapable of doing so. Furthermore, he was sick of being accused of things he had not said by 'imbeciles and malicious people'. The insults rumbled on for a while, then finally fell silent. But they left a taste of animosity which would never go away.

For a moment, by his death, Dalla Chiesa appeared to achieve what, alive, he had been unable to do. Along with La Torre's new laws, an all-out offensive against the Mafia was launched. Thousands of arrests followed, even if, of all the major figures implicated only the profoundly tainted Vito Ciancimino and the Salvo cousins really suffered. All too soon, however, the mood in Palermo returned to one of weary indifference. The rivers of heroin flowed on.

In the spring of 1983, the Moro Commission was ready to report. Its findings were muted, exonerating many of those involved and leaving many issues unsolved. Sciascia was scathing. In his minority report, twenty-four pages written on *Camera dei Deputati* – Chamber of Deputies – paper, he tried to answer what he saw as the fundamental question: why was Moro not saved? Was it because of the *compromesso storico*? Why were the clues given by Moro himself not followed up? Why did the police and carabinieri not combine their forces to explore the leads that they were given? It was, he said, a sorry tale of 'omissions and dysfunction', and he had been filled with despair listening to the lies and evasions presented by the forces of law and order and by the Christian Democrats. Then he repeated the conclusion he had come to in his book. It had been worse, far worse, to suggest that Moro as a prisoner was a different man from the shrewd, calculating politician he had always been. Because Moro had so badly wanted to be rescued, he had had to be painted as having become 'someone else'. It had been a clear form of torture. Handing in his minority report, he observed that Pirandello had often spoken of the dead as the 'pensioners of memory'. We must, Sciascia now said, be very careful to pension them off truthfully, not with lies, which were as 'offensive to the dead as to the living'.

In *L'Espresso*, Sciascia wrote that despite the hundreds of hours he had spent listening to evidence, despite the millions of words he had been forced to read, it had not been wasted time, though one of the great problems with such commissions was the tedium. Nor did he feel that his time in Parliament had been wasted. Having written so much about Italian political life over the years, he had needed to look at it close up: it was simply a matter of experience and having been there in turbulent times – Sindona's arrest, the discovery of the P2 Masonic lodge, the rise and fall and rise again of Andreotti, the deaths of Giuliano, Terranova, Costa, Mattarella and Dalla Chiesa – he had learnt much. But now *'basta'* – enough. He had been 'absolutely useless' as a parliamentarian and it was time to go home. He would not be standing again.

At the gathering for his departure in March 1983, at which he was presented with a gold pen, he made his fellow deputies laugh when he pointed out that he had the honour of having been the briefest speaker in Italian history. He had spoken, he reminded them, just nineteen times, mostly on Mafia matters, and he repeated a Sicilian proverb: 'The best word is the one that is not spoken.' However, he told them, he was leaving with all his prejudices confirmed: Parliament clearly had no power, which resided entirely with the civil servants and the secret services, along with a judiciary which seemed to him to have 'excessive authority'. Parliament, he told his friends, was simply a mirror of Italy, a country that contained more good people than bad, but that did not stop politics, which had always been dirty and were becoming dirtier, from being a 'mediocre activity carried out by mediocre people' who had to pretend that they were being useful. It had all seemed pretty 'desolate'.

Sciascia intended to return to devote his time to writing, splitting his days between Palermo and Racalmuto. He left Rome with relief. But he was a sadder man. Challenged, as he always was, about his legendary pessimism, he no longer brushed it off. 'I live in Sicily and I'm a writer: how could I not be pessimistic?'

14

Hungry and thirsty for justice

No Italian writer has ever been as concerned as Sciascia about justice. Ever since the lies and obfuscations surrounding the capture and death of the bandit Giuliano in 1950, Italy, he said, had been a country 'without truth' and certainly not a democracy. Indeed, it had been without truth long before, when the torture carried out by the Inquisition had been not a corrective for heresy but an instrument of repression. The way Italy administered justice was 'terrifying', a coming together of inefficiency, compromise and violence, its reality lying somewhere between 'creativity and illegality', while Italians seemed absolutely indifferent to its many shortcomings. Courtrooms filled him with anguish. Asked what he would put at the top of a list of Italy's ills, he repeatedly replied: the 'failings and dysfunctions' of its legal system. As Sciascia grew older, so these questions came to haunt and obsess him.

If pressed, he would say that his feelings stemmed from growing up Sicilian, on an island dominated by centuries of oppression, in which there were two kinds of justice: State justice, which was seen as arbitrary and imposed by force and in which no one believed, and Mafia justice, based on *omertà*, bribery and cronyism, in which they did. He never forgot his days working for the rationing office in Racalmuto. The clear premise of justice – that all men were equal before the law – did not apply. On the one side were the weak; on the other the powerful who knew that they could violate any law with impunity.

There were certainly, he accepted, honest magistrates; but too often they were thwarted by political interference and intimidation. And who judged the judges? The best were those, he claimed, who found judging repellent and saw it as a solitary and painful necessity, who tempered their sentencing with compassion and felt condemned to lives of doubt and unease. But there were very few of them, and the rest, the majority, suffered from a kind of fanaticism and refractoriness and were unwilling to suffer criticism. He was hugely relieved that he had never been called for jury duty.

It was no coincidence, he thought, that the word '*dietrologia*' – conspiracy – was such a part of Sicilian thinking, since most Sicilians were convinced that the politics they saw and heard were not actually the truth, because truth was a matter of secrecy and hidden agendas. Writing about Moro, he had been struck by his words: 'Perhaps man's destiny is not how to bring about permanent justice, but to be perpetually hungry and thirsty for it.' Sciascia's hunger and thirst had grown steadily with the years.

After his first book, *Fables from the Dictatorship*, Sciascia wrote almost nothing that did not in some way contain an idea about justice; all his books in the end are about its malleability. His heroes are just men ultimately defeated by a failure of the law brought about by powerful interests, who reach conclusions that are invariably ambiguous. Lies, deception, manipulation are threads that run through all his books, both the *inchieste* and the *gialli*. Like Lampedusa, he came to think that change in Sicily was probably impossible; unlike him, he refused to stop delving, analysing and pushing, in the belief that if justice is indeed unattainable, then it was his duty as a writer to denounce injustice wherever he saw it. It fed into his conviction that literature is ultimately the only way to truth and that memory is a corrector of falsehood: in fact, literature is a superior form of justice in that it provides both witness and the possibility of exoneration. As he moved into his sixties, Sciascia told an interviewer that the words 'investigation, pardon, sentence and judgment' were those that resonated most with him. They sparked off thoughts, he said, about philosophy, literature and politics, and in the process turned into metaphors, dreams and fantasies, themselves the mulch of literature. He talked about *garantismo* – respect for human rights and the rights of the accused – for him a daily reminder of 'the law', but for too many others an excuse for evasion.

The 1980s in Italy, and especially in Sicily, would see the law challenged as never before. Sciascia did not waver, reiterating his commitment to a 'just justice' and his deep mistrust in the authorities to deliver it, even when it became very awkward and very unpleasant for him. Echoing Primo Levi and the need to be ever vigilant, he said: 'You can never go on holiday.' He became, as people said, implacable.

It was not long before Sciascia's fervour and outspokenness were once again tested. On 17 June 1983 police in Naples launched a dawn manhunt for people suspected of belonging to the local version of the Mafia, the Camorra. One of the men they picked up was a popular television presenter in his mid fifties called Enzo Tortora. Sciascia had met him in Caltanissetta at the end of the 1950s when Tortora, having read and admired *Gli zii di Sicilia*, asked to meet him. The two became friends, talked at length about Stendhal and watercolours; Anna Maria and Laura were delighted when Tortora wrote affectionate messages in their autograph books.

The trial that followed caused a furore: 856 people had been caught in the police net and two hundred were soon freed because of mistaken identities or watertight alibis, but not before spending anxious days in custody. Tortora was sentenced – on the, as it turned out, false testimony of a *pentito*, a suspect turned state witness – to ten years in prison for drug offences and for belonging to the Camorra. Sent first to the Regina Coeli prison in Rome then to a jail in Bergamo, he wrote to Sciascia that he felt as if he were in an 'absurd tunnel, demented'. He had never, he added, 'betrayed the esteem that you showed me'. Tortora's treatment outraged Sciascia. 'I don't ask myself: what if Tortora is innocent?' he wrote in the *Corriere della Sera*. 'I am certain that he is.' Then he appeared on television to repeat it. His words were seized on by journalists all over Italy.

After this he picked up his pen and wrote to President Pertini. He was appealing, he said, to the man who had himself as a partisan been unjustly imprisoned, only in his case he was able to keep his idealism intact. As President, he was the custodian not just of the Italian constitution, but of justice, without which, Sciascia suggested, public life could not exist. Would he intervene? Pertini, perhaps remembering the awkward and chilly lunch, did not reply. Sciascia's bitter comment was that it was now clear that in Italy liberty, democracy and justice were nothing but words.

The following year Tortora was absolved and released. When they met again, he and Sciascia talked about the fragility of justice. Tortora, wrote Sciascia, had shown exemplary dignity. He now proposed that judges at the beginning of their careers should spend at least three days in one of Sicily's more terrible prisons, which would give them time to reflect on the consequences of the power they wielded. Tortora died of cancer soon after, telling Sciascia that he would like to think that what had happened to him might prove instructive. Sciascia was sceptical. Judges handed down verdicts in the same way that priests gave communion, he remarked, as an act of transubstantiation. It was power, legitimising itself.

But there was something else, for him, at play. The idea of the *pentito* – the man who offers to provide evidence in return for absolution or a lower sentence – was moving to the very centre of Mafia matters. Sciascia felt not just repugnance, but deep wariness that turncoats could ever really be trusted to tell the truth.

Sciascia was not well. Doctors seemed baffled by the slowness of his recovery from his fractured vertebra. He looked tired, his expression wary, though interviewers remarked on his smile, and the way that it started slowly then creased his whole face. A young friend, Antonio Motta, noted that his eyes suggested measureless depths, a 'sort of Homeric blindness'. Sciascia was always happiest when at *La Noce*, surrounded by Maria, his daughters and four grandchildren, with Vito, the youngest, by his side.

Sciascia with his grandson, Vito

A SICILIAN MAN

Racalmuto, having lost many inhabitants after the closure of the sulphur mines, was growing again. The theatre in which Sciascia had spent so many boyhood hours had long since closed and become derelict. Hearing that a Venetian architect, Antonio Foscari, had restored an ancient village on a promontory in Sicily, imaginatively using the discarded stones to create an amphitheatre, Sciascia invited him to Racalmuto and persuaded him to take on the restoration of the little theatre, with all its former gilt and red plush. The two men walked slowly and purposefully up and down the main street until Sciascia judged that enough people had seen them together. Now, he told Foscari, you will get all the help you need. Not quite a question of the Mafia, perhaps: but undoubtedly in the spirit of Sicily.

Having resolved never to catch an aeroplane, Sciascia ventured abroad only by train, travelling to Paris as often as he could, to wander the streets and remember the *Encyclopédistes*, refusing to speak French though he knew it well, requiring his companions to do the talking, and correcting them when they got it wrong. He continued to stalk the back streets in search of antiquarian booksellers, riffling through cabinets, poking into dark corners in search of etchings and engravings. With Maria, and often with Ferdinando Scianna taking photographs, he paid visits to Barcelona, Madrid and Salamanca, cities with ancestral ties to Sicily, and to the sites of the civil war that had 'given voice to our hopes'. These journeys reminded him of his younger days, when he could roam, look, without commitments; now, everyone wanted his attention. For a Sicilian like himself, he said, Spain was historical memory. As he had written in *Parrocchie*, he had Spain 'in his heart'.

He wrote ceaselessly. He had finished putting together an alphabet of expressions in Sicilian dialect, *Occhio di capra*, full of sayings and proverbs from his childhood, which sent him on expeditions into Racalmuto's past, telling his grandchildren, to whom it was dedicated, that it was essential to preserve memory and that a single word was often enough to bring back whole passages of time. Primo Levi wrote to tell him that his book was 'as rich as a mine'. Memory was much on Sciascia's mind. After meeting Susan Sontag in Turin, where she was directing a play of Pirandello's *Come tu mi vuoi* (*As You Desire Me*), about an amnesiac, he turned to another *inchiesta*, *The Theatre of Memory*, about a man who forgets who he is. It made him think of Moro, and the way his friends had chosen to deny him his true self.

The three volumes of anthology for schools had taken five years to complete, the editorial sessions held in the Sellerio offices, where Sciascia continued to entertain his fellow editors with his soliloquies on Proust and Joyce – he disliked Proust's 'narrow and particular space' and preferred *Dubliners* to *Ulysses*. Marx, he told them, had taught him about the past, but he owed to psychoanalysis some of his understanding of the present. He insisted that nothing of his own writing be included in the anthology and that all the proceeds go to needy students. He was disappointed when the books failed to sell.

The Sellerios had separated but continued to live in adjoining flats in the Viale Scaduto. After *The Moro Affair* had given the publishing house a considerable boost, Sciascia introduced Elvira to Andrea Camilleri, though at first professing some doubt about his books. It proved a providential encounter and the Sellerio finances were secured. A grateful Camilleri would later say that he took several of his hero Montalbano's traits from Sciascia, not least his acute embarrassment at public speaking. Elvira was widely referred to as '*la signora dei libri*' in Palermo, but her long friendship with Sciascia had become strained, in the way of intense Sicilian relationships, in which intimacy carries such a weight of expectation and disappointment. Like that with Guttuso, their very Sicilian friendship had been a part of him; broken, it was gone.

Sciascia was spending more time in his other '*circolo*', the Arte al Borgo gallery, with painter friends who had contributed jackets for the Sellerio books and who now did portraits of him. He loved the subtle colours of their works, their handling of Sicily's arid landscapes and brilliant skies, but for his ever-growing collection of engravings and prints he continued to prefer black and white. Talking of their meetings, their shared 'mistrust of man and faith in art' and their attempts to struggle with the violent reality of Palermo in the early 1980s, the painter Gaetano Tranchino would later say: 'We grew rich on his words ... He gave us openings for thoughts that went on for ever.' Some of their meetings involved shopping in the nearby street market, ferreting out delicacies. Passers-by addressed him as '*u'prufissuri*'.

Consciously avoiding the contentious subjects that invariably led him into polemics, Sciascia put together a series of essays on the interconnectedness of things, people and ideas, delighting in his favourite literary game, allowing his imagination to soar among coincidences until they fell naturally into horizontal and vertical patterns and thus became a crossword, a *cruciverba*. This weaving of literature and history was, he said, the very mulch of our times. Then he produced an homage to Manzoni on the two hundredth anniversary of his birth, *La Strega e il capitano*, about an innocent woman burnt at the stake for witchcraft, which brought into play all his disgust at the falsehoods and shenanigans wielded by the powerful. This was sparked by a cache of unseen papers sent to him by a stranger, as was now often the case, with members of the public delivering folders of long-buried legal cases to his house. After this came another homage, *1912+1*, this time to Pirandello's endless jostling between appearances and reality, the story of an army captain's wife who in 1913 shot her husband's aide-de-camp. He wrote it in twenty-two days. In their review, the *TLS* noted that Sciascia was a 'master at the height of his powers'.

Sciascia had spent much of his writing life thinking about Pirandello, sometimes moving towards him, at other times drawing back. Now, finally, he seemed to come to terms with him, both as a man and as a writer, accepting that much of his own aversion towards the herd, his fear of ridicule and his irony and spirit of contradiction came from him. It was Pirandello, he said, who had shown him the 'too human' face of Sicily, in its 'most exasperating, extreme, murderous form'. He saw 'in men's hearts', below the tranquil surface, a 'convulsed, insane world'. He had adopted Pirandello's habit of giving audiences to his characters on Sunday mornings, listening to their discontents and trying to penetrate their 'souls with a long and subtle enquiry'.

Sciascia had finally met the Argentinian writer Jorge Luis Borges, whom he had admired – revered – all his life, saying that he had merged theology into aesthetics and made the 'conversation about God' into a 'conversation about literature': Borges was an 'atheist theologian', 'another me', of the kind he had always felt himself to be, using labyrinths and paradoxes to provide a sense of shock before presenting his readers with evidence from which they could deduce some kind of reality. The two writers met in a hotel in Rome. Borges spoke in Spanish, Sciascia in Italian; they understood each other perfectly, knowing that each shared a sense that literature could approximate happiness, and that this lay in trying to decipher the truth. He only wished, said Sciascia, that he could meet him every day. He decided to dedicate to him *Cronachette*, a collection of seven brief tales, 'little events of the past', each built around a mystery to be solved by literature. Published by Sellerio, it became the hundredth title in their *Memoria* series.

Early in the 1980s, Sciascia returned once again to the all-consuming question of justice. He regarded the death penalty as an 'eternal Inquisition', more macabre and atrocious than any lynching since it was carried out in cold blood. His new book was timely. After being off the statute books for nearly forty years, the death penalty was again under discussion for terrorist offences. Like torture, the death penalty went far beyond the idea of justice; for Sciascia it was itself a crime, the 'greatest infamy' to which a state could descend.

Porte aperte – *Open Doors* – the phrase taken from Mussolini's claim that Italy was so safe under Fascism that Italians could leave their doors unlocked – has as its protagonist '*il piccolo giudice*', the little judge – little not in stature but as in David and Goliath. He is one of Sciascia's most endearing characters. It is set in 1937, when Fascism had passed its peak and was beginning to struggle to hold on to its authority, and Sciascia said that he had known just such a judge, in Racalmuto, when he was growing up. Called on to preside over the trial of a triple murderer, whose guilt is beyond question, the little judge is informed that the Fascist authorities are expecting a death sentence. Implacably opposed to it, he manages to sway the jury with his eloquence and recourse to Montaigne, Tolstoy and Dostoevsky. When they return a verdict that spares the murderer's life, the little judge knows that his career is over, and that in any case his ruling will soon be overturned on appeal. The one really noble judge in all Sciascia's books, he is left reflecting that literature has the power to awaken people to a better world. Justice, at least for a few brief minutes, had been underpinned by 'the human heart'; but it was not enough to drive away fear and horror.

With sales of his books growing steadily, new foreign editions appearing all the time and constantly pressed by newspapers for his opinion on subjects of every kind, Sciascia was now the great sage, orator and interpreter of all things Sicilian. Interviewed for the women's magazine *Amica*, in the summer of 1982, which described him as a 'shy, timid, solitary man', he said that his pleasures had shrunk to enjoying good food and good books. 'The more the years pass, the closer I feel to the written word.' His forays into the past continued to give Sciascia great pleasure. But Sicily was submerged in Mafia matters, and Sciascia was about to take a step that would cloud the remaining years of his life.

Giovanni Falcone and Paolo Borsellino grew up in the Kalsa district of Palermo, among the decaying palazzi scheduled for demolition during the sack of the city. As boys they played football in the Piazza Magione, a grassy field behind one of the prettiest small churches in the old town. Falcone's father was the director of a chemical laboratory, Borsellino's a pharmacist. Falcone's family was religious, but like Sciascia he drifted towards the Communists while never becoming a member of the party. Borsellino turned towards the monarchists. What the two men had in common was that they were drawn to the dark side of Sicilian life. After university in Palermo both went into the magistrature; after stints in the provinces they arrived back in the capital at the end of the 1970s. Borsellino was a family man, with three children, extrovert, charming, with strong faith; he often spoke in dialect. Falcone, whose wife had recently left him, was more austere, reserved, with an ironical smile which did not invite intimacy, though with friends he could be witty and tender. His tenaciousness was proverbial, as was his obsession with not making mistakes. He liked to win and could be aggressive when faced with incompetence. At much the same time, the two young magistrates joined Judge Rocco Chinnici in the Judicial Investigation Office in the Tribunal in Palermo. Both Falcone and Borsellino were stubborn men.

General Dalla Chiesa had not been the last *cadavere eccellente*. A judge called Giangiacomo Montalto, tracking shipments of heroin in Marsala, had told his wife that he had the feeling that those around him were trying to isolate him: he was shot dead in January 1983. Money from the drug market continued to pour in and Palermo remained a city in crisis, with tens of millions of lire lost every year to kickbacks. In the space of a little less than five years, four judges or prosecutors, one prefect, one member of parliament, the President of the Sicilian Region, one policeman and a journalist had been killed, along with several carabinieri, a clear warning to a political class not to tamper with the status quo. Chinnici, a big, rumpled, somewhat dour man, had taken the decision to direct his magistrates to pursue hitherto neglected bank controls. Falcone, who had been with the bankruptcy court, now did what Sciascia had been urging for almost a quarter of a century: he applied his financial knowledge to the Mafia. In his diary, Chinnici noted that the President of the Court of Appeal, Giovanni Pizzillo, was most concerned about 'this young magistrate who was ruining the Sicilian economy'.

On 29 July 1983 Chinnici, his driver, two bodyguards and a bystander were killed when a radio-controlled car bomb blew up his car. His wife was watching from the window. Another brave judge, Antonio Caponnetto, who had been serving in Florence, agreed to take his place. His immediate idea was to form a 'pool' of the men working under him, sharing everything, so as to ensure that no single individual was uniquely vulnerable. Caponnetto, like Falcone a man of few words, moved into the Treasury barracks for safety. The ten-man pool, with Falcone the acknowledged leader, started work on the upper floor of the Court of Appeal, because the offices below, giving on to the street, were deemed too exposed. Their rooms lay behind bullet-proof steel doors. They called them 'our little bunker'.

Visitors found Falcone to be a wry, friendly figure, with a generous moustache and a slight double chin, not unlike Sciascia in manner; he looked exhausted. Papers filled every corner of his office. Little by little he was putting together a great map of Cosa Nostra, exchanging information and photographs with police forces all over the world. As he saw it, the Mafia was so deeply embedded in Sicilian life that it had become its very fabric. It made him angry when colleagues still asked him: 'Does the Mafia really exist?' Like Sciascia, he had grown up 'breathing, day after day, the air of the Mafia, of violence, extortion and murder'; and like Sciascia he felt able to identify with the *mafiosi*. It was Sciascia, he said, who had made him understand what it was to be Sicilian. 'I learned to understand the Mafia from his books.'

In 1984 Falcone flew to Brazil to meet Tommaso Buscetta, a former Mafia boss recently arrested and accused of coordinating a world-wide cocaine ring. Buscetta was the fourteenth child of a glazier, who had grown up in Palermo, married at sixteen, become a father at seventeen and a *'uomo d'onore'* – a made man – in the Porta Nuova clan at eighteen, having killed, as Cosa Nostra demanded, his first man. Brazil, with its thousands of miles of deserted coastline, lying at the heart of the world's major cocaine producers, had been extremely lucrative.

The encounter between Falcone and Buscetta proved decisive. Buscetta was returned to Italy and in exchange for turning State witness, he was offered the prospect of eventual resettlement in a witness programme in the US. He told Falcone that he did not, however, see himself as a *pentito*, saying that the Mafia had betrayed itself by turning into a very different animal from the one he had known as a boy. And he was angry. Since his arrest and collaboration with the authorities in Brazil, his two sons, his brother Vincenzo, nephew Benedetto and Vincenzo's brother-in-law had all been assassinated.

Buscetta was not the first important *pentito*. In 1973, a man of honour called Leonardo Vitale had come forward after a religious conversion and given detailed information about the Corleonesi and about the illegal activities of Ciancimino and Lima; but he had been ignored, not least because he had kept changing his story. Declared insane, he was sent to a mental asylum; when freed he was promptly murdered. Another *mafioso*, Giuseppe Di Cristina, fearing that he too was about to be killed, had since provided useful information to the police about Mafia killings and in particular about Luciano Leggio's great wealth, but he too had been ignored and quickly murdered on a busy Palermo street. The last policeman to see him remarked that he looked like a terrified, cornered animal.

But Buscetta was different. He had been high in the command structure of Cosa Nostra. What he did now was to break, very publically, the unwritten Mafia code by which you did not deal with the State but rather take your punishment, go to jail, then return home with enhanced prestige.

Pentiti were anathema to Sciascia. He was haunted by the idea of people accusing each other, sometimes for crimes they had not committed, drawn to give names in order to improve their own positions. In the *Corriere della Sera* he railed against the new law offering deals to those who came forward, writing that it was 'horrendous and ignoble . . . encouraging lies, opportunism and moral indignity . . . corrupting the sense of justice and civilisation'. It was nothing but more 'stupidity and pain' in the Mafia's 'spider's web'. But Buscetta, who had tried but failed to take his own life in his US jail, was about to hand the State something that it had never had: not just confirmation of everything Vitale and Di Cristina had said but a precise, detailed portrait of Cosa Nostra, its inner workings, its criminal activities, its victims, its major players. Further evidence came when the police discovered the world's biggest heroin factory in Trapani. With the wall of *omertà* apparently cracking, it was just possible that at last the fight against the Mafia had turned a corner.

In Rome, Benedetto Craxi, fighting the election on a promise to end corruption, had just become the first Socialist prime minister in Italy's history. The Ministries of Justice and the Interior were in the hands of reforming Christian Democrats. In Sicily an association of women against the Mafia, led by the widows of murdered magistrates and policemen, was spreading from town to town, while the Centro Giuseppe Impastato in Palermo, named after a young man who had denounced the Mafia on the radio and been tied to the rails of the Trapani–Palermo line and crushed by a train, was sponsoring thirty-eight separate anti-Mafia initiatives. Cardinal Pappalardo was pushing for a new resolve against the 'barbarities of the Mafia' and calling on the 'assassins' to 'abandon the way of eternal perdition'. A crusading new mayor, Leoluca Orlando, was elected, defiant and full of plans. Twenty-five years after Sciascia had spelt out its perimeters in *The Day of the Owl*, it was finally impossible to deny the existence of the Mafia. As Sciascia said, it had become suddenly visible 'in people's expressions that they believed it did and were afraid'.

But Cosa Nostra was not yet defeated. To signal their continuing grip on power, it now arranged for a train to be blown up between Milan and Naples, killing sixteen people and wounding a further 266 in late December 1984. The following August, a young, elegant, much-liked deputy chairman of Palermo's police, Antonio Cassarà, who had been exploring Mafia deals in Catania, was shot dead by ten men with Kalashnikovs while paying a secret visit to his family. Falcone believed that he had been betrayed by a colleague. If the Mafia had hoped to scare off the pool of magistrates, however, they had made a mistake: it only seemed to galvanise them to work harder and faster. Palermo was now full of journalists, 'scavenger birds waiting for the next illustrious corpse'.

Falcone was sometimes accused of treating Buscetta – and the other *pentiti* who, following his example, were coming forward – with too much respect. But it was his method. He was courteous, blunt, sceptical, never familiar, but he did not resort to bullying and he never lied. He insisted that they look him in the eye. Bit by bit, he extracted from Buscetta the key to unlock the pyramidal structure of the modern Mafia, with its epicentre in Palermo, where the ruling Cupola met to decide what to infiltrate and who to kill. The Corleonesi, Buscetta told him, wished to become a 'dictatorial monarchy', though Sciascia, hearing the term, preferred the image of a galaxy with families floating in the same orbit, sometimes working together, sometimes apart. Falcone knew that he was not getting the whole story, but it was enough. 'The Mafia,' he said, 'appeared before me as an enormous world, boundless, unexplored.' He knew that 'we had come to the edge of the precipice, where no one has dared to go before'. It was like a set of Russian dolls, each one opening on to a smaller one, exposing the inner fabric of Mafia business. One of the things Buscetta told him was that the Mafia had been standing by to help in the aborted Borghese coup in Rome. It was as Sciascia had said: the line of palm trees had long since moved north.

As the pool of magistrates worked, tapping telephones, controlling passenger lists, hotel stays and board meetings, examining bank accounts and the movement of funds, analysing building contracts, travelling from London to Bangkok, New York to Istanbul, so they began to attract the help of police forces all over the world. The picture they were putting together was chilling, that of a parallel state, living in perfect symbiosis with a myriad of protectors, accomplices and informers from every stratum of society who had been bribed, intimidated or blackmailed. Sciascia's repeated warning that the Mafia possessed an infinite capacity to adapt, to change, yet remain true to itself, had been correct. Compared to the Italian State, as Falcone said, it was both extremely agile and very pragmatic. But he added that it would be wrong to see it as a monster or the devil. That was the problem: 'We must recognise that it resembles ourselves.' Listening to the tapped telephone calls, Falcone was struck by the conservatism of the bosses, their intense love for their children, their prohibition on divorce, gambling or prostitution, even while they admired 'men who lived like lions and died on their feet'. Echoing Sciascia, he repeated that the great failure of the State had been to underestimate the reach of the Mafia at every moment in its history. 'Investigating the Mafia is like crossing a minefield: you never know when you're going to step on a mine.'

None of this work came without extreme peril. A senior officer came from Rome to bump up security and Falcone's neighbours complained bitterly about the police cars with blazing sirens that sped ceaselessly up and down their street; and there was a terrible moment when Borsellino's car killed two students in the street. Even so, as the magistrates began assembling their great jigsaw for the trial they were planning, threats against them mounted. Messages arrived with the words 'You work too hard, you should rest'. Postcards were delivered with the dates of birth and death of the individual magistrates. A phone call came in: 'The coffin is ready.' The summer of 1985 was spent putting the finishing touches to the prosecution, a vast and elaborate chessboard built on laws, procedures and norms. Falcone and Borsellino and their families retired to the prison island of Asinara off Sardinia, the only place where it was judged they could be kept safe. Asked whether he feared being killed, Falcone said that he carried the idea of death about with him everywhere. 'In my position, either you pray or you organise. I am incapable of praying.'

The *maxi-processo* – the trial of 471 *mafiosi*, with a number of them in absentia – opened in Palermo on 10 February 1986. It was the largest such trial in history and quickly dubbed a 'judicial monster'. Its preamble was sonorous and almost poetic. 'This is the trial of the Mafia organisation named Cosa Nostra, a highly dangerous criminal association, which through violence and intimidation has sown and continues to sow death and terror.' In the dock were representatives from all the most important Mafia families from the province of Palermo, together with a few from Catania. Ciancimino, Palermo's former mayor was there, as was the tax-gathering Ignazio Salvo, his cousin and fellow conspirator

Nino having died of lung cancer just as the trial began. Ignazio was charged not with drug trafficking but with polluting Sicily with his tangle of interests in building and politics and his political chicanery. Behind these defendants there were thought to be at least 5,000 other men of honour, criminals and killers chosen by a harsh selection process and obedient to a rigid set of rules. Their ghostly presence hung heavily over the court.

The *maxi-processo*

The oldest person on trial was in his eighties, the youngest twenty-one. Many of them wore dark suits. Just four of them were women. All but thirty were Sicilian. The 1,342 charges against them included 1,280 for murder, the others for kidnapping, rape, drug trafficking, money laundering and bearing false witness. What was important to Falcone, as it was to Sciascia, was that it was not just the Mafia that was on trial, but the State itself, with its long record of violence, obfuscation and shady deals. Six hundred journalists from all over the world attended the opening day. Most of them were in support of the trial, but in Sicily there had been attempts by a number of newspapers to undermine it, with dire warnings about spiralling costs and the abuse of civil rights, in which few had ever shown much interest before.

To house this spectacular undertaking, a special bunker

courtroom had been built, in record time, onto the walls of the Ucciardone, Palermo's central prison, with tunnels underneath to convey the defendants back and forth to their cells. The roof and walls were bullet proof. Outside the walls were stationed two tanks and a number of armoured cars, turning the area into what looked like a war zone. Three thousand extra policemen were drafted in to increase security. Inside the immense pale green octagonal hall had been constructed thirty steel cages with thick bars, in which the defendants were grouped. To the right of the raised dais for the presiding judge and magistrates was a square, bullet-proof box made of clear plastic for the witnesses. Luciano Leggio, in tracksuit and Adidas trainers, brought from his maximum security prison in Sardinia, had a cage to himself, in which he sat solemnly smoking a black Tuscan cigar and reading the newspaper. From his own cage, Michele Greco, the gentlemanly host to many parties of well-connected huntsmen, charged now with the murder of Rocco Chinnici and many others, seemed magisterial and aloof. In his canary-coloured cardigan, he looked like a country grandee, his features pleasant but his expression watchful.

Two full sets of judges and jurors had been appointed by government decree, so that any sudden death would not interrupt proceedings. Seven different magistrates had declined the job of presiding judge before a more courageous eighth, Alfonso Giordano, was prevailed on to accept it. The prosecutors and court officials moved to live either inside the courthouse or in police barracks, cut off from their families. If they had to leave the Ucciardone, they travelled with escorts in bullet-proof Alfa Romeos. The indictments drafted by Falcone, Borsellino and the pool ran to 8,607 pages and covered the years 1975 to 1985, during which, they intended to prove, the Sicilian Mafia had become the primary source for narcotics and an international criminal cartel.

From the first moment, proceedings were repeatedly interrupted by jeers, shouts and protests as the defendants in their cages rattled the bars. One defendant had sown his lips together, another had swallowed nails. There were noisy interventions from the visitors' gallery, and constant attempts by the police to keep down the din. A small, plump, elderly lady with a handbag wandered up and down the cages with a portrait of her son, killed by the Corleonesi. She was one of several wives and mothers bringing civil suits against the Mafia killers and she described the way that, when it was known she had been to the police, she had been ostracised. No one visited her shop and her neighbours no longer spoke to her. She lived, she said, behind a 'wall of silence'. Other witnesses, who had told magistrates that they would testify, proved too frightened when the moment came or took back what they had said before. Michela Buscemi, whose two brothers had been killed, withdrew after receiving a message saying that her six-year-old son would be killed. But one woman, Vita Rognetta, spoke out. Her only son had been killed. 'Come and kill me too,' she announced, 'if you want to. I have no one left.'

In early April, Buscetta was brought into court. He was a slight, dapper figure in a pale grey jacket, dark trousers and white shirt, his very black hair low on his forehead. With his dark skin and pencil-thin moustache, he looked sly and knowing. Guarding him closely were six exceptionally tall carabinieri, their height and bulk almost obscuring him from view. From the cages came oaths and threats and more rattling of the bars. Over the following days, sitting with his back to the men he was accusing, Buscetta outlined the great pyramid of the Cupola, from the bosses down to the foot soldiers recruited from a vast reservoir of men from the island's interior. He gave their names and described their crimes. Greco and Leggio watched impassively as he insisted that no killing had ever been carried out without their explicit authorisation. Leggio, he said, had also been involved in the kidnapping of John Paul Getty III, grandson of the American oil tycoon, who was abducted and held for ransom and whose severed ear was sent to his grandfather, who eventually paid up.

For the first time since it had come into being in the middle of the nineteenth century, the Sicilian Mafia was being laid out, absolutely bare to public view, with all its violence, greed and vengefulness, its culture of death and anguish. Describing its members, Buscetta said: 'They are like you and me', much as Don Mariano in *The Day of the Owl* said that he thought of himself not as a criminal but as part of the only culture and world he knew.

In mid April Sciascia joined the reporters in the press gallery to write an article for the *Corriere della Sera*. He listened to Buscetta being questioned by Falcone. In his article he described him as being on the whole credible but warned that it would be a mistake to see him as an exterminating angel bent on bringing down the entire Mafia. Buscetta was, he wrote, simply a man who had seen his family murdered and wanted revenge. He noted that he refused to produce any name of a political figure, concluding that this must have been for his own personal protection, and remarked wryly on Buscetta's apparent nostalgia for the values and 'nobility' of the earlier Mafia. His conclusion was approving: with this trial, the myth and immunity enjoyed for so long by the Mafia seemed at last to be coming to a close.

For a moment, Palermo itself seemed to enjoy a 'spring': the violence was down, the city was being cleaned up, the garbage collected. But it was all a bit deceptive. Falcone and Borsellino were constantly under attack by hostile journalists trying to discredit the trial, mocking the magistrates for their flak jackets and helicopters, passing themselves off as brave when they were really very cowardly.

On 16 December 1987, having heard 1,314 witnesses, considered 676,000 documents and listened to the confessions of twenty-one *pentiti*, the Court of Palermo handed down its verdicts. The trial had lasted 638 days. Nineteen men were given life sentences, among them Michele Greco, Bernardo Provenzano and Toto Riina, the two Corleone bosses, both currently on the run. Greco, charged with seventy-eight separate murders, shouted out one of the Mafia's most used threats: 'I hope that peace may be with you for the rest of your lives.' There were well over eleven million lire in fines and a total of many centuries in prison for 323 of the defendants. Buscetta received a three-and-a-half-year prison sentence.

One of the four women, Antonietta Giustolisi, received a twelve-year prison sentence on drug trafficking charges; another, Anna Ianni, got two years and six months for acting as a courier between *mafiosi* bosses and for receiving drugs. The other two were acquitted. Though the full extent of the involvement of mothers, wives and sisters in Mafia business would not be clear until later, Falcone was building up a picture of women running heroin businesses, hiding weapons, dealing with kickbacks, delivering drugs and taking over clans when their men were killed or arrested, ruling with no more mercy than the men. Most importantly, Sciascia's secret, perverse, 'subterranean and dangerous' female power had been put on the map. The idea of a powerful and influential 'matriarchy', for which he had been so criticised, was spelt out in some of the indictments, mothers bringing up their sons to embrace violence and carry out vendettas while arranging dynastic marriages within the Mafia community. Here too his message had been prescient; it would never again be possible to ignore their role in the Mafia world, nor for women to escape justice by claiming, as Ninetta Bagarella did some years before, that she was a 'woman in love'. The trial also gave a boost to a movement which had been taking shape for some time, the 'illustrious widows' – wives of murdered policemen and magistrates – coming together to form a common cause against the Mafia, joined by brave widows and mothers of *mafiosi* men, now sickened by the violence.

The problem with past Mafia trials was that the cases invariably ended in acquittals, if not at the time, then at appeal. The *maxi-processo* promised to be different. Violence did break out immediately when one of the acquitted defendants, Antonio Gulla, was shot dead within hours of his release, as were seventeen others who were allowed to go free. But Sciascia was right: something extraordinary had taken place. The 8,607 pages of findings – 4,000 of them relating to bank deposits, transactions and money laundering – had given a vivid picture of a vast web of criminality and collusion underpinning the whole of Sicilian society, in which politicians, civil servants, the local authorities and the business world were seen to be deeply involved. The Mafia had been robbed of its aura of impunity and invincibility, and it could no longer be dismissed as folklore or a state of mind. Ciancimino's days as a squalid purveyor of illicit building permits was over, as was Ignazio Salvo's reign over the deeply corrupt tax world. Sciascia had indeed been prescient. The Mafia had, at last, been proved to be, beyond all possible doubt, a criminal association, and as such could finally be investigated further and more deeply. There was, of course, still much to be done, more bosses to hunt down, more men of honour to be identified, more illegal bank transactions to follow up, and successes followed by reversals would continue to mark every step in the battle between the Italian State and its criminal underworld. Lima, no less unscrupulous than his friend Ciancimino, was hanging on to power, and one of the most tantalising threads to have emerged throughout the trial was Andreotti's ghostly presence at many crucial meetings.

15

God's policeman

'My greatest worry,' Falcone told an interviewer, 'is that the Mafia will always manage to stay ahead of us.' He was not wrong. Though it had indeed been battered and many of its *capi* were now serving long prison sentences, it was not beaten. Drugs continued to flow, fortunes were made and corruption thrived. Palermo was again on edge. Unemployed workers, seeing illicit labour practices, which had benefited them, under threat staged a march with banners saying: 'Long live the Mafia'. With their 'cocktail of slogans', the anti-Mafia movement was itself in disarray. And Sciascia, inadvertently, perhaps foolishly and to some extent misinterpreted, was about to provide the Mafia with a small boost, one which would sadden and sour what little remained of his life.

Fearful for his safety, with his daughter traumatised by the menaces to which the magistrates had been subjected, Borsellino's family had persuaded him to apply for the vacant job of prosecutor at Marsala. According to the rules of seniority in the Italian judiciary, the post should have gone to an older colleague, next in line for promotion. But given that Marsala was in the grip of a wave of Mafia crimes and that Borsellino had an unrivalled knowledge of its workings, the magistrates' presiding body (the CSM) decided to appoint him instead.

On 10 January 1987 Sciascia wrote a long review of two books on the Mafia for the *Corriere della Sera*. Towards the end of it – possibly having seen documents leaked to him by envious magistrates – he took aim at Borsellino's appointment, naming him and warning against the use of the anti-Mafia as an instrument of power in the service of politics. 'Nothing in Sicily,' he wrote, 'is more valuable to a career in the magistrature than to take part in Mafia trials.' He also criticised, though without naming him, the reforming mayor Leoluca Orlando for spending his time on television and at conferences – 'out of either conviction or calculation' – boasting about his work against the Mafia, rather than attending to the many basic problems of the city of Palermo. An editor at the *Corriere* provided the headline: '*I professionisti della mafia*' – 'the Mafia professionals'. The meaning was clear. People should not delude themselves that they govern better and are more important if they label themselves anti-Mafia. And by now everything that Sciascia said, even in a whisper, sounded like a trumpet.

It would be impossible to exaggerate the furore that exploded around Sciascia's head. As his daughter Anna Maria said later, it was as if the end of the world had come, even though in essence it was not so very different from what he had said before: that there must never be two legal systems, one for the Mafia, another for everyone else. A radio commentator, Claudio Fava, declared that Sciascia was suffering from 'acrimonious senility'. Others spoke of 'moralists without morals' and called Sciascia's article the manifesto of the enemies of the 'pool'. Eugenio Scalfari, editor-in-chief of *La Repubblica*, which led the attacks, said that it was no surprise to hear him speak this way since his 'personal vanity' was often stronger than his sense of civic responsibility. He was said to have shown 'overwhelming exhibitionism'. Orlando called him a '*quaquaraqua*', Sciascia's own term in *The Day of the Owl* for a braggart, adding that he had now exposed both Borsellino and himself to considerable danger. Furthermore, wrote the sociologist Pino Arlacchi, referring back to the time when Sciascia had admitted feeling he had to impose some sort of self-censorship when writing *The Day of the Owl*, Sciascia was obviously a coward. He coined the word '*Sciascismo*' to denote a tendency to be 'bewitched by the monster'.

Where, asked Giampaolo Pansa, also in *La Repubblica*, was the old Sciascia, with his talent for 'trenchant analysis'? Like Moro in the hands of the Red Brigades he had become 'unrecognisable', mysteriously metamorphosed into someone else. None of it would matter, he went on, had Sciascia not been Sicily's most revered writer, but as he was, it was catastrophic. The men he had chosen to attack, Borsellino and Orlando, were 'heroes' and should be treated as such. Then a young law student, Francesco Petruzzella, spearheaded a *Coordinamento*, a group of three hundred academics, magistrates and the relations of people murdered by the Mafia, and issued a communiqué claiming that this once 'enlightened and civilised man' must be relegated, 'with all the strength we possess' to the 'very margins of civil society'.

In Milan, a few days after the article appeared, a meeting was called to debate Sciascia's role in the 'power and culture of the Mafia and the anti-Mafia'. It turned into a kangaroo court. Despite heavy rain, dozens of political figures and journalists arrived to compete with each other with vitriolic accusations. Sciascia, it was agreed, had become a writer who no longer saw things straight and he had done the cause of fighting the Mafia immense harm. Their reactions were indeed excessive and unbridled, but it was undeniably true that Sciascia had provided ideological respectability to people who wanted to discredit the judges. Mafia lawyers, corrupt politicians, people who had never heard of Sciascia were now quick to praise him.

In Palermo, Sciascia was under siege. As Rino Nicolosi, President of the Sicilian Region, put it, 'everything here turns into a drama'. The telephone never stopped ringing with friends warning of further attacks to come. Characteristically, Sciascia did not back down. In a series of articles he repeated the credo he had held to all his life: that the only solution to fighting the Mafia was to hold fast to justice and legality, and that if you bent the rules you wound up by becoming another kind of mafia. His attack, he insisted, was not against Borsellino personally, a fine magistrate he much admired, but against the behaviour of the CSM, who instead of promoting Borsellino and saying nothing, should have had the courage of their convictions and formally altered the rule about seniority. As for the *Coordinamento*, he went on, it was nothing but a fanatical fringe group, castrating, as in a western, with 'rapid summary justice', those who disagreed with them. The headline, he repeated again and again, though deeply unfortunate, had not been his, but he did not distance himself from the meaning of its words.

To Pansa and Scalfari, he replied wearily that he had spent thirty years defending himself, first from those who accused him of defaming Sicily, then from those who said that he did not criticise it enough; from physicists who claimed that he had vilified science; then from Communists who suggested that he had joked about

Stalin and from clerics who said that he was godless. 'I am not infallible,' he wrote, 'but I believe I have said some incontrovertible truths ... I am sixty-seven and can regret and reproach myself for many things' but never for 'acting in bad faith or in the service of particular interests ... I do not possess, I recognise, the gift of expediency or prudence. But one is as one is.' The violence to which he was being subjected only convinced him that he had been right. To reject out of hand all doubt and dissent was to return to the evil days of Fascism, and once you exchanged the scales of justice for a pair of handcuffs you were 'irredeemably lost'; it was both sad and deeply wrong when to criticise was to risk being labelled *mafioso*. Italy, Sciascia told an interviewer angrily, was a state without ideology, run by puppets. Asked to list positive things about Sicily, he replied: 'I don't know that I can any longer find any.'

The attacks continued, commentators vying with each other for who could be most accusatory. Ministers joined in, then many politicians, then priests, trade unionists, magistrates. Friends rallied. Giorgio Bocca spoke about Sciascia's sixth sense for ambiguity in public life and his talent for perceiving the demons 'crouched above the heads of virtuous men'. Others whom he thought of as friends joined in the attacks, to his great sorrow. Though the *Corriere della Sera* publicly supported him, he left the paper and took his articles to *La Stampa*. Even close friends agreed that though his uneasiness about how the battle against the Mafia was being waged might well be justified – as indeed it was later proved to be – his timing and his choice of targets, with Palermo living under a state of fear about repercussions from the *maxi-processo*, had been disastrous. Sciascia held firm. Saying that in Sicily writers had always been dismissed as heretics and spies, he repeated, with not a little stubbornness and hauteur: 'I am above all the custodian of the truth.'

Then came what was perhaps an even more unfortunate development. When Antonino Caponnetto, who had steered the 'pool' for four very tough years, announced that he would now return to Florence, he assumed that Falcone, who had applied for his job, would naturally get it. There was still much to be done, new trials to organise, more leads to follow up. But in the CSM, Falcone's enemies were quick to play on the confusions caused by Sciascia's article, and when it came to the vote, opted to give the post to Antonino Meli, a sixty-seven-year-old egotistic and irascible magistrate nearing retirement, with no experience of Mafia matters, but intent on seeking glory of his own. It took Meli, who immediately declared that he preferred generalists to specialists, just over a month to dismantle the pool, decide that the winning strategy against the Mafia so painstakingly put together over the years by Falcone, Borsellino and their colleagues would be abandoned, and to hand out the new cases to magistrates who had never had anything to do with the Mafia. Anonymous attacks on Falcone poured in. He was accused of putting his nose into matters – such as Ciancimino and Lima's affairs – where he had no business to be, and of lacking the humility that should go with the job of magistrate. The Palace of Justice in Palermo became known as the 'palace of poison'.

Appalled by Meli's decision, Borsellino gave a number of angry and perhaps injudicious interviews. He declared that with the loss of Falcone at the helm, the battle against the Mafia would rapidly run into the sand. Cosa Nostra was already reorganising itself 'as before, better than before'. The CSM opened a disciplinary hearing against him and months of acrimonious exchanges followed before the decision was taken to issue no formal censure.

Borsellino himself remained sanguine and generous towards Sciascia, saying that he had always admired him and would continue to do so. But in private he worried that the 'fight against the Mafia no longer exists' and that Falcone was now painfully isolated. It was, he said, a 'tragedy'. His wife would later say that he 'suffered enormously' and felt that Sciascia had stabbed him in the back. Orlando told an acquaintance that what had really upset both him and Borsellino was that they had always regarded themselves as Sciascia's disciples. Caponnetto, back in Florence and watching, dismayed, events unfold, commented that Falcone 'began to die' after the CSM, by appointing Meli, gave a clear and loud signal to the Mafia that the investigative patrimony of the pool was being 'reduced to dust'. As Attilio Bolzoni commented in *La Repubblica*, there was now a 'dangerous void'. There would no longer be any need for Falcone and Borsellino's enemies to hide in the shadows.

Though by now well accustomed to provoking considerable annoyance with his 'polemics', Sciascia had not expected such a degree of hostility. He felt himself to be truly *un uomo solo*, like his best heroes, though he insisted that his role in Sicilian life, refusing to stay silent and speaking what he considered to be the truth, would not change. But, as his grandson Vito said later, he did not talk about what had happened. It was the same as with the other great painful experience of his life, the suicide of his brother Giuseppe: '*dolore*' – pain – was something that you did not discuss. Sciascia's daughter Anna Maria was one of the few people who saw how very deeply he had been affected. Always wary of interviews, he now insisted that they take the form of written questions and answers, saying that otherwise his words were invariably distorted. He told *Panorama* that what was said about him – the lies – were attempts to 'deprive me of one identity and give me another, which resembles death' just as people had done with Moro. The difference was that, unlike Moro, he continued to live, and 'to be the person I have always been'. More deeply gloomy than ever before, he was becoming increasingly intolerant of *cretini*, and his irritation was sometimes accompanied by flashes of arrogance and perversity, as if indifferent to how swayed people were by his words.

Sciascia's health was growing poorer. His eyesight was bad and friends noticed that he grew tired very quickly. Specialists from all over Italy and even Switzerland continued to find nothing wrong beyond the legacy of his fractured vertebra and the ill effects of a lifetime of heavy smoking. But he looked wan and pale and his deep-set eyes appeared sunken in his face. He told Foscari that the doctors had described his problems as 'light chains', but 'I can tell you: they are not light at all'.

In any case, there was still much he wanted to write. In the summer of 1988, to escape the endless round of medical visits which seemed to yield nothing, Sciascia took Maria and his daughters to stay with friends, producers of grappa, in Percoto near Udine. Having failed to take his Olivetti typewriter with him, he spent the mornings in the garden, writing by hand. He had started what would be his most personal novel, returning to his never-ending theme of corruption and absolute power and including a dig at a world in which all dissent was marginalised. His hero, the unnamed '*Vice*', is a man 'who lacked all hope but wanted the truth'.

Inspired by an engraving of Dürer's called *The Knight, Death and the Devil* that he had hanging in his study, Sciascia set his new novel not in Sicily but somewhere in the north of Italy, saying that there was no longer any point in asking for whom the bell tolled, since 'the bell of the Mafia tolls for everyone'. The *Vice*, suffering from melancholy and with a terminal illness casting its shadow, investigates the murder of a lawyer. He is the Knight, the champion battling evil in a flawed moral world. Rapidly solving the case, identifying the murderer as the elegant and arrogant president of a corporation in which the lawyer has uncovered corruption, the *Vice*, in true Sciascia fashion, is prevented from bringing the culprit to justice. He ruminates on keeping at bay pain, which he likens to an animal, 'small, ferocious and filthy'; ever attached to clarity and reality, he refuses morphine.

Much of *Il cavaliere e la morte* (*The Knight and Death*) – Sciascia dropped the devil, saying that he is useless in a world in which evil competes with man – is a soliloquy on dying. Nearing the end, the *Vice* meditates on truth and lies, dignity and indignity and the folly of a world willing to risk its own extinction. A vision of the Apocalypse leaves him feeling that a spider's 'viscous filthy web' shrouds his face. '*Che confusione*,' he thinks as he dies – not of his illness but murdered, his discovery of the truth coinciding neatly with his death. 'Truth,' he thinks, 'instead of life is death.' In Sciascia's study in Racalmuto, near the Dürer engraving, he had hung a Goya etching, '*Murio La Verdad*' – truth is dead.

Il cavaliere, written in lesson books on his knee, came out somewhat long and often illegible. Sciascia returned home to his Olivetti and did what he had never done before: he rewrote it, cutting it by a third to produce what became, at eighty pages, one of his shortest novels. In a decidedly despairing interview with *La Repubblica*, he said that 'this is, for me, a book of closure', in the sense that it closed his experience of life, his thoughts on existence and on Italy, his 'sense of being alive and the sense of death'. The Italy he now saw around him was suffocating under conformity, and Italians had been reduced to a state of permanent insecurity by financial malfeasance and subversive iniquity, tolerated by the State because it suited them. Returning for a last time to Lampedusa's words, he declared that 'nothing will now change, at least not in the span of my short life'. The criminality of the times, creeping and disguised, had come to seem to him worse than 'the wholly criminal nature of Fascism'. *Il cavaliere* attracted much praise, with some people saying that it was Sciascia's finest book.

Not always so approving of Sciascia, the journalist and editor Indro Montanelli used the occasion of his own eightieth birthday to declare that whenever he was confronted by an awkward question of conscience, he asked himself what Sciascia would do in his place. Sciascia, he said, was a man who would never, ever, say something that he did not believe. To an interviewer, Sciascia said that posterity was not important to him; nor, up to a point, success. 'My goal is not to bore: that is my first and only precept', though he should perhaps have added his insistence on higher principles. He had recently become friends with the French critic Claude Ambroise, who had begun editing a collection of Sciascia's work, and Sciascia had embarked on a conversation with an old friend, Domenico Porzio, with the idea of turning it eventually into a book. Porzio sent him a list of topics they should discuss, written in Latin. There was *de anima* (on the soul), *de studio* (on books), *de litteris* (on literature more generally), *de mulieribus* (on women) and *de rebus siculis* (on Sicilian affairs). They started their talks, two old friends musing amiably and without haste, with Cicero. And he was deriving great pleasure from assembling an exhibition of his many portraits of the writers he had loved and collected.

Over the years, Sciascia's work had become more accusatory. But his heroes had remained essentially the same, different versions of Captain Bellodi in *The Day of the Owl*. They were men very like Sciascia himself, solitary, obsessive, erudite, modest, brave and outspoken, uninterested in fashionable causes, men of ideas and philosophy, not action. They were cultured and heroic. They battled with enigmas, snares and coincidences and once they had reached down into the very roots of their investigations, they opened them up and turned them into meditations on justice and truth. They were rebels and heretics, as he was, refractory to ideology, profoundly opposed to chicanery and accommodations; often they were ill-tempered and intractable. As his friend Bufalino said, they were 'God's policemen', grand inquisitors who asked not, 'Who is the killer?' but, 'Why death?'

Though after finishing *Candido* he had written no more fiction for ten years, he never ceased to believe that his *gialli* were the most honest way to deliver the truth, even when they were woven through with asides and full of labyrinths and mirrors. His investigators were never the most senior, and invariably someone above them sooner or later thwarted them. Sciascia's literary universe had been peopled by men in uniform, policemen, carabinieri, lawyers, judges. They had been set up to fail, to solve cases and yet be defeated by the malign forces lined up against them. Doubt was their weapon. Like all proper Sicilians, they were sceptical about everything and especially about the people around them who, while apparently upholding the law, were in fact intent on subverting it.

They read the world using their considerable intelligence, deciphering, distilling, unravelling secret, buried things even when these were capricious and contradictory, and where every trail led deeper into the undergrowth. And then, when every clue had been assembled, when every 'hidden mineral of the soul' properly mined and the subsoil laid bare, then the conclusion had to be submitted to yet another strainer of doubt. If no light had been brought, and the obscurity remained impassable, at least it had become clear that the truth was impossible to know. Asked whether he was a satirist, he replied that yes, 'satire is a form of criticism', a 'mirror in which you can see the world's distortions'. Everything he had ever written, he said, had contained a vein of satire.

Disliking pigeonholes, he was irritated when people referred to him as an intellectual. But he was in fact the very essence of an intellectual, bringing his agile mind, vast culture and almost uncannily deep memory to bear on everything around him. In a country which admired such people, he was a rare public intellectual, an uncomfortable and prescient interpreter not just of *Sicilianità* but of Italian affairs generally. Increasingly, he was called on to have views and to deliver them in newspaper columns, in books, on university platforms and before television cameras, though his famous long silences continued to unnerve interviewers and listeners alike. He took this duty seriously, though he liked to quote Machiavelli as saying that intellectuals had so little power that they could not even turn over a stone and that writers were merely decorative. He saw no meaning in the phrase 'intellectual in an ivory tower': writing, by definition, was for him a political, public act. He described himself as a conservative, in the sense that he wanted to conserve all that was best and then act in the light of it.

By the end of the 1980s, Sciascia had as a writer been all things: novelist, detective story writer, essayist, literary critic, historian, pamphleteer and autobiographer, trying at every turn to extract simplicity from complication. At one time or another, he had written for every major newspaper and magazine, but he could not be lured by money to do anything he did not want to do, saying that in order to be truly free you could not be attached to money. Asked for a comment, as he repeatedly was, he would pick up a piece of paper, barely pause to think, then write at great speed, neither altering nor correcting, reducing his views to their very essence so that the words felt, as his biographer and friend Matteo Collura put it, 'dried by the sun'.

In *Il Consiglio*, Sciascia had invited his readers to reflect on bad faith and the ignorance of those who allowed themselves to be duped. *Il contesto* and *Todo modo*, metaphors for the vacuum of immorality into which Italy had fallen, had described creeping injustice and corruption, a world in which no one was safe. In his collection of short stories, *The Wine Dark Sea*, he had laid out his life's interests: the Mafia, the power of the family, miscarriage of justice, historical curiosities. Candido had been the ultimate rebel, the man who said no to the Italian way of life. In each book, ever more loudly, he had attacked the Italian State, the Catholic Church, the judiciary and the world of big business. There was almost nothing that had happened in Italy during his lifetime on which he had not pronounced, and almost nothing that he wrote that did not somewhere at its heart carry the crushing legacy of sulphur in Western Sicily. Nor did he ever stop regarding the Mafia, 'a total dimension of evil,' as one way of being Sicilian. No other writer, perhaps, has had such a profound influence on creating a consciousness of doubt, and his many pages on justice, on politics, on the death penalty, are among the most resonant in literary history.

Critics sometimes complained that Sciascia was impossible to define, and some found his irony too disturbing, his morality too exacting, his punctiliousness too scholarly and his many references and paradoxes too recondite. Over the years, a persistent little band of angry opponents, a clique of academic critics, repeatedly accused him of being a 'provincial Voltaire', of using the Mafia to get readers and enrich himself, saying that his 'monotonous denigrations' of Sicily had driven away tourists and potential investors. There was nothing, his most acerbic and mindless critic, Santi Correnti, wrote, at which 'he has not thrown mud'. Some of the attacks Sciascia found painful; many he just pushed away.

But among his legions of readers there were few who did not admire his endless quest for knowledge and truth, his battles for a 'just justice', his persistent desire to keep digging, his willingness to contradict himself, which was, as he said himself, a proof that he was human and aware that contradiction lay at the very heart of moral existence. 'I have never been able to love Sicily wholeheartedly,' Sciascia admitted to an interviewer, 'without feeling a counterpart of impatience, resentment and dislike.' One gloomy winter day he told a French journalist that his personal story was 'one of defeat, or more exactly, disappointment'.

It did not stop people thinking this melancholy, obstinate, uncomfortable man was right when he declared the 'incandescent nucleus of *Sicilitudine*' was apprehension, a constant battle between physical beauty and fear felt by people steeped in 'natural and tragic solitude'. And they proved their great admiration for him by buying, in great number, his books and inundating him with requests for interviews, of which he gave many hundreds, complaining that he kept repeating himself and provoking interviewers into describing him as very friendly and apparently very open but actually saying very little. There was talk of the Nobel Prize. By now *The Day of the Owl* alone had sold over half a million copies. Sciascia, normally very wary of the many major prizes awarded to him over the years, was delighted when he was given the Premio Amici di Latino at a dinner in Florence, saying that what really pleased him was the prize of an enormous ham.

For all the renewed wave of killings, the *maxi-processo*, it was agreed, had achieved one very important result: it had robbed the Mafia of its aura of impunity and invincibility and brought the crime of belonging to the Mafia firmly into the legal system. But the Mafia had not wasted its time. It had regrouped, moved its centre of operations to Trapani, and embarked on a new round of *cadaveri eccellenti*. Within a year of the *maxi-processo*, two hundred people had been murdered, among them two judges and a former mayor, a man much liked by Sciascia who had been tainted by allegations of involvement with the Mafia then murdered for going to the police. On 25 September 1988, Antonino Saetta, who as a magistrate had achieved notable successes against the Mafia, was shot dead with his son as they were returning to Caltanissetta from the christening of a grandchild. And though hardly a *cadavere eccellente*, Michele Sindona was found dead in his prison cell in Voghera, having drunk an espresso laced with strychnine.

A new Anti-Mafia Commission warned that three of Italy's regions – Campania, Calabria and Sicily – were no longer under police control. Over 12 per cent of the national GDP was estimated to be coming from Mafia crime, half of it from drugs, the rest from extortion and bribery. A criminal federation of vast proportions was taking shape across the world, bringing into play Turkey's Grey Wolves and China's Triads, along with Kurds and Puerto Ricans.

Sciascia made his peace with Borsellino. Finding themselves at the same conference, they lunched, together with their wives. Borsellino accepted Sciascia's assurances that he had never intended to attack him personally and declared that Sciascia 'had always been and remained a "master"'. The two men met again and were friendly: a photograph was taken and widely published to prove it. Falcone had also been heard to say that Sciascia was probably right in his warnings.

Falcone and Borsellino had guaranteed that there would be further Mafia trials, saying that a *'terzo livello'* – an upper echelon – of politicians, businessmen and civil servants working with the Mafia was still at large and pulling the strings. But the political world was turning against their resolve. The elections of July 1987, fought by candidates on all sides on promises to weaken what they saw as the overweening power of the magistrature – some went as far as to call it 'the judicial road to Communism' – had brought to prominence men little committed to their particular and passionate fight against the Mafia. To many delighted *mafiosi*, it now seemed as if the Socialists and the Radicals could be just as helpful to them as the Christian Democrats. In Rome, civil servants continued to be swayed by financial rewards and political favours; serious proposals for reform were endlessly negotiated and watered down. Shady Mafia power was everywhere.

Though a special law had been passed during the *maxi-processo* to prevent most of those convicted from going free on appeal, many were once again on the loose, benefiting from the legal loopholes with which the system was peppered. Among them were Antonietta Giustolisi and Anna Ianni. By early 1989 only sixty of the 342 convicted *mafiosi* remained in jail. In Palermo, where intimidation, arson and murder were once again on the rise, the police were demoralised and ineffective. Under the prickly, stubborn Antonino Meli, seemingly bent on undoing eight years of progress in Mafia prosecutions, the war against the Mafia had stalled. Investigations dwindled, not least because a decision had been taken to abandon the witness protection programme, which meant that the number of new *pentiti* coming forward had dried up. Falcone, for his admirers, was spoken of as a mythical hero, but his critics redoubled their vitriol. His much repeated motto – 'We can always do something' – was beginning to sound a little hollow.

Before the trial was over, Falcone had married Francesca Morvillo, a judge on the Court of Appeal. Blocked from his usual prosecutions, denied another promotion he had expected, he had turned his attention to recycled money as a way to attack Cosa Nostra internationally. He was at his villa on the Gulf of Mondella with two Swiss colleagues when, on 21 June 1989, one of his bodyguards noticed a large, black bag on the rocks just below the house. It was found to contain fifty-five sticks of dynamite, primed for a telephone command. Falcone's opponents immediately declared that he must have planted it himself; anonymous messages arrived with the words 'a squalid opportunist' with 'messianic tendencies'.

Falcone was also at odds with Mayor Orlando, who very publicly – and absurdly – accused him of standing up for Andreotti and Lima. He understood only too well, Falcone told an interviewer, how dangerously isolated he had become. 'In Sicily, the Mafia kills the servants of the State that the State has not been able to protect.' Saying that he could no longer work in such compromised circumstances, he asked the CSM for an immediate transfer. His plan now was to take up a job in Rome, offered by the Socialist Minister of Justice, Claudio Martelli, with a view to forming a new and much larger anti-Mafia pool, involving the whole of Italy, with a Mafia '*superprocura*' at its head. Though Borsellino sympathised with his decision, Falcone's departure, he declared, would be a tragedy, since he was the man the Sicilian Mafia really feared. 'First,' he told his friend, 'they'll kill *me*. Then it will be *your* turn. And they won't give up until they succeed.'

Sciascia, consulted as usual for his views, said that while in the early days he had indeed understood the Mafia in his bones, it had turned into an entirely new and unrecognisable animal. He had no more to say. His expertise had ended. But he was only too familiar with the calumnies now descending on Falcone's head. He wrote sadly to his friend Giuseppe Scaraffia: 'Like Stendhal I have a feeling of inadequacy, of the banality of things I have said and the importance of things that I haven't.' As Anna Maria would say later, the memory of her father's brush with Borsellino was never allowed to fade, kept constantly alive by journalists whenever his name was mentioned.

Sciascia was now rereading the authors he loved. He sat at his desk in Palermo, surrounded by his portraits of writers, Zola in baggy trousers and jacket, Pirandello on his death bed looking sly and knowing, Stendhal in a top hat, Rousseau in a fur one, Apollinaire booted and in military dress, D'Annunzio standing martial and triumphant. He reread *Don Quixote*, the *Divine Comedy*, *Dead Souls* and *I promessi sposi*, saying that books do not exist in themselves, but are read differently by every generation of readers, and by the same readers at different times of their life. Reading them repeatedly gave him the impression of winding up a clock so that it did not stop next day, and he considered that anyone who did not read and reread Stendhal was *'un povero infelice'* – a very unhappy person; though given Stendhal's preoccupations with human emotions, and his own apparent need to keep them at bay, Sciascia's love for Stendhal was not easy to understand. Montaigne remained his master, with his scepticism, his acceptance of contradictions, his belief that truth itself had many faces, his feeling that the better one was prepared for death, the more things became unimportant. Having for many years read no poetry, he turned back to it saying that he could once again 'see its horizon, which I thought I had lost'. Asked by a reporter what it felt like to be considered the 'conscience of an entire nation', he replied: 'Bad. And alone.'

Sciascia had told an interviewer on Italian Swiss radio that there came a time in life when you restricted yourself to a small circle of friends. As his health slowly grew worse, Bufalino, Consolo, Cavallaro and Scimè, with whom he had put on a play in the Regina Margherita in Racalmuto almost half a century before, and Scianna, whose collection of portraits of Sciascia was now nearing 1,500 photographs, gathered close around him. There were still good days when the group moved from anecdote to anecdote, laughing, smoking, remembering. A new battery of tests carried out in Milan in the spring of 1989 finally revealed that he had a rare form of cancer, a *mieloma micromolecolare*. Maria was told that he had five to nine months to live, but the family decided not to tell Sciascia. It was clear that he knew, but the pretence was kept up. He agreed to chemotherapy and dialysis.

Elvira had lent the Sciascias her flat in Milan, where his doctor, Giovanni Fogazzi, kept a diary of his visits. They exchanged presents of books and bookplates. One day the doctor asked him why it was that people took such pleasure in collecting books. Because, said Sciascia, 'they help us to live'. When he could, he walked very slowly to Manzoni's church, the San Fedele, to breathe the air that Manzoni had breathed, then strolled past Manzoni's house. The film director Giuseppe Tornatore had recently completed *Nuova Cinema Paradiso*, his story of a small boy, Toto, in impoverished post-war Sicily, who has fallen in love with films and helps project them in a small, gilded cinema. Consolo was able to arrange a special screening, at which Sciascia was allowed to smoke. Afterwards, Sciascia wept.

Though he told Bufalino that he felt that he was now 'sharpening a pencil to an ever finer point' but that it would not write, he was in fact hard at work, saying that 'I will stop writing only when I stop living'. He had started a new *giallo*, this time about a former diplomat returning to his country house after long years abroad to search for some letters written to his great-grandfather by Pirandello and Garibaldi. In the shuttered house he finds a valuable painting, stolen from a church and hidden there. He calls the police. Next day, his friends turn up to find him dead, a bullet to his temple. They assume that, since, like the *Vice*, the diplomat suffers from a terminal illness, he died by suicide. But, in true Sciascia fashion, he has in fact been murdered by the policeman who answered his call and who is part of a criminal band. The last of Sciascia's 'men alone', the diplomat is another reader of books, another lover of the *Encyclopédistes*, solitary, rueful, conscious of his impending death and, as with the *Vice*, obsessed with confusion and corruption, his metaphor for the moral catastrophe of modern society. He called it *A Simple Story* and said that writing it made him feel more cheerful. Indifferent as ever to money, he turned down an offer from Mondadori to buy the rights to all his work for $5 million, saying that he preferred to be free. Even as his health faded, his curiosity remained as keen, his appetite for new stories as unquenchable, needing always to learn, to understand.

He was also helping to put together one collection of his articles, *A futura memoria*, many of which were about the polemics that had coloured and embittered his recent years, and another, his forty-third book, of stories and articles. Memory continued to fill his mind; as Bufalino said, it was a particular kind of memory, invariably steeped in morality. And Sciascia was starting to think about a new *inchiesta*, about a renowned Fascist journalist called Telesio Interlandi, improbably saved by his Socialist lawyer during the violent reprisals of the immediate post-war months. It was to be another Moro, a plea for tolerance and compassion. Visiting the lawyer's adopted son in February 1989, Sciascia coughed incessantly. His eyes looked anguished.

Early in September, Sciascia and Maria returned to Palermo by plane, with Sciascia on a drip and in a wheelchair. For a while, he attended dialysis three times a week, and then a machine was installed in the flat in the Viale Francesco Scaduto. He listened to old Neapolitan songs. Unlike his *Vice*, he agreed to take morphine for the increasing pain. The pretence was kept up that he would soon get well. He was never alone. Maria, Laura and Anna Maria were constantly at his side; friends took it in turns to keep him company. Vito, his ten-year-old grandson, seldom left him. One day Orlando paid a visit. After he left, with a flash of his old irony, Sciascia asked Anna Maria: 'What do you think he wanted?'

Claude Ambroise, during one of their long talks, had asked Sciascia whether one aspect of his writing was a desire to make of death 'a narratable experience'. Yes, Sciascia had said, 'I want to tell it.' He said that he had reduced the thought of death to an 'ultimately supremely intellectual matter', and in so doing made it 'less heavy, less obsessive, as with any wait which is accompanied by a feeling of curiosity'. But that, once you stop thinking about death, you give up thinking. He was not afraid: would it not, after all, be restful? Over the telephone he told Matteo Collura: 'I have already disembarked on a deserted island.' He could give the appearance of being well, he said, 'but I am very ill'.

There was not much time left. Though it seemed clear that he knew that he was dying, there were days when he asked Maria whether new specialists could not be consulted. Roberto Galasso, his friend and editor at Adelphi, was rushing *A Simple Story* into print, with Sciascia giving his corrections over the phone in a small, quiet, exhausted voice. He was able to see a finished copy and to choose red type for the jacket of *A futura memoria*.

In mid November, Sciascia decided to stop dialysis, telling Maria that the pain of living like this, not only physically but in the way that his illness flowed into every part of his life, had become too much. Four days later, on 20 November, the day 100,000 copies of *A Simple Story* reached the bookshops, Sciascia died. He was sixty-eight. In the Chamber of Deputies in Rome, the President rose and announced his death; there was a minute's silence. A little before, he had said to Anna Maria: 'It should not have ended like this.' He had left a page of typewritten wishes. There should be no speeches, no eulogies, and no one should waste any time defending his memory or correcting anything that he had said or written, for he would no longer be in a position to reconsider. He hoped his 'fears' and the battles he had fought would give him 'a small immortality'. Then he had added, with a characteristic touch of pride, that in time his warnings, his observations and his many unpopular arguments would all come to be proved true.

Sciascia had long professed a horror of not being really dead when placed in his coffin. He had asked his family to wait a bit, so as to be 'beyond all possible doubt', before it was sealed. One by one, his friends came to say goodbye. An eighteenth-century silver cross had been placed by Maria between his folded hands and he wore a grey suit and a new tie. In a farewell open letter to *Il Giornale*, Bufalino remembered his friend as the 'most charming, generous, disarming ... master', a true recorder of injustice, below the 'veneer of a contrarian'. All over Italy, the front pages of newspapers were filled with tributes. 'He voiced our doubts,' wrote Michele Perreira, 'even our prickly ones. We will miss his spine.'

Nisticò, the tough-minded Communist editor of *L'Ora*, later came to the flat and kissed Sciascia's typewriter.

Two days later, a long funeral cortège left Palermo for the drive to Racalmuto. Seven thousand people were waiting, among them mayors in their tricolour sashes, senators and deputies from Rome, the Archbishop of Agrigento, writers, painters, politicians, friends from all over Europe. The schools had closed and the shops were shuttered. *Malgrado Tutto*, the local paper he had helped to launch, brought out a special fourteen-page issue with the headline: 'Addio Maestro'. Bells from the old sulphur mines were rung.

Sciascia had agreed, to many people's surprise, and perhaps to please Maria, to have his funeral in the church by the *zie*'s house, the Madonna del Monte, saying that it was his prerogative to contradict himself and that loving truth and accepting all the risks that this entailed had conferred on him a certain religiosity. He certainly did not believe in the devil, but as certainly he did believe in evil. Though an 'absolute sceptic' all his life, he had felt a certain piety about life and above all about death, regarding religion as an aspiration, a longing for the absolute, in a world permanently in torment and anxiety. Father Domenico Cuffaro, an old friend who had married both Laura and Anna Maria, said that not long before Sciascia had quoted to him Pascal's words: 'God, I look for you because I know that you are there.' On his desk, by his typewriter, lay a small silver crucifix. As with so much about Sciascia, and for all the clarity of his words, it is sometimes hard to know exactly what he was thinking. At different times he had said many things about faith, and, like Graham Greene, sometimes he believed and sometimes he did not. He would like to ask God, he once said, precisely why he had chosen to give people life and death.

Sciascia's coffin was carried to the cemetery on the hill to one side of Racalmuto, to lie close to the graves of his brother, his parents, his grandparents and the *zie*, by the pupils whose hunger he had so poignantly described thirty years before. Few had read his books, but they had loved him. He had spent almost his entire life in the small triangle formed by Racalmuto, Caltanissetta and Palermo, always fearing in his bones exile from Sicily and repeating 'neither with you nor without you can I live'. He had asked that his plain white marble tombstone bear the inscription, '*Ce ne ricorderemo di questo pianeta'* – we will remember this planet – words written by the nineteenth-century French author Villiers de l'Isle-Adam, a man known for his mysterious and cruel tales. While many puzzled as to what Sciascia meant by them, and friends took them to say that there was much happiness in life to remember and that the world had proved so interesting to him that he would never forget it, the words also carried the perfect Sciascia ring of irony and enigma.

Afterword

Eleven days after Sciascia's death, the Berlin Wall came down and with it many of the equations between the left and the right that had held Italy together for half a century. The impact on the strong Italian Communist Party was enormous. But other currents were beginning to flow, some of which Sciascia had uncannily foreseen, others that would have delighted him, others again that would have saddened him greatly.

In January 1993, Judge Corrado Carnevale, the *'ammazza sentenza'* – sentence killer – suspected of being in league with the Mafia, who overturned a high number of convictions on appeal which allowed many *mafiosi* to go free, was suspended from his current position in the Supreme Court on grounds of breaching judicial ethics. This enabled his replacement to uphold the convictions of the major Mafia bosses in the *maxi-processo*. But the Mafia was not done. It had recently silenced a maker of pyjamas and dressing gowns called Libero Grassi, shot dead on a hot summer afternoon in Palermo after refusing to pay the *'pizzo'* – the sum extorted from many, possibly most, businesses in the city. A placard was put up where he fell. Here lies, it said, a man killed 'by the Mafia, by the *omertà* . . . of the industrialists, by the indifference of the political parties and by the absence of the State'. Grassi was certainly *un uomo solo*.

In March 1992 Salvatore Lima, the most powerful and tainted Christian Democrat politician in Sicily, crony of Prime Minister Giulio Andreotti, was also shot dead on the streets of Palermo. It was punishment for his failure to get the Mafia sentences overturned on appeal, but it was also a sign that the age-old alliance between the Mafia and the Christian Democrats was at last breaking down. Sicily remained an essential power base for the Christian Democrats and Andreotti arrived in time to attend Lima's funeral. He looked visibly shaken. Rumours about his links to the Sicilian Mafia had long abounded. They grew louder when a remarkable picture taken by Letizia Battaglia, a photographer famous for her stories on Mafia violence, came to light showing Andreotti embracing both Lima and Toto Riina, the Corleonesi boss, at a banquet held in the Salvos' luxury hotel, the Zagarella, in the summer of 1987, when Andreotti was Foreign Secretary. The 'kiss' seemed to capture perfectly a seal between two heads of state.

Andreotti, lizard like, a little stooped, with his black hair and pebble glasses, memorably described by one reporter as an 'aged tortoise retracting into his shell', had spent his life in the corridors of power, ingratiating himself, eliminating his opponents, rotating from post to post through seven prime ministerships and nineteen governments. Andreotti was the man Sciascia had in mind when he wrote about corruption in high places in *Todo modo*. Challenged to respond to the photograph of the 'kiss', Andreotti claimed that he had no knowledge of the occasion. He remained silent and imperturbable. But this time he was not allowed to wriggle away. Accusations of collusion with the Mafia, and ultimately a charge for the murder of the journalist Mino Pecorelli at the time of the Moro kidnapping, led to a series of trials. Though always insisting that he knew nothing about anything and constantly acquitted on technicalities, over the next few years he would find himself repeatedly in the dock; people spoke of him as 'the Italian politician most accused and most absolved'. Sciascia would have enjoyed it greatly; though he would have been angered by the legal shenanigans that kept Andreotti out of jail.

With the Communist threat laid to rest, the ugly stench of malfeasance was becoming unbearable. The Italians who had for so long wilfully chosen to ignore decades of political sleaze now became zealous champions of probity. In February 1992 a Socialist politician called Mario Chiesa was arrested in Milan as he was flushing a $7,000 bribe for a cleaning contract for a nursing home down the lavatory. Under questioning, he revealed that he also had $10 million in a Swiss bank. Craxi, his party leader, dismissed him as a 'bad apple'; infuriated, Chiesa agreed to supply the investigating magistrates with a full picture of kickbacks in Milan. What began as a very small puddle grew into an enormous lake, pulling in politicians and judges, industrialists and bankers. A group of magistrates set themselves up as *'Mani Pulite'* – clean hands. Over the next two years they uncovered an immense web of criminality, reaching into every corner of Italy as one after another people in positions of power were discovered to have lived off kickbacks and favours, millions of lire destined for public works having flowed seamlessly into their pockets. In this shadowy world, it became apparent, a parallel rule had been operating, feeding on illicit money, backed by fraudulent accounting, tolerated because the State itself was absent. Sciascia had again been right.

The public reacted with new verve. The pork barrel politics that had dominated Italy, and made Sicily under Lima and Ciancimino the world's largest consumer of cement, were effectively over. Soon over 10,000 people from across the whole of Italy were under investigation, nine of them senior magistrates. Proceedings were launched against forty prominent Sicilians – a former minister, four members of parliament, twelve regional councillors, along with a number of mayors and prominent industrialists. *'Tangentopoli'*, as it became known, after the word for bribe or kickback, did not solve corruption entirely, but it removed immunity from those who had long thrived on it. The Socialist leader, Benedetto Craxi, found to have been deeply implicated, managed to escape to Tunisia to avoid a jail sentence.

The parliamentary elections of April 1992 and 1993 saw the traditional governing parties humbled: the Christian Democrat vote fell to 26 per cent. The President of the Republic, Francesco Cossiga, resigned. By the beginning of 1994, 296 people had been charged with illicit funding, 207 with corruption, 157 with extortion, 95 with receiving stolen goods; and some of them with multiple charges. The way was paved for Silvio Berlusconi and his populist party, Forza Italia; but his rule is another story altogether.

By now, however, a second series of disasters had taken place. Assassination had returned to the streets of Palermo.

It was later said that it was at a Mafia summit held in 1987, at the time of the *maxi-processo*, that Toto Riina handed down three death sentences: the first for Falcone, the second for Borsellino, the third for Mayor Leoluca Orlando. On Saturday 23 May 1992

AFTERWORD

Falcone and his wife Francesca caught a plane in Rome to fly back to Palermo for the weekend. He had made considerable progress with his plans for a new penal code for *pentiti* and a coordinated anti-Mafia programme, but neither he nor Borsellino had many doubts about the danger they were in. The Falcones told no one they were travelling. A seven-man escort and three cars were waiting on the runway when they landed. Falcone decided to take the wheel of the middle car, with his driver sitting in the back. The usual helicopter was missing as a decision had been taken to reduce expenditure. Three hundred kilograms of dynamite had been concealed in a drainage tunnel under the motorway at Capaci, a Mafia stronghold on the way into Palermo, and men were waiting with detonators. The explosion killed three bodyguards outright. Falcone and Francesca were taken to hospital. He died soon after; she regained consciousness, learnt of his death, and slipped away.

It would be hard to exaggerate the sense of outrage, anger and grief that followed. As the funeral cortège passed down the streets of Palermo, women hung white sheets from their windows. The silent, shuttered city took on a ghostly air. The five closed coffins lay in state in the marble lobby of the Palermo Palace of Justice. The Italian Parliament declared a day of mourning. As politicians and senior legal figures tried to slip past the crowd into the church unperceived, there were shouts of 'Jackals!' and 'Murderers!' Rosaria Schifani, the twenty-three-year-old widow of one of the bodyguards, spoke, delicate and implacable. Falcone's death, remarked the philosopher Norberto Bobbio, 'made me ashamed to be Italian'. At a great public memorial held before 40,000 people two days later, Borsellino spoke bitterly about the 'Judases' who had betrayed his friend. A chain of mourners joined hands across the centre of Palermo and flowers and tributes were laid at the foot of the banyan tree outside his house. To this day, it remains a site of pilgrimage.

Borsellino had just fifty-seven days left to live. He took precautions but rushed around, telling friends that there was so much to do. On 19 July he rang his mother to tell her that he was coming to visit her. It was later discovered that in the previous few days, 3,000 unexplained and peculiar calls had been logged between Sicily, the US, Poland, Switzerland and Slovenia. Borsellino arrived in the Via d'Amelio with five bodyguards. As he pressed his mother's bell, a car bomb exploded, killing them all instantly. Anna

Maria and her son Vito were in their flat not far away: they went out on to the balcony and tried to locate the noise. One can only guess what Sciascia would have felt. Antonio Caponnetto, founder of the original anti-Mafia pool, wept as he surveyed the carnage. The crowds at the funerals showed no restraint. Pushing their way through the cordons of policemen, they jeered and jostled the arriving politicians. A number of women went on hunger strike. Eight prosecutors resigned, saying that they could no longer carry out their jobs properly. Now fearing himself to be the next target, Orlando moved for safety into a carabinieri barracks. In London, the *Observer* described Italy as in a state of war. The exchange rate of the lira plummeted.

Not long before, Borsellino had befriended seventeen-year-old Rita Atria, whose father and much-loved brother had been killed by a Mafia clan to which both belonged. Rita had gone to Borsellino to give evidence against their killers. After her mother discovered what she had done and issued threats against her, Borsellino put her into protective custody in Rome, visiting her whenever he could get away. Rita kept a diary. A week after his death, she threw herself from her third-floor balcony window. 'There is no one left to protect me,' she had written. Her mother did not attend her funeral, though many women from Palermo did. But some time later she took a hammer, went to the cemetery and smashed Rita's picture on her grave. It was only around this time that it was properly recognised that Mafia wives and mothers were playing crucial roles in the criminal organisation, not simply, as Sciascia had warned, by perpetuating its values but by replacing their imprisoned or mudered men in day-to-day operations.

Now, at last, concerted action was taken. Five thousand soldiers were drafted into Sicily and some detailed to guard the graves of Falcone and Borsellino. The Vatican, noticeably silent over the years, weighed in. At a special mass held in the Greek temples at Agrigento, Pope Paul II declared that *mafiosi* were living in mortal sin. The effect of the murders was not, as many had feared, to warn off witnesses and deter magistrates. On the contrary, many *pentiti* came forward, and with them came a new resolve to investigate and bring to trial further *mafiosi*. Networks were dismantled; billions of illicit dollars seized; the murder rate fell by 42 per cent. After twenty-three years on the run, during which time he married and had three children apparently undetected, Toto Riina was arrested. A short, stocky man, with small piggy eyes buried in folds of flesh, he had been betrayed by other bosses, keen to placate and deflect the authorities. Riina, it was said, was responsible for at least eight hundred killings. By 1996, the number of *pentiti* across Italy had risen to 1,177. Bit by bit, the murderous power of the Sicilian Mafia was at least partially curbed. Palermo ceased to be the city where tourists went to enjoy a frisson of danger. Work began on restoring 158 churches and four hundred palazzi. The anti-Mafia movement embarked on a concerted programme of education in schools. Foundations were set up in the names of Falcone and Borsellino. The airport was renamed after them.

As Sciascia had understood, the Mafia was no longer the organisation he had so minutely described in 1961, but something different, an international cartel of drug traffickers and money launderers with outposts all over the world and vast profits coming from people smuggling, prostitution and eventually the Bitcoin market. They were no longer 'men of honour' but ruthless killers bent on making fortunes. Sicily and Cosa Nostra had ceased to be leaders in the field, much of their vigour shifting to the Camorra in Naples and the 'Ndranghetta in Calabria. It was as Sciascia had said. Palm trees were growing everywhere.

Sciascia did not live to see the collapse of the old order but, perhaps more than any other of his contemporaries, he chronicled the steps that led to it. He was no longer alive when Cossiga, Minister of the Interior when Moro was kidnapped and adamant in his insistence that in captivity Moro was no longer Moro, admitted that Sciascia had been right all along, and that he regretted failing to follow up the clues his coded letters provided. Nor was he alive when it was discovered that secret sources in Czechoslovakia had indeed been giving aid to the Italian terrorists, so firmly denied by Berlinguer and then Guttuso. Nor did he witness the revelations about the seediness and corruption in high places that he so vividly described in *Todo modo*. When Ciancimino died in 2002, he left a vast fortune in cars, yachts and properties in Spain, Romania, Russia and Kazakhstan, but it was said that some sixty million in euros were never found. And nor, most sadly, was Sciascia able to visit the Palazzo Serri when Anna Maria's husband Nino unveiled yet another palimpsest of graffiti done by the Inquisition's prisoners. That, he would have enjoyed. As he would have enjoyed the campaign being mounted by a group of lawyers to have magistrates experience for themselves a few days in prison, so that they might better understand the *terribiltà* of the power they wield.

Many questions remained, not least where Borsellino's red diary had gone, vanished from his briefcase at the time of his murder, or why Falcone's computer had been mysteriously wiped clean. And who had been the 'third level' mentioned in the *maxi-processo*? Had the Italian secret services, working with the Americans, tried to keep the Communist Party from power? Sciascia would have enjoyed them all and turned them into elegant *inchieste*. As he once said, 'The writer is curiosity and it is from curiosity that a writer is born.' Asked why he became an investigator, the *Vice* replies: 'In order to learn a little more.'

Sciascia spent his entire life learning. He felt that he had been put on earth to question, to dig, to appraise, to challenge, to seek the truth wherever it led him, using literature and history as his interpreters, accepting that he would never know the full answer to anything. There was never the option of standing back or abdicating.

The span of his life, from the beginnings of Fascism to the coming down of the Berlin Wall, was a period of almost incessant turmoil and violence in Italy. He dealt with it by refusing to acknowledge compromise, by speaking uncomfortable truths, by believing that justice, the law and rights were the things that mattered most. He was one of that very small number of European intellectuals, along with Simone Weil, Hannah Arendt and Albert Camus, who testified, in their beliefs as in their actions, to what they saw as truth, free of ideology or politics, and witnesses to much that had been forgotten or lost. The energy of Sciascia's conscience was remarkable.

History has judged him well. Even if his timing and his targets were sometimes ill chosen, he turned out to be correct over almost everything that he said. The anti-Mafia movement *did* prove flawed; Moro *was* vindicated. Even the most vitriolic of his critics came to admit how prophetic he had been. In Italy, Sciascia's sales remain very high – 25 to 27 thousand copies of *The Day of the Owl* alone are sold each year – and he continues to be widely credited with being the first writer to describe in fiction the links between the Mafia and the political world and to make of the *giallo* a book of social commentary. There are streets, piazzas, schools and institutions all over Italy named after him. In Racalmuto, a *'percorso'* – a trail – takes the visitor past the *zie*'s house to the school where a classroom has been kept as a shrine to his memory; then to the theatre in which he learnt to love cinema, to the ruined remains of his grandfather's tile factory and to the grotto in which Fra Diego hid. The old electricity plant has become a foundation to house his archive and his collection of writers' portraits. In the Casa Sciascia, where as a boy he sat under the aunts' table and learnt to read the world, a philanthropist keeps every edition of his books, in their many languages, along with a vast library of Sicilian writers and artists. The house has been restored with the furniture and decorations of his childhood. A local biscuit has been named after him.

In Palermo, Vito, his grandson, keeps the flat in the Viale Scaduto as it was the day Sciascia died, almost forty years ago now, with the desk calendar open at the date of his death. Visitors come to pay their respects. Almost no other Sicilian writer has enjoyed such lasting fame. Controversial and contrary all his life, he is now revered for his lucidity and loved for his subtle linguistic games, conjectures and flights of elegant fantasy, his mordant criticism and his gift for disturbing the stagnant waters of society, all of it flecked with Sicilian baroque, digressions and allusions. Roberto Scarpinato, Prosecutor General at the Court of Appeal in Palermo, has said that as time went by, he increasingly came to 'live inside Sciascia's world, inside the kind of degenerated power that he described', the world of Mafia bosses and corrupt ministers, bankers and priests and the inner sanctums they inhabited. Soon after his death, George Steiner declared: 'if you had told me in the past that there would be a new Stendhal, I would not have believed it. And yet Leonardo Sciascia, for me, is the Stendhal of our times.'

As Sciascia said himself, there was for him a question: what did it mean to be Sicilian, even before Sicily became a metaphor for the ills of the world? It meant using memory, history and literature and borrowing from the French eighteenth-century writers he loved their scepticism and rationality. It meant deciphering the violent, hidden, capricious, anxious, bold and tormented nature of Sicilians, with their culture of death and pessimism, living their world from within, 'as if every person every thing every fact were a book you can open and read'. Many other writers saw more of the world. But few have written with greater political intelligence and the clarity to see who we are, what we inherit from the past and the distortions of the present. How did a boy born in one of the poorest and most backward villages in Sicily grow up so prophetic, so deeply understanding of the infinite and subtle varieties of power, what he called 'the whole mosaic of evil', so fearless in denouncing it, so perceptive in mapping out the evolution of contemporary history? And had his warnings been listened to, might it have made a difference? There is, of course, no answer.

Acknowledgements

Many people helped me with this book. But first and foremost I want to thank, warmly and gratefully, Sciascia's family: his daughter Anna Maria, her husband Antonino Catalano and their son Vito. They talked to me at length, provided material and photographs, introduced me to friends and colleagues and steered me through Sciascia's vast archive. Sciascia's cousins, Maria Martorelli and Angelo Sciascia, and his niece, Mila Rossi, were very helpful and very hospitable. Sciascia's Italian biographer, Matteo Collura, and Joseph Farrell, author of a scholarly work on Sciascia, *Leonardo Sciascia: The Man and the Writer*, and translator of several of his books, gave me enormous assistance.

Edith Cutaia at the Fondazione Leonardo Sciascia in Racalmuto went out of her way to provide books, papers and letters, and Francesco Izzo and Penny Brucculeri at the Associazione Amici di Leonardo Sciascia were very generous with their time. I thank them very much. My gratitude also goes to the librarians and staff of the British Library, the Archivio di Stato and Biblioteca Centrale della Regione Siciliana in Palermo and most particularly to Umberto Santino and Anna Puglisi at the Centro Siciliano di Documentazione Giuseppe Impastato, in whose archive I spent many hours reading and who patiently answered my numerous questions.

I would also like to thank the following people for taking the time to talk to me: Nicola d'Alessandro, Vincenzo Barbarotto, Emma Bonino, Luciana Castellina, Felice Cavallaro, Anna Chimenti, Pippo di Falco, Antonio Foscari, Simonetta Hornby, Christopher Maclehose, Dacia Maraini, Nando Dalla Chiesa, Leoluca Orlando, Aaron Pettinari, Francesco Petruzzella, Salvatore Picone, Nicoletta

Polo, David Porter, Claudio Riolo, Gaetano Savatteri, Ferdinando Scianna, Olivia Sellerio, Marcello Sorgi, Massimo Teodori, Ian Thomson, Gaetano Tranchino. Ian Thomson has also translated some of Sciascia's books into English.

Some of the research for this book was done during the months of Covid lockdown. I am very grateful to the London Library for the loan of their books and to Peter Baring for his help in getting them.

I would also like to thank my travelling companion Patricia Williams. As ever, my warmest thanks go to Anne Chisholm, my first reader, and to Joseph Farrell, who kindly agreed to read the manuscript. The translations are all my own.

As ever, many thanks go to my editor, Molly Slight, and to Asia Choudhry, Lucy Chaudhuri, Alison Tulett and Jessica Spivey at Chatto; and to my wonderful agent, Clare Alexander.

List of Illustrations

pp. x, xi   Maps of Sicily and Racalmuto (courtesy of Bill Donohoe)
p. xv   Statue of Sciascia in Racalmuto (Bettmann/Getty Images)
p. 2   Leonardo Sr, with his wife and children (from the Sciascia family archive)
p. 3   Leonardo, Anna and Giuseppe (from the Sciascia family archive)
p. 5   Sulphur miners (Hulton Archive/Getty Images)
p. 6   *La Noce* (photo taken by Leonardo Sciascia)
p. 9   Sciascia, aged four (from the Sciascia family archive)
p. 22   Don Calò
p. 25   Cesare Mori (Smith Archive/Alamy)
p. 29   Racalmuto
p. 30   Sciascia with Giuseppe (from the Sciascia family archive)
p. 35   Young Sciascia with his family (from the Sciascia family archive)
p. 37   Luigi Pirandello (Bettmann/Getty Images)
p. 42   Sciascia, aged fourteen or fifteen (from the Sciascia family archive)
p. 62   Sciascia with wife Maria and daughter Laura (from the Sciascia family archive)
p. 69   Salvatore Giuliano (Chronicle/Alamy)
p. 80   Pier Paolo Pasolini (ullstein bild/Getty Images)
p. 88   Maria (from the Sciascia family archive)
p. 99   Sciascia with Calvino (LaPresse/Alamy)
p. 114   Sciascia and Scianna (photo taken by Nino Catalano, used by kind permission of the Sciascia family archive)
p. 117   Sciascia with Guttuso (photo taken by Letizia Battaglia © Archivio Letizia Battaglia)

p. 119 Elvira Sellerio (© Effigie. All rights reserved 2025/Bridgeman Images)

p. 132 Nica with Genoveffa (from the Sciascia family archive)

p. 165 Aldo Moro photographed by the Red Brigades (Hulton Archive/Getty Images)

p. 179 Aldo Moro's body (Associated Press/Alamy)

p. 203 Falcone at Chiesa's funeral (photo taken by Letizia Battaglia © Archivio Letizia Battaglia)

p. 204 Andreotti and Lima (ZUMA Press, Inc./Alamy)

p. 211 Sciascia with his grandson, Vito (from the Sciascia family archive)

p. 222 The *maxi-processo* (Universal Images Group North America LLC/Alamy)

p. 245 Portrait of Sciascia (© Ferdinando Scianna/Magnum Photos)

Every effort has been made by the publishers to trace the holders of copyright. Any inadvertent omissions of acknowledgement or permission can be rectified in future editions.

Select Bibliography

Aglianò, Sebastiano, *Questa Sicilia*, Milan, 1949
Agosti, Aldo, *Palmiro Togliatti*, Turin, 1996
d'Alessio, Luigi, *Lo zolfo come metafora*, Rome, 1997
Amaduri, R. & Carta, A., *La donna, le donne nell'opera (e nella Sicilia) di Leonardo Sciascia*, Rome, 2012
Amodio, Ennio & Catalano, Elena Maria (eds), *La sconfitta della ragione: Leonardo Sciascia e la giustizia penale*, Palermo, 2022
Ambroise, Claude, *Invito alla letteratura di Sciascia*, Milan, 1983
Ambroise, Claude, *14 domande a Leonardo Sciascia, Opere 1956–87*, Milan, 1987
Gli Amici della Noce, Fondazione Leonardo Sciascia, Racalmuto, 2010
Arlacchi, Pino, *Gli uomini del disonore*, Milan, 1992
Associazione Cosa Vostra, *Morire di mafia*, Milan, 2020
Attanasio, Sandro, *Gli anni della rabbia: Sicilia 1943–47*, Milan, 1984
Baris, Tommaso & Vetri, Carlo, *I Siciliani nella resistenza*, Palermo, 2019
Bartoletti, Loredana & Wlodek Goldkorn (eds), *L'Espresso Pasolini*, Rome, 2015
Battaglia, Letizia, *Il dolore della memoria*, Rome, 2002
Benfari, Michele (ed.), *Figli della stessa terra*, Agrigento, 2022
Bischie, Gian Italo & Calanchi, Alessandra, *Arrivano! Sciascia e gli Americani*, Fano, 2021
Bocca, Giorgio, *L'inferno: profondo Sud, male oscuro*, Milan, 1992
Bolzoni, Attilio, *White Shotgun*, Milan, 2008
Bolzoni, Attilio & d'Avanzo, Giuseppe, *Il capo dei capi*, Milan, 2007
Bolzoni, Attilio & Lodato, Saverio, *C'era una volta la lotta alla mafia*, Rome, 1998
Brydone, P., *A Tour Through Sicily and Malta in a Series of Letters to William Beckford*, London, 1773
Bufalino, Gesualdo, *Opere 1981–1988*, Milan, 1992
Caico, Louise, *Sicilian Ways and Days*, London, 1910
Calvi, Fabrizio, *La vie quotidienne de la mafia de 1950 à nos jours*, Paris, 1986
Calvino, Italo & Sciascia, Leonardo, *L'illuminismo mio e tuo: Carteggio 1953–1985*, Milan, 2003

SELECT BIBLIOGRAPHY

Camilleri, Andrea, *Un'onorevole siciliano: le interpellanze parlamentari di Leonardo Sciascia*, Milan, 2011
Cancila, Orazio, *Palermo*, Rome, 1988
Cancila, Orazio, *Baroni e popolo nella Sicilia del grano*, Palermo, 1983
Candida, Renato, *Questa mafia*, Caltanissetta, 1962
Cannon, Joanna, *The Novel as Investigation: Leonardo Sciascia, Dacia Maraini and Antonio Tabucchi*, Toronto, 2006
Caruso, Bruno, *Le giornate romane di Leonardo Sciascia*, Milan, 1997
Cavallaro, Felice, *Sciascia l'eretico*, Milan, 2021
Cavidi, Augusto, *Quel maledetto 1992*, Trapani, 2022
Chinnici, Giorgio et al., *Gabbie vuote: processi per omicidio a Palermo dal 1983 al maxi-processo*, Milan, 1992
Ciconte, Enzo & Torre, Giovanna (eds), *Giovanni Falcone: l'uomo, il giudice, il testimone*, Pavia, 2019
Colajanni, Napoleone, *Nel regno della mafia 1847–1921*, Milan, 2013
Cole, David, *Rough Road to Rome*, London, 1983
Collura, Matteo, *Il maestro di Regalpetra: vita e opere di Leonardo Sciascia*, Milan, 2019
Collura, Matteo, *La memoria, il futuro*, Milan, 1999
Collura, Matteo, *Alfabeto Sciascia*, Milan, 2002
Coluccello, Rino, *Challenging the Mafia Mystique*, London, 2016
Cornwell, Rupert, *God's Banker: An account of the life and death of Roberto Calvi*, London, 1983
Correnti, Santi, *La Sicilia di Sciascia*, Catania, 1977
Costantino, Salvatore & Zanca, Aldo (eds), *Convegno in Palma di Montechiaro 27–29 April 1960*, Milan, 2014
Curcuruto, Michele, *Signori dello zolfo*, Caltanissetta, 2001
Dalla Chiesa, Carlo Alberto, *In nome del popolo Italiano*, Milan, 1997
Dalla Chiesa, Nando, *Mafia, onore e potere*, Quaderni storici, Bologna, April 1984
Dalla Chiesa, Nando, *Delitto imperfetto: il generale, la mafia, la società Italiana*, Milan, 1984
Dalla Chiesa, Nando, *La legalità è un sentimento*, Milan, 2023
Dickie, John, *Mafia Republic*, London, 2013
Distefano, Barbara, *Sciascia maestro di scuola*, Rome, 2019
Dolci, Danilo, *Banditi a Partinico*, Bari, 1955
Dolci, Danilo, *Inchiesta a Palermo*, Turin, 1956
Duggan, Christopher, *The Sicilian Origins of the Mafia*, Conflict Studies, 203, 1987
Duggan, Christopher, *Fascism and the Mafia*, London, 1989
Faenza, Roberto & Fini, Marco, *Gli Americani in Italia*, Milan, 1976
Falcone, Giovanni with Padovani, Marcelle, *Men of Honour: The truth about the Mafia*, London, 1992
Farrell, Joseph, *Leonardo Sciascia: The man and the writer*, Florence, 2022
Ferrero, Ernesto, *I migliori anni della nostra vita*, Milan, 2003
Finley, M. I., Mack Smith, D. & Duggan, C., *A History of Sicily*, London, 1986

SELECT BIBLIOGRAPHY

Fiocco, Gianluca, *L'Italia prima del miracolo economico 1951–54*. PhD thesis, Siena, 2002
Franchetti, Leopoldo & Sonnino, Sidney, *La Sicilia in 1876*, 2 vols, Florence, 1877
Freni, Melo, *Verso la vacanza: la morte di Sciascia*, Marina di Patti, 1992
Frosini, V., Renda, F., Sciascia, L., *La mafia: quattro studi*, Bologna, 1970
Gentile, Giovanni, *Il tramonto della cultura Siciliana*, Bologna, 1917
Gilmour, David, *The Last Leopard: A life of Giuseppe Tomasi di Lampedusa*, London, 1988
Ginsborg, Paul, *A History of Contemporary Italy 1943–1980*, London, 1990
Ginsborg, Paul, *Italy and its Discontents: Family, civil society, state 1980–2001*, London, 2002
Gotor, Miguel (ed.), *Aldo Moro: Lettere dalla prigionia*, Turin, 2008
Giudice, Gaspare, *Pirandello: A biography*, London, 1975
Goethe, Johann Wolfgang von, *Travels in Sicily*, London, 1885
Gower Chapman, Charlotte, *Milocca: A Sicilian village*, London, 1930
Grammatico, Dino, *La rivolta Siciliana del 1958*, Palermo, 1966
Hess, Henner, *Mafia and Mafiosi: Origin, power and myth*, Tübingen, 1970
Hobsbawn, E. J., *Primitive Rebels*, Manchester, 1959
Holland, James, *Sicily '43: The first assault on Fortress Europe*, London, 2020
Innocenti, Marco, *L'Italia nel 1943*, Milan, 1993
Kahn, Milka & Veron, Anne, *Women of Honour*, London, 2017
La Duca, Rosario, *I veleni di Palermo*, Palermo, 1970
Lajolo, Davide (ed.), *Conversazione in una stanza chiusa*, Varese, 1981
La Porta, Filippo (ed.), *Pasolini e Sciascia: uomini eretici*, Venice, 2021
Levi, Carlo, *Le parole sono pietre*, Turin, 1955
Lewis, Norman, *The Honoured Society: The Sicilian Mafia observed*, London, 1964
Lewis, Norman, *In Sicily*, London, 2000
Lodato, Saverio, *Trent'anni di mafia*, Milan, 2006
Lo Iacono, Domenico, *Il fascismo clandestino in Sicilia 1943–46*, Palermo, 2015
Macaluso, Emanuele, *Leonardo Sciascia e i comunisti*, Milan, 2010
Mack Smith, Denis, *Storia di cento anni di vita Italiana – visti attraverso il Corriere della Sera*, Milan, 1978
Mafai, Simone et al., *Essere donna in Sicilia*, Rome, 1976
Mangiameli, Rosario (ed.), *Sicily Zone Handbook*, Caltanissetta, 1994
Mangiameli, Rosario, *Misurarsi con il regime*, Rome, 2008
Mangiameli, Rosario & Nicastro, Franco (eds), *Arrivano!: gli Americani a Vittoria nell'estate del '43*, Ragusa, 2003
Maraini, Dacia, *Bagheria*, Milan, 1993
Maraini, Dacia con Joseph Farrell, *La mia vita. Le mie battaglie*, Pisa, 2015
Matteo, Salvo di, *Anni roventi: la Sicilia dal 1943 al 1947*, Palermo, 1968
Mazzalari, Primo, *Viaggio in Sicilia*, Palermo, 1992
Mazzamuto, P., *La mafia nella letteratura, Nuovi quaderni del meridione*, Vol. 5, 1964

SELECT BIBLIOGRAPHY

Meccia, Andrea (ed.), *Media Mafia: Cosa Nostra fra cinema e TV*, Trapani, 2014
Mercuri, Lamberto, *La Sicilia e gli alleati*, *Storia Contemporanea*, March 1972
Messana, Eugenio Napoleone, *Racalmuto nella storia di Sicilia*, Canicatti, 1969
Monti, Giommaria, *Falcone e Borsellino*, Rome, 1996
Moro, Aldo, *Il memoriale di Aldo Moro*, Rome, 1979
Motta, Antonio, *Giorni felici con Leonardo Sciascia*, Bellinzona, 2004
Motta, Antonio, *Sulle orme di Leonardo Sciascia*, Soveria Mannelli, 2023
Mughini, Gianpiero (ed.), *Il mezzogiorno negli anni della Repubblica*, Rome, 1977
Mughini, Gianpiero, *Il grande disordine: i nostri indimenticabili anni settanta*, Milan, 1998
Mughini, Gianpiero, *Gli intellettuali e il Caso Moro*, Bologna, 1978
Mullen, Anne, *Inquisition and Inquiry: Sciascia's inchiesta*, Market Harborough, 2000
Nigro, Salvatore Silvano, *Leonardo Sciascia: scrittore, editore ovvero la felicità di fare libri*, Palermo, 2019
Nisticò, Vittorio, *L'ora dei ricordi*, Palermo, 2004
Nocilla, Nicola (ed.), *Leonardo Sciascia: la civiltà della tavola*, Palermo, 2022
Onofri, Massimo, *Storia di Sciascia*, Rome-Bari, 1994
Orlando, Leoluca, *Fighting the Mafia and Renewing Sicilian Culture*, New York, 2001
Palazzolo, Lanfranco, *Leonardo Sciascia deputato radicale 1978–1983*, Milan, 2004
Pantaleone, Michele, *Mafia e politica 1943–1962*, Turin, 1962
Perreira, Michele, *Romanzo d'amore*, Palermo, 2002
Petacco, Arrigo, *1943: giorno per giorno attraverso i bollettini del comando supremo*, Milan, 1993
Petacco, Arrigo, *Il prefetto di ferro*, Rome, 1975
Pezzotti, Barbara, *Politics and Society in Italian Crime Fiction*, Jefferson, 2014
Picone, Salvatore (ed.), *Tra i banchi di Regalpetra: Leonardo Sciascia e la sua scuola*, Agrigento, 2007
Picone, Salvatore & Restivo, Gigi, *Dalle parti di Leonardo Sciascia*, Milan, 2021
Pitré, Giuseppe, *Usi e costumi: credenze e pregiudizi del popolo Italiano*, Palermo, 1889
Pogliaghi, Luigi, *Giustizia come ossessione. Forme della giustizia nelle pagine di Leonardo Sciascia*, Milan, 2005
Poma, Rosario & Perrone, Enzo, *Quelli della lupara*, Palermo, 1964
Porzio, Domenico, *Fuoco all'anima: conversazione con Leonardo Sciascia*, Milan, 2021
Pyle, Ernie, *Brave Men*, New York, 1944
Pyle, Ernie, *Ernie's War: The best of Ernie Pyle's WW2 dispatches*, New York, 1986
Rago, Michele, *Pagine di diario 1951–1996*, Rome, 2021

Reeder, Linda, *Widows in White: Migration and the transformation of rural Italian women, Sicily 1880–1920*, Toronto, 2003
Renda, Francesco, *Storia della Sicilia dal 1860 al 1970*, Palermo, 1987
Robb, Peter, *Midnight in Sicily*, Sydney, 1996
Saladino, Giuliana, *Terra di rapina*, Turin, 1977
Santagati, Luigi, *Storia di Caltanissetta*, Caltanissetta, 1989
Santino, Umberto, *Mafia e maxi-processo*, Milan, 1992
Santino, Umberto, *Storia del movimento anti-mafia*, Rome, 2009
Santino, Umberto, *La mafia dimenticata*, Milan, 2017
Santino, Umberto & Puglisi, Anna, *La memoria e il progetto del Centro Impastato al No Mafia memorial*, Trapani, 2020
Savatteri, Gaetano, *I Siciliani*, Rome, 2005
Saviano, Roberto, *Beauty and the Inferno*, London, 2010
Schirripa, Vincenzo, *Borgo di Dio: La Sicilia di Danilo Dolci 1952–1956*, Milan, 2010
Schneider, Jane & Schneider, Peter, *Mafia, Anti-Mafia and the Question of Sicilian culture, Politics and Society*, Vol. 22, No. 2, June 1994
Sciascia, Anna Maria, *Il gioco dei padri: Pirandello e Sciascia*, Rome, 2009
Sciascia, Anna Maria, *Tra Racalmuto e Caltanissetta*, Foggia, 2013
Scrivere la Sicilia: Vittorini ed oltre. Atti del Convegno di Studi, Siracusa, 1983
Sechi, Salvatore (ed.), *Le vene aperte del delitto Moro*, Florence, 2009
Secomandi, Alessandro, *Potere e memoria*, Severia Mannelli, 2023
Sgroi, Salvatore Claudio, *Per la lingua di Pirandello e Sciascia*, Caltanissetta, 1990
Silj, Alessandro, *Brigate Rosse-Stato*, Florence, 1978
Silj, Alessandro, *Malpaese*, Rome, 1994
Sorgi, Marcello, *Le sconfitte non contano*, Milan, 2013
Sorgi, Marcello, *La testa ci fa dire: dialogo con Andrea Camilleri*, Rome, 2019
Spalanca, Lavinia (ed.), *Ladri di luce: Leonardo Sciascia e Piero Guccione tra bellezza e verità,*, Florence, 2023
Spataforma, Nunziatina, *Sciascia: le donne, la mafia*, Catania, 2000
Stajano, Corrado (ed.), *Mafia: l'atto d'accusa dei giudici di Palermo*, Milan, 1986
Sterling, Claire, *The Mafia: The long reach of the international Sicilian Mafia*, London, 1990
Stille, Alexander, *Excellent Cadavers: The Mafia and the death of the first Italian republic*, London, 1995
Tani, Stefano, *The Doomed Detective*, South Illinois, 1984
Cesare Terranova in memoria, with a preface by Leonardo Sciascia, Palermo, 1982
Thomson, Ian, *Sicilian Writers and the Mafia*, London Magazine, April/May 1987
Torrealta, Maurizio, *Processo allo stato*, Milan, 2012
Traina, Giuseppe, *Siciliani ultimi? Tre studi su Sciascia, Bufalino, Consolo e oltre*, Modena, 2014
Tranfaglia, Nicola, *Come nasce la Repubblica 1943–1947*, Milan, 2004

SELECT BIBLIOGRAPHY

Tranfaglia, Nicola, *Perché la mafia ha vinto*, Turin, 2008
Trevelyan, Raleigh, *Princes under the Volcano*, London, 1972
Ursetta, Umberto, *Mafia e potere alla sbarra*, Cosenza, 2010
Ursetta, Umberto, *Processo agli intoccabili*, Cosenza, 2013
Vecellio, Valter (ed.), *L'uomo solo: L'Affaire Moro di Leonardo Sciascia*. Atti di Convegno, Camera dei Deputati, 5–6 December 2001, Milan, 2002
Vecellio, Valter, *Leonardo Sciascia: la politica, il coraggio della solitudine*, Rome, 2019
Vilardo, Stefano, *A scuola con Leonardo Sciascia*, Palermo, 2022
Violante, Piero, *Swinging Palermo*, Palermo, 2015
Vittorini, Elio, *Conversazione in Sicilia*, Florence, 1941
Viviano, Francesco, *Mauro De Mauro: la verità scomoda*, Reggio Emilia, 2009
Williams, Isobel, *Allies and Italians under Occupation*, London, 2013
Zaloga, Steven J., *Sicily 1943*, Oxford, 2013
Zilletti, Lorenzo & Scuto, Salvatore, *Ispezioni della terribiltà: Leonardo Sciascia e la giustizia*, Florence, 2022

Endnotes

The books, papers, memoirs and biographies written about Sciascia in Italy are too numerous to list. The Associazione Amici di Leonardo Sciascia, founded by Francesco Izzo, put out a yearly one- or two-volume journal of Sciascia studies called *Todo modo*. It includes research papers, appreciations, reviews, personal memoirs, literary criticism by scholars from all over the world. These have been invaluable for my own research.

Sciascia wrote an excellent memoir of growing up and later teaching in Racalmuto, *Le parrocchie di Regalpetra (Salt in the Wound)*, and much personal material is to be found in his journalism, *Nero su nero* and scattered throughout his essays. He had many correspondents, all over the world, and the letters are to be found in the Fondazione Leonardo Sciascia in Racalmuto.

There are several excellent books on Sciascia in Italian and particularly that of Matteo Collura, *Il maestro di Regalpetra*. In English, Joseph Farrell has written a scholarly account of Sciascia's work, *Leonardo Sciascia: The Man and the Writer*. There are many collections of his works: I have used the three volumes superbly edited by Paolo Squillaciotti: *Opere*, and published by Adelphi in Milan. His notes at the end of each volume are essential reading.

Foreword

p. xiii The statue of Leonardo Sciascia, unveiled by his publisher Giulio Einaudi in 1997 and standing on Racalmuto's Corso Garibaldi is by Giuseppe Agnello.
p. xiv 'Sciascia attended the trial ...' *Corriere della Sera*, 18 April 1986
p. xiv 'I met Giovanni Falcone ...' interview with author, 15 May 1986

Chapter 1

There are many good histories of Sicily through the ages, in particular Finley, M. I., Mack Smith, D. & Duggan, C., *A History of Sicily*, and the early years

ENDNOTES

of the Mafia have been covered by scores of writers. See in particular Pantaleone, M., *Mafia e politica 1943–1962*; Poma, R. & Perrone, E., *Quelli della lupara*; Coluccello, R., *Challenging the Mafia Mystique*; Duggan, C., *The Sicilian Origins of the Mafia*; Robb, P., *Midnight in Sicily* .

p. 1   'It all began . . .' Anna Maria Sciascia and Vito Catalano, interviews with author
p. 4   'From its smelters . . .' Messana, E. N., *Racalmuto nella storia di Sicilia*
p. 7   'Sciascia, all his life . . .' See *Le parrocchie di Regalpetra*
p. 8   'Racalmuto's dignitaries . . .' See *Le parrocchie di Regalpetra*
p. 10   '. . . the "nurse at whose breast . . ."' Finley et al., *A History of Sicily*, p. 33
p. 11   '. . . tutor to a Scottish nobleman . . . Brydone, P., *A Tour Through Sicily and Malta*, Vol. 2, p. 39
p. 13   'Then, early in 1876 . . .' see Franchetti, L. & Sonnino, S., *La Sicilia in 1876*
p. 14   'Amid much talk . . .' Coluccello, R., *Challenging the Mafia Mystique*, p. 69
p. 16   'Many writers make . . .' Farrell, J., *Leonardo Sciascia*
p. 16   '. . . with an atavistic fear . . .' Aglianò, S., *Questa Sicilia*, p. 12
p. 16   'To be a Sicilian . . .' Sciascia, L., *La corda pazza*, p. 235

Chapter 2

Sicily's years under Fascism are well covered by Duggan, C., *Fascism and the Mafia*.

p. 19   'Sciascia had been very fond . . .' Sciascia, L., *La Sicilia come metafora*, p. 13
p. 20   'Calling a doctor . . .' See Sciascia, L., *Cruciverba*
p. 20   'Sciascia was a poor . . .' Sciascia, L., *Le parrocchie di Regalpetra*, p. 42
p. 20   'Year four . . .' see Picone, S. (ed.), a *Tra i banchi di Regalpetra*
p. 22   'The first *capo* . . .' Pantaleone, M., *Mafia e politica 1943–1962*, p. 43
p. 23   'Mori remains . . .' see Petacco, A., *Il prefetto di ferro*
p. 24   'The Sicilian criminal . . .' Sterling, C., *The Mafia*
p. 26   '. . . in 1927 Mussolini . . .' Lewis, N., *The Honoured Society*, p. 63
p. 27   'In Racalmuto, Fascism . . .' Messana, E. N., *Racalmuto nella storia di Sicilia*, p. 371
p. 28   'Racalmuto had several . . .' Messana, E. N., *Racalmuto nella storia di Sicilia*, p. 371
p. 28   'Giorgio Agosti . . .' *Todo modo*, Vol. XII, p. 167
p. 28   'Macaluso was capricious . . .' see Sciascia, L., *Cruciverba*
p. 30   'He saw the actor . . .' *Todo modo*, Vol. VII, p. 31
p. 30   'He filled the days . . .' Collura, M., *Il maestro di Regalpetra*, p. 89
p. 31   '. . . the *belle époque* . . .' see Violante, P., *Swinging Palermo*

ENDNOTES

Chapter 3

For memories of Sciascia's boyhood, see *Le parrocchie di Regalpetra*. Over the years, he also wrote extensively about the cinema, in essays and newspaper articles. See *Cruciverba, La Sicilia come metafora, Nero su nero*.

- p. 34   'For boys like ...' Vilardo, S., *A scuola con Leonardo Sciascia*, p. 82
- p. 36   'One of Sciascia's ...' Sciascia, L., *Pirandello e la Sicilia*, p. 66
- p. 38   '... the French Enlightenment ...' see Dauphiné, J., interview with LS, 1987
- p. 39   'But as part of ...' Pezzotti, B., *Politics and Society in Italian Crime Fiction*, p. 14
- p. 40   'Sciascia himself preferred ...' LS interview with *Annabella*, 2 January 1982
- p. 41   'Brancati's work ...' LS interview with *Popolo d'Italia*, 18 June 1983
- p. 41   '"I want to die," ...' Collura, M., *La Memoria, il futuro*, p. 113
- p. 44   '... in one of his most powerful ...' Sciascia, L., *Le parrocchie di Regalpetra*, p. 49
- p. 44   'It was here that Caltanissetta's ...' Vilardo, S., *A scuola con Leonardo Sciascia*, p. 46
- p. 45   'Elio Vittorini ...' see *Scrivere la Sicilia*
- p. 47   'The oranges fell early ...' Brancati, V., *La noia del '937*, in *Tutti i racconti*, Milan 2016

Chapter 4

Many historians have written about the Allied landings in Sicily on 9 July 1943. Sciascia himself wrote a description in *Kermesse*, later reprinted as *Occhio di capra*.

- p. 54   'Aristocratic Sicilian women ...' Mangiameli, R. (ed.), *Sicily Zone Handbook*, p. 17
- p. 55   'It would also ... be brutal ...' Lo Iacono, D., *Il fascismo clandestino in Sicilia*, p. 29
- p. 55   'Having been told to expect ...' Holland, J., *Sicily '43*, p. 314
- p. 55   'There were soon so many ...' Pyle, E., *Brave Men*, p. 28; Buchanan, A., *Journal of Contemporary History*, London, 2008, p. 43
- p. 55   '... "are a rotten crowd ..."' Cole, D., *Rough Road to Rome*, p. 84
- p. 57   'City centres had been reduced ...' Attanasio, S., *Gli anni della rabbia*, p. 61
- p. 57   'Absurd rumours ...' Mercuri, L., *La Sicilia e gli alleati*, Storia Contemporanea, p. 917
- p. 57   'When their requests ...' Luconi, S., *Italian Americana*, Vol. 25, 2007
- p. 58   'There is a story ...' There are many versions, see Lewis, N., *The Honoured Society*; Sterling, C., *The Mafia*; Robb, P., *Midnight in Sicily*

ENDNOTES

p. 60 'Don Calò ... was able ...' see Mangiameli, R. & Nicastro, F. (eds), *Arrivano!*
p. 60 'It was not made easier by ...' Williams, I., *Allies and Italians under Occupation*, p. 119
p. 63 'Of its 150 members ...' Collura, M., *Il maestro di Regalpetra*, p. 127
p. 63 'Tinebra was the manager ...' Cavallaro, F., *Sciascia l'eretico*, p. 9
p. 64 'Between them, they had lost ...' Holland, J., *Sicily '43*, p. 586
p. 65 'When the last AMGOT ...' see Ginsborg, P., *A History of Contemporary Italy 1943–1980*
p. 68 'Bandits, as the historian ...' Santino, U., *Storia del movimento antimafia*, p. 172
p. 68 'In many places, these bandits ...' see Matteo, Salvo di, *Anni roventi*
p. 70 '... appointed Giuliano lieutenant-colonel ...' A great deal has been written about Giuliano: see Tranfaglia, N., *Perché la mafia ha vinto*; Robb, P., *Midnight in Sicily*; Lewis, N., *The Honoured Society*
p. 71 'As for Pisciotta, he was not ...' Pantaleone, M., *Mafia e politica 1943–1962*, p. 156

Chapter 5

p. 75 'On 12 October ...' see Sciascia, L., *Le parrocchie di Regalpetra*
p. 76 'The boys were hungry ...' *Todo modo*, Vol. XII, p. 38
p. 77 'At break, the teachers ...' See Picone, S. (ed.), *Tra i banchi di Regalpetra*
p. 80 'Sciascia returned the ...' see La Porta, F. (ed.), *Pasolini e Sciascia*
p. 82 'Sicily suffered, wrote ...' Mughini, G., *Il grande disordine*, p. xix
p. 82 'After the regional government ...' Ginsborg, P., *A History of Contemporary Italy 1943–1980*, p. 187
p. 86 'Laterza was delighted ..."' letter to LS, 29 February 1955
p. 86 '... "true, strong, heartfelt ..."' Pasolini letter to LS, 31 March 1956
p. 87 'For him, as for Pirandello ...' Collura, M., *Il maestro di Regalpetra*, p. 152
p. 87 'Spain was also ...' *Todo modo*, Vol. II, pp. 14–15
p. 90 'Pasquale had been a hard ...' Porzio, D., *Fuoco all'anima*, p. 28
p. 92 '"Pascal was right ..."' LS letter to Vilardo, 8 December 1957

Chapter 6

A very great deal has been written about the Sicilian Mafia and its move into drugs. The books I have consulted most are the following: Bolzoni, A., *White Shotgun*; Bolzoni, A. & Lodato, S., *C'era una volta la lotta alla mafia*; Candida, R., *Questa mafia*; Pantaleone, M., *Mafia e politica 1943–1962*; Santino, U., *Storia del movimento anti-mafia*; Sterling, C., *The Mafia: The long reach of the international Sicilian Mafia*; Lewis, N., *The Honoured Society: The Sicilian Mafia observed*; Coluccello, R., *Challenging the Mafia Mystique*.

p. 95 'It was a summit for the two mafias ...' See Santino, U., *Storia del movimento anti-mafia*
p. 96 'The Mafia spirit was ...' see Savatteri, G., *I Siciliani*
p. 98 'The Sicilian Mafia ...' Sciascia, L., *Pirandello e la Sicilia*, p. 208
p. 99 'The *giallo*, he decided ...' *Todo modo*, Vol. II, p. 74
p. 101 'The book written ...' LS letter to Laterza, 9 December 1959
p. 101 'There was some dispute ...' see Squillaciotti, P., 'Notes on *Civetta*', in *Opere*, Vol. 1 (Milan 2012), p. 1765
p. 102 'In *The New York Times* ...' 22 February 1964
p. 102 'Sicily, Sciascia told ...' LS letter to Roversi, 23 April 1962
p. 103 'Sciascia had become ...' LS interview with Marcelle Padovani, *La Sicilia come metafora*
p. 103 'No one sued ...' Collura, M., *Il maestro di Regalpetra*, p. 182

Chapter 7

p. 106 'Few contemporary novels ...' interview Franco Loi, 8 April 1989, in *Todo modo*, Vol. VII, p. 7
p. 106 '..."one of the most miserable ..."' See Coluccello, R., *Challenging the Mafia Mystique*
p. 107 'Then, having watched ...' Sorgi, M., *Le sconfitte non contano*, p. 88
p. 107 'The world needed to know ...' Renda, F., *Storia della Sicilia dal 1860 al 1970*
p. 108 'Sciascia had written ...' *L'Ora*, 22 February 1967
p. 109 'Later, Anna Maria ...' Anna Maria Sciascia, interview with author
p. 109 'Maria, influenced by the aunts ...' Mila Rossi, interview with author
p. 109 '"The family," he told ...' interview *Linea d'Ombra*, 1989/1990
p. 111 'Knowing that there would be ...' Sciascia, L., in *Nuovo Mondo*, 12 June 1960
p. 113 'The Church was outraged ...' Cavallaro, F., *Sciascia l'eretico*, p. 99
p. 113 'For the twenty-year-old ...' Ferdinando Scianna, interview with author
p. 114 'In *The New York Times* ...' *The New York Times*, 11 May 1968

Chapter 8

p. 116 'He told Einaudi ...' LS letter to Einaudi, 19 April 1968
p. 116 'Occasionally he added ...' see *Todo modo*, Vol. VI, p. 313
p. 117 'What bound them ...' Guttuso letter to LS, January 7 1967
p. 118 'The three of them agreed ...' see Nigro, S. S., *Leonardo Sciascia, scrittore, editore ovvero la felicità di fare libri*
p. 120 'The Sellerio office became ...' Ottavia Sellerio, interview with author
p. 120 'It was a thread ...' Collura, M., *Alfabeto Sciascia*, p. 18
p. 121 'He was increasingly ...' see *Todo modo*, Vol. VIII, p. 73
p. 121 '... the "sack of Palermo" ...' Cancila, O., *Baroni e popolo nella Sicilia del grano*, p. 330

ENDNOTES

p. 122 'In his report . . .' see Dolci, D., *Inchiesta a Palermo*
p. 122 'They lived and slept . . .' Lewis, N., *In Sicily*, p. 72
p. 123 'One of his strongest . . .' see Sciascia, L., *Nero su nero*
p. 123 'The offices of *L'Ora* . . .' see Nisticò, V., *L'Ora dei ricordi*
p. 124 'The late 1960s . . .' Violante, P., *Swinging Palermo*, p. 243
p. 124 'Punctual, reticent . . .' Marcello Sorgi, interview with author
p. 126 'At the heart of everything . . .' see Zilletti, L. & Scuto, S., *Ispezioni della terribiltà*
p. 126 '"Everything," Sciascia declared . . .' see Ambroise, C., *14 Domande a Leonardo Sciascia*
p. 129 'Soon after the publication . . .' Calvino, letter to LS, 26 October 1964
p. 129 'Straddling history, fiction . . .' see Mullen, A., *Inquisition and Inquiry*
p. 133 'Irony was his way . . .' Collura, M., *La memoria, il futuro*, p. 81
p. 133 '"I prefer to lose . . ."' See Ambroise, C., *Invito alla letteratura di Sciascia*

Chapter 9

p. 135 'In the investigations . . .' Ginsborg, P., *Italy and its Discontents*, p. 332
p. 139 'Sciascia had been right . . .' *L'Unità*, 5 February 1972
p. 139 'In the pages of *Avanti!* . . .' 2 January 1972
p. 139 'One of Sciascia's few . . .' *L'Unità*, 1 February 1972
p. 140 'As for the vehemence . . .' *Panorama*, 8 November 1973
p. 140 'Privately, he told . . .' LS letter to Mario La Cava, 11 January 1973
p. 141 '"I have attempted" . . .' LS interview, *Europeo*, 16 January 1975
p. 142 'Like Voltaire . . .' *L'Ora*, 5–6 May 1976
p. 142 'Soon after the war . . .' *Combat*, 19 November 1946
p. 145 'Feminism came late . . .' see Mafai, S. et al., *Essere donna in Sicilia*; also Dacia Maraini, interview with author
p. 147 'In *Il Giorno* . . .' Carla Ravaioli, 1 February 1974
p. 147 'His reply . . . in *Panorama* . . .' 27 February 1974
p. 149 'Pasolini was, by far . . .' Bartoletti, L. & Goldkorn, W., *L'Espresso Pasolini*, p. 102
p. 149 'Reviewing *Todo modo* . . .' see La Porta, F. (ed.), *Pasolini e Sciascia*

Chapter 10

p. 152 'Sciascia excused himself . . .' Marcello Sorgi, interview with author
p. 155 'At Sellerio, he, Elvira . . .' *Todo modo*, Vol. XII, p. 47
p. 156 'Then the word went out . . .' Felice Cavallaro, interview with author
p. 157 'He said that he liked to model . . .' Collura, M., *Il maestro di Regalpetra*, p. 42
p. 157 '. . . Maria continued to cook . . .' Vilardo, S., *A scuola con Leonardo Sciascia*, p. 73
p. 158 '*Todo modo* . . . was accused . . .' *Corriere della Sera*, 1 May 1976
p. 161 'The mid 1970s had seen . . .' see Silj, A., *Malpaese*

ENDNOTES

Chapter 11

There have been many books on the kidnapping of Aldo Moro, written soon after and later, and it has been analysed repeatedly. Sciascia's own book, *L'Affaire Moro*, is essential reading. See also Gotor, M. (ed.), *Aldo Moro: Lettere dalla prigionia*.

p. 165 'The *Corriere della Sera* described...' Silj, A., *Brigate Rosse-Stato*, p. 13
p. 166 'The Christian Democrats, he repeated...' see Vecellio, V. (ed.), *L'uomo solo* & Vecellio, V., *Leonardo Sciascia, la politica, il coraggio della solitudine*
p. 166 'He began to be...' Camilleri, A., *Un'onorevole siciliano*, p. 13
p. 173 'With his death, he told a reporter...' *L'Epoca*, 25 June 1978
p. 176 'In mid August, Sciascia told...' *La Sicilia*, 15 August, 1978
p. 176 '...this book was making him uneasy...' *Corriere della Sera*, 6 September 1978
p. 177 'Though there was nothing...' Silj, A., *Malpaese*, p. 272
p. 178 'Moro's description of a rotten...' *Le Monde*, February 1979

Chapter 12

p. 180 '...Pasolini had remarked...' see La Porta, F. (ed.), *Pasolini e Sciascia*
p. 180 '...the political fallout...' Ginsborg, P., *A History of Contemporary Italy 1943–1980*, p. 386
p. 180 '..."the little elementary..."' Zilletti, L. & Scuto, S., *Ispezioni della terribiltà*, p. 244
p. 182 'As he saw it now...' Palazzolo, L., *Leonardo Sciascia deputato radicale*, p.16
p. 183 'Emma Bonino, a fellow...' Emma Bonino, conversation with author
p. 183 'On the rare occasions...' Luciana Castelani, conversation with author
p. 183 'His friends greatly enjoyed...' Marcello Sorgi, conversation with author
p. 185 '...he used the metaphor...' see Collura, M., *Alfabeta Sciascia*
p. 186 'Guttuso, flustered...' Caruso, B., *Le giornate romane di Leonardo Sciascia*, p. 58
p. 188 'Its current chairman...' for good accounts, see Cornwell, R., *God's Banker* and Silj, A., *Malpaese*
p. 188 'One of his ports of call...' Cavallaro, F., *Sciascia l'eretico*, p. 217

Chapter 13

p. 197 'Leggio had arrived...' Sterling, C., *The Mafia*, p. 64
p. 199 'Before leaving Rome...' Orlando, L., *Fighting the Mafia and Renewing Sicilian Culture*, p. 70
p. 200 'As he told a reporter...' *L'Unità*, 6 August 1982

p. 201 'The Dalla Chiesa family ...' see Dalla Chiesa, N., *Delitto imperfetto*; also Nando Dalla Chiesa, conversation with author
p. 204 'Then Sciascia joined in ...' *Corriere della Sera*, 19 September 1982
p. 204 '... "if someone behind me ..."' *L'Espresso*, 20 February 1983
p. 205 'Sciascia's intervention ...' *La Repubblica*, 20 February 1983
p. 206 'Parliament ... was simply a mirror ...' Palazzolo, L., *Leonardo Sciascia deputato radicale*, p. 248
p. 207 'Sciascia intended to return ...' *La Domenica del Corriere*, 3 April 1982
p. 207 'Challenged, as he always ...' see Lajolo, D. (ed.), *Conversazione in una stanza chiusa*

Chapter 14

Many books have been written about Sciascia's passion for justice. See, in particular, Pogliaghi, L., *Giustizia come ossessione. Forme della giustizia nelle pagine di Leonardo Sciascia*; Zilletti, L. & Scuto, S., *Ispezioni della terribiltà*. The lives and deaths of Falcone and Borsellino have also been written about in detail. See Ciconte, E. & Torre, G. (eds), *Giovanni Falcone*; Monti, G., *Falcone e Borsellino*.

p. 208 'And who judged the judges? ...' *Corriere della Sera*, 14 October 1983
p. 209 '... "Perhaps man's destiny ..."' See Zilletti, L. & Scuto, S., *Ispezioni della terribiltà*
p. 210 'Tortora's treatment outraged ...' *Corriere della Sera*, 7 August 1983
p. 211 'A young friend ...' see Motta, A., *Giorni felici con Leonardo Sciascia*
p. 213 'Talking of their meetings ...' Gaetano Tranchino, interview with author
p. 214 'It was Pirandello ...' Ambroise, C., *Invito alla letteratura di Sciascia*, p. 14
p. 218 '*Pentiti* were anathema ...' *Corriere della Sera*, 3 April 1982
p. 219 'In Sicily an association ...' see Santino, U., *Storia del movimento anti-mafia* and Santino, U. & Puglisi, A., *La memoria e il progetto del Centro Impastato al No Mafia memorial*; also Umberto Santini, conversation with author
p. 219 'To signal ...' Stille, A., *Excellent Cadavers*, p. 90
p. 220 'Falcone knew that he was not ...' Sterling, C., *The Mafia*, p. 198
p. 220 'That was the problem ...' Sciascia, L., *La Sicilia come metafora*, p. 92
p. 221 '"In my position ..."' Ciconte, E. & Torre, G. (eds), *Giovanni Falcone*, p. 81
p. 221 'The *maxi-processo* ...' see Stajano, C. (ed.), *Mafia: l'atto d'accusa dei giudici di Palermo*
p. 224 'He listened to Buscetta ...' *Corriere della Sera*, 18 April 1986
p. 225 '... under attack by hostile journalists ...' *Giornale di Sicilia*, 30 June and 5 July 1986

ENDNOTES

Chapter 15

p. 228 'As his daughter Anna Maria ...' Anna Maria Sciascia, interview with author
p. 228 'Where, asked Giampaolo Pansa ...' *La Repubblica*, 15 January 1987
p. 230 'Even close friends ...' Claudio Riolo, interview with author
p. 230 'Then came what ...' Ciconte, E. & Torre, G. (eds), *Giovanni Falcone*, p. 21
p. 231 'As Attilio Bolzoni ...' *La Repubblica*, 20 July 1988
p. 232 'He told Foscari ...' Antonio Foscari, interview with author
P. 233 'In a decidedly despairing ...' *La Repubblica*, 2 December 1988
p. 234 'Not always so approving ...' Collura, M., *La memoria, il futoro*, p.113
p. 238 'Though a special law ...' Stille, A., *Excellent Cadavers*, p. 275
p. 240 'Sciascia, consulted as usual ...' *La Repubblica*, 2 December 1988
p. 240 '... his feeling that the better ...' see Porzio, D., *Fuoco all'anima*
p. 240 'Sciascia had told an interviewer ...' Swiss radio, 23 May 1988
p. 241 'As his health ...' Gaetano Tranchino, interview with author
p. 242 'Visiting the lawyer's ...' Freni, M., *Verso la vacanza*, p. 55
p. 242 'One day Orlando ...' Anna Maria Sciascia, interview with author
p. 243 'In a farewell open letter ...' *Il Giornale*, 21 November 1989
p. 244 'Two days later ...' Anna Maria Sciascia and Vito Catalano, interviews with author

Afterword

p. 246 'But the Mafia was not done ...' Santino, U., *La mafia dimenticata*, pp. 202 and 360
p. 247 'Andreotti, lizard like ...' Robb, P., *Midnight in Sicily*, p. 12
p. 249 'He had made considerable ...' Ciconte, E. & Torre, G. (eds), *Giovanni Falcone*, p. 31
p. 250 'Now, at last ...' Silj, A., *Malpaese*, p.407

Principal works by Leonardo Sciascia

Favole della dittatura, Rome, 1950 (*Fables from the Dictatorship*, 2021)
La Sicilia, il suo cuore, Rome, 1952
Pirandello e il Pirandellismo, Caltanissetta, 1953
Le parrocchie di Regalpetra, Bari, 1956 (*Salt in the Wound*, 1969)
Gli zii di Sicilia, Turin, 1956 (*Sicilian Uncles*, 1986)
Il giorno della civetta, Turin, 1961 (*The Day of the Owl*, 1984)
Il Consiglio d'Egitto, Turin, 1963 (*The Council of Egypt*, 1966)
Morte dell'Inquisitore, Bari, 1964 (*Death of the Inquisitor*, 1969)
L'Onorevole, Turin, 1965
A ciascuno il suo, Turin, 1966 (*To Each his Own*, 1992)
Recitazione della controversia liparitana dedicata ad A.D., Turin, 1969
Il contesto, Turin, 1971 (*Equal Danger*, 1973)
Atti relativi alla morte di Raymond Roussel, Palermo, 1971
Il mare colore del vino, Turin, 1973 (*The Wine Dark Sea*, 1985)
Todo modo, Turin, 1974 (*One Way or Another*, 1977)
La scomparsa di Majorana, Turin, 1975 (*The Mystery of Majorana*, 1987)
I pugnalatori, Turin, 1976
Candido ovvero un sogno fatto in Sicilia, Turin, 1977 (*Candido or A Dream Dreamed in Sicily*, 1979)
L'affaire Moro, Palermo, 1978 (*The Moro Affair*, 1987)
Nero su nero, Turin, 1979
La Sicilia come metafora (con Marcelle Padovani), Milan, 1979
Dalle parti degli infideli, Palermo, 1979
Il teatro della memoria, Turin, 1981
La palma va al Nord, Rome, 1981
La sentenza memorabile, Palermo, 1982
Cruciverba, Turin, 1983
Occhio di capra, Turin, 1984
Stendhal e la Sicilia, Palermo, 1984
Cronachette, Palermo, 1985 (*Little Chronicles*, 1990)
Per un ritratto dello scrittore da giovane, Palermo, 1985
La strega e il capitano, Milan, 1986 (*The Captain and the Witch*, 1990)
1912+1, Milan, 1986 (*1912+1*, 1989)

PRINCIPAL WORKS BY LEONARDO SCIASCIA

Porte Aperte, Milan, 1987 (*Open Doors*, 1991)
Il cavaliere e la morte, Milan, 1988 (*The Knight and Death*, 1991)
Ore di Spagna, Marina di Patti, 1988
Alfabeto pirandelliano, Milan, 1989
Una storia semplice, Milan, 1989 (*A Straightforward Tale*, 1991)
A futura memoria (se la memoria ha un futuro), Milan, 1989

Index

A ciascuno il suo (Sciascia), 112–13, 133, 145
A futura memoria (1989), 242, 243
Acquasanta, Palermo, 110
Adelphi, 243
L'Affaire Moro (Sciascia), 173–9, 209, 213
Agosti, Giorgio, 28
agriculture
   Fascist period (1922–43), 27, 47–8, 54, 57
   feudalism, 10, 15, 34, 67, 82–3
   land reform, 66–7, 69, 70, 72
   Second World War (1940–45), 47–8, 54, 57, 60–61
Agrigento, Sicily, xiii, 1, 18, 37, 50, 54, 65, 98, 250
d'Ajeta, Marquese, 31
Albini, Umberto, 27
d'Alessandro, Nicolo, 157
Alessi, Giuseppe, 44, 110
Alicia, 197
Allied occupied Sicily (1943–4), 56–65, 94, 188
Allingham, Margery, 39
Ambroise, Claude, 234, 242
Ambrosoli, Giorgio, 188, 190
Amendola, Giorgio, 163–4, 180
AMGOT, 56, 59, 63, 64–5, 66, 188
Amica, 216
ammasso, 47–8, 57
Amnesty International, 172
anarchism, 8, 30, 135

Andreotti, Giulio, 122, 166, 177, 180, 183, 186, 189, *204*, 206, 246–7
   Lima's death (1992), 247
   Mafia war (1981–3), 196–205
   maxi-processo (1986–92), 226, 239
Andronico, Maria, 48, 61–2, *62*, 74, 88, 108–9, 140, 141, 156, 211
   cooking, 157
   earthquake (1968), 114
   first reader, 108, 132
   Leonardo's death (1989), 241, 242, 243
   Paris trips, 87
   wedding (1944), 61
Animal Farm (Orwell), 79
animal theft, 22, 26, 65, 68, 95–6
d'Annunzio, Gabriele, 149, 185, 240
anti-communism, 57, 65–6, 73, 81, 123, 135, 136, 189
anti-Fascist movement, 28, 44–5, 46, 47, 49, 63–4, 80–81, 149
anti-Mafia campaign (1925–9), 23–6, 32, 33–4, 41, 94
Anti-Mafia Commission (1962–82), 110, 153, 185, 192, 194, 196
anti-separatism, 66–7
L'Antimonio (Sciascia), 44, 158
Antonello da Messina, 118
Aprile, Andrea Finocchiaro, 66
Arabs; Arabic, 2, 4, 10, 11, 31, 55, 60, 128
Aragonese Sicily (1282–1479), 10, 16, 130, 208

INDEX

Arendt, Hannah, xv, 252
Argentina, 53, 189
Arlacchi, Pino, 228
Armistice of Cassibile (1943), 64
Artom, Camillo, 43
As You Desire Me (Pirandello), 212
Asinara, 221
Assoro, Sicily, 32, 73
Atria, Rita, 250
Avanti!, 139

Baader-Meinhof Gang, 172
baccala, 47
Badalamenti, Gaetano, 197
Bagarella, Ninetta, 226
Bagheria, Sicily, 122–3
balilla, 20, 21
Balliol College, Oxford, 53
Banco Ambrosiano, 187–91
bandits, 16, 21, 23, 24, 68–73, 75, 103, 107, 112, 208
Bangkok, Thailand, 220
Bank of Italy, 188
Bank of Sicily, 14
Barcelona, Catalonia, 87, 212
Bardi, 79
Bari, Puglia, 84, 185
Barthes, Roland, 163
Barzini, Luigi, 158
Basile, Emanuele, 194
Bassani, Giorgio, 106
Battaglia, Letizia, 247
Battle for Grain (1925), 27
Battle of Caporetto (1917), 53
Baudelaire, Charles, 93
Beckett, Samuel, 124
Beckford, William, 11
Belgium, 84
Belice, Sicily, 114
belle époque (c. 1871–1914), 31, 116
Bennardo, Lilly, 35–6
Bentinck, William, 11
Bergamo, Lombardy, 210
Bergman, Ingrid, 184
Berlin Wall, 246, 252
Berlinguer, Enrico, 152–3, 166, 180, 181, 186, 251
Berlusconi, Silvio, 248
Bernhardt, Sarah, 31

Bersaglieri, 51
Betrothed, The (Manzoni), 18, 127, 240
biddina, 4, 140
Bitcoin, 251
Black Hand, 22
Blackfriars Bridge, London, 190
Bobbio, Norberto, 249
Bocca, Giorgio, 230
Bologna, Emilia-Romagna, 80, 163
  bombing (1980), 191
Bolshevism, 21–2, 136
Bolzoni, Attilio, 231
Bonfadini, Romualdo, 12
Bonino, Emma, 183
Bontate, Stefano, 197, 198
Borges, Jorge Luis, 129, 176, 214–15
Borghese, Giulio Valerio, 135–6, 220
Borgias, 183
Borsellino, Paolo, xiv, xv, 216, 221, 225, 227–31, 238–40, 248
  assassination (1992), 249–50, 251, 252
Boston, Massachusetts, 54
Bourbon Sicily (1735–1860), 2, 9–12, 128–9, 131, 196
Brancati, Vitaliano, xiii, 40–41, 45, 46, 47, 63, 84, 133–4
Braudel, Fernand, 68
Brazil, 53, 189, 217–18
bribery, 15, 71, 85, 168, 208, 220, 238, 247
Brigate Rosse, *see* Red Brigades
Brindisi, Apulia, 53
British occupied Sicily (1806–15), 7, 11
Brydone, Patrick, 11
Bufalino, Gesualdo, 120, 178, 182, 184, 241, 242, 243
Burgos, Spain, 87
Burma, 193
Burruano, Carmelo, 90
Buscemi, Michela, 224
Buscetta, Benedetto, 218
Buscetta, Tommaso, xiv, 217–20, 224–5
Buscetta, Vincenzo, 218
Buttitta, Antonino, 119
Byzantine Sicily (535–902), 10, 31

277

INDEX

cadaveri eccellenti, xiv, 14, 192–5, 216, 220, 237–8
Cadaveri eccellenti (1976 film), 158
Caffè Greco, Rome, 185
Cagol, Margherita, 136
Calabria, 238, 251
Callas, Maria, 149
Caltanissetta, Sicily, 32, 34–49, 54, 109
    anti-Fascists in, 44–5, 46, 47
    Mafia in, 59, 96
    Saetta assassination (1988), 238
    Sciascia's bookshop, 44–5, 78
    Second World War (1940–45), 46, 48, 56, 59
    sulphur mines, 32, 34, 46
Calvi, Roberto, 188, 189, 190
Calvino, Italo, 99, 152, 163
    Einaudi editor, 101–2, 112, 118, 129, 139, 142
    Palermo conference (1953), 82
    as reader, 84, 89, 99, 108
Camilleri, Andrea, 213
Camorra, 13, 210, 251
Campania, 238
Camus, Albert, 142, 152, 252
Candida, Renato, 98, 99
Candido (Sciascia), 159–61, 174, 234
Capaci, Sicily, 249
capi, 21, 94, 95, 96, 227
capo di tutti i capi, 22
Caponnetto, Antonino, 217, 230, 231, 250
Capote, Truman, 78
Capuana, Luigi, 14, 36
Capuchin Order, 96–7, 122, 158
carabinieri, 19, 21, 48, 52, 60, 98
    Anti-Terrorist section, 161
    cadaveri eccellenti, xiv, 14, 192–5
    Giuliano's banditry, 69, 71
    Mafia war (1981–3), 199–205
    Moro kidnapping (1978), 167, 169, 176–8
Cardinale, Claudia, 102
Carnevale, Corrado, 246
Carraro, Emanuela Setti, 201–2
Caruso, Bruno, 118, 124, 131, 184–5

Casablanca Conference (1943), 50
Casanova, Giacomo, 38–9
Casaroli, Agostino, 172
Cascio Ferro, Vito, 22, 25
Cassa per il Mezzogiorno, 83, 95
Cassarà, Antonio, 219
cassetta, 25
Castelvetrano, Sicily, 71, 72
Castiglione di Sicilia, 56
Catalano, Antonino, 140
Catalano, Vito, 181, 211, *211*, 250, 253
Catania, Sicily, 10, 15, 102, 141, 201, 219, 221
Cather, Willa, 48
Catholic Church, xv, 76, 85, 108, 112, 113, 122, 123, 140–42, 158, 236
    Banco Ambrosiano, and 187–91
    Mafia, relations with, 96–7, 108, 112, 113, 122, 123, 196
    Mazzarino extortion affair (1959–60), 96–7, 122
cattle horns, 75
cattle rustling, 22, 26, 65, 95–6
Catullus, 74
Cavaliere e la morte, Il (Sciascia), 232–4
Cavallaro, Felice, 241
Cefalù, Sicily, 24, 118
Centro Giuseppe Impastato, Palermo, 219
Cernuda, Luis, 87
Cervantes, Miguel, 240
Cesareo, Giovanni Alfredo, 14
Chaplin, Charlie, 29
Chesterton, Gilbert Keith, 98
Chiavarelli, Eleonora, 168, 172
Chicago, Illinois, 22, 54, 95
Chiesa, Mario, 247
China, 238
Chinnici, Rocco, 216, 217, 223
cholera, 32
Christian Democracy, 68, 73, 81, 83, 85, 121, 122, 137, 148, 155
    Anti-Mafia Commission (1962–82), 110, 153, 185, 192, 194, 196

INDEX

Communist Party, relations with, 166–7, 169–70, 172, 175, 180, 186
  divorce referendum (1974), 145
  Mafia, relations with, 73, 166, 191–2, 197, 199, 203–4, 246–7
  Moro kidnapping and murder (1978), xv, 165–79, 180, 182–3, 186–7, 205–6, 209, 251
  Operazione Milazzo (1958–9), 121
  Pasolini murder (1975), 150
  razza padrona, 187
  Sciascia's views on, 81, 123, 137, 140, 141, 142, 160, 166–79
Christie, Agatha, 39, 150
Christmas, 85
Churchill, Winston, 50, 64, 66
Ciaculli, Sicily, 110
Ciancimino, Vito, 121–2, 124, 153, 154, 196, 200, 205, 226, 248
  maxi-processo (1986–92), 221, 231
  Sciascia, petitioning of, 191
  Vitale's evidence (1973), 218
Cicero, 234
cigarettes, *see* tobacco
Cinecittà, Rome, 184
cinema, *see* film
Circolo Unione, Racalmuto, 62–3, 86
Civil War (1944–5), 53, 63, 64, 65, 135
clubs, 62–3
coal mining, 84
Cobb, Lee, 102
cocaine, 218
Colajanni, Napoleone, 139
Colajanni, Pompeo, 44
Colbert, Claudette, 32
Cold War (1947–91), 72–3, 81
Collura, Matteo, 199, 236, 243
Come tu mi vuoi (Pirandello), 212
Communists, 8, 75, 80, 81, 90, 121, 138–40, 160, 161, 162, 182
  Allied occupation (1943–4), 57, 63, 65–6
  anti-communism and, 57, 65–6, 73, 81, 123, 135, 136, 189
  anti-separatism, 66, 70
  Berlin Wall, fall of (1989), 246, 252
  Christian Democracy, relations with, 166–7, 169–70, 172, 175, 178, 180, 186
  Eurocommunism, 166
  Fascist period (1922–43), 28
  Mafia and, 103, 108, 110, 122, 123, 198
  Moro Commission (1979–2018), 186–7
  Moro kidnapping and murder (1978), 169, 172, 175, 178, 180
  Operation Gladio (1952–90), 135, 177, 252
  Pasolini murder (1975), 150
  Red Brigades trial (1974), 163
  regional elections (1947), 69
  regional elections (1975), 152–4
compromesso storico, 167, 186, 205
Conca d'Oro, Palermo, 31, 95
confino, 196
conformity, 149, 160
Congress of Sicilian Women (1953), 145
Consiglio d' Egitto, Il (Sciascia), 128–9, 236
Consolo, Vincenzo, 183, 241
Consorzio Agrario, 47, 57, 60
conspiracy, 209
Contesto, Il (Sciascia), 138–40, 158, 163, 166, 182, 236
contraception, 147
Cooper, Gary, 44
Coordinamento, 229
Corleone, Sicily, 95–6, 121, 185, 197, 198, 218, 220, 223, 225
Correnti, Santi, 237
Corriere della Sera, 150, 165, 169, 171, 186, 194, 210, 218–19
  maxi-processo (1986–92), xiv, 224, 227–31
corruption, xiii, xv, 14, 32, 68, 73, 104, 162, 166, 238, 246–7
  Andreotti and, 189, 196, 197, 199, 203–4, 239, 246–7

INDEX

corruption, *(Cont'd)*
  Banco Ambrosiano and, 189, 190, 191
  bribery, 15, 71, 85, 168, 208, 220, 238, 247
  Chiesa case (1992), 247–8
  Mani Pulite investigations (1992–4), 248
  Palizzolo trial (1893–1904), 14
  Sack of Palermo (1950s–80s), 95, 121–3, 124, 148, 153, 248
Corso Umberto, Caltanissetta, 44
Cortese, Luigi, 44
cosca, 96
Cossiga, Francesco, 168, 186, 248
Costa, Gaetano, 44, 194, 198, 206
Council of Egypt, The (Sciascia), 128–9, 236
Courier, Paul Louis, 38, 86
Craxi, Benedetto, 169, 219, 247, 248
crêpe Georgette, 40
di Cristina, Giuseppe, 218, 219
Croce, Elena, 105–6
Cronache Letterarie (Capuana), 36
Cronachette (Sciascia), 215
CSM, 227, 229, 230, 231, 239
Cuba, 95, 161
Cuccio, Francesco 'Ciccio', 24
Cuffaro, Domenico, 244
Cupola, 196, 220, 224
Curcio, Renato, 136
Czechoslovakia (1918–92), 186, 251

Dalla Chiesa, Carlo Alberto, 96, 161, 169, 176–8, 184, 199–205
Dalla Chiesa, Nando, 201, 203, 205
Dalle parti degli infedeli (Sciascia), 186
Dante, 240
Day of the Owl, The (Sciascia), xiv, 99–104, 111, 113, 147, 219, 224, 234
  Catholic Church in, 108
  Dalla Chiesa and, 204
  film adaptation (1968), 102
  justice in, 126, 127
  quaquaraqua, 228
  reception, 102–4, 110
  sales, 237, 252
  self-censorship and, 228
  Sirchio and, 192
  women in, 145
Dead Souls (Gogol), 240
Death Comes for the Archbishop (Cather), 48
Death of an inquisitor (Sciascia), 130–31
Death of Stalin, The (Sciascia), 89, 229–30
death, 20, 37, 149, 175, 233
death penalty, 127, 170, 215
Decima MAS, 125, 135
defascistazione, 58
Dell'Arco, Mario, 79, 84
DeMille, Cecil Blount, 32
democracy, 24, 100, 123, 169, 198, 200, 208
dialect, 4, 80–81, 148, 212
Diderot, Denis, 18, 38, 87, 124, 158
dishwashers, 137
Divine Comedy (Dante), 240
divine providence, 20
divorce, 145, 148, 153, 181, 221
doctors, 20
Dolci, Danilo, 106–8, 122, 123
Dominican Order, 190
Don Quixote (Cervantes), 240
dopolavoro, 62
Dorso, Guido, 82
Dos Passos, John, 44
Dostoevsky, Fyodor, 215
Doyle, Arthur Conan, 39
Dreyfus affair (1894–1906), 14, 174
drug trade, 95, 153, 188, 193, 196, 197, 205, 216, 219, 238, 251
  maxi-processo and, 222, 223, 225, 227
Dubliners (Joyce), 213
Dunne, Irene, 40
Dürer, Albrecht, 232–3
dysentery, 54

earthquake (1968), 114–15
economic miracle (1958–63), 137
Eden, Anthony, 43

INDEX

Einaudi, 89–90, 101–2, 118, 138, 160
Einaudi, Giulio, 160
Einaudi, Luigi, 83
elections, 85
  1925 local elections, 27
  1947 regional elections, 68–9
  1948 general election, 71
  1953 general election, 81
  1975 regional elections, 152–4
  1976 general election, 166
  1979 general election, 181
  1987 general election, 238
  1992 general election, 248
  1993 local elections, 248
electricity, 28
emigration, 2–3, 52, 53–4, 84, 85, 86–7, 89, 90, 181
Encyclopédistes, 38, 124, 158–9, 212, 242
English people, 7
ENI, 125
Enlightenment (*c.* 1685–1815), 10, 16, 38–9, 87, 98, 116, 121
L'Epoca, 161, 173
Equal Danger (Sciascia), 138–40, 158, 163, 166, 182, 236
Esercizio Volontario d'Independenza Siciliana (EVIS), 70
L'Espresso, 82, 146, 162, 163, 176
Ethiopia, 42–3
Eurocommunism, 166
European Parliament, 181
European Union (EU), 181, 197
evil eye, 76
excellent corpses, xiv, 14, 192–5, 216, 220, 237–8
extortion, 22–3, 26, 68, 95, 96–7, 122, 217, 238, 246

Fables from the Dictatorship (Sciascia), 79–80, 126, 209
Falange, 88
Falcone, Giovanni, xiv, 191, 196, 203, 216, 217–21, 223, 227, 230–31, 239
  assassination (1992), 248–9, 251, 252
Fanfani, Amintore, 121–2

Fantauzzo, Rosalia, 31
Fascism, 20, 24, 27–8, 40, 79, 90, 125, 163, 230, 252
  Allied invasion and, 51, 52–3, 55, 57–8, 63–4, 85, 242
  anti-Fascism, 28, 44–5, 46, 47, 49, 79, 80–81, 149
  Mafia and, 21, 24, 67
  Pasolini and, 149, 150
  Pirandello and, 37, 38, 44, 173
  post-war years, 79, 81, 121, 127, 135–6, 190
Fascist Italy (1922–43), xiii, 8–9, 16, 19, 20–21, 26–8, 36, 40, 41, 77, 90, 252
  Allied invasion (1943), 51, 52–3, 55, 57–8, 63–4, 85, 242
  anti-Fascist movement, 28, 44–5, 46, 47, 49
  anti-Mafia campaign (1925–9), 23–6, 32, 33–4, 41, 94
  balilla, 20, 21, 28
  Battle for Grain (1925), 27
  censorship in, 39, 40
  dopolavoro, 62
  emigration restrictions (1931), 53
  Ethiopian War (1935–7), 42–3
  Jews, persecution of, 43
  literary style, 43
  March on Rome (1922), 8
  Matteotti assassination (1924), 9, 28, 132
  Mussolini's Sicily visit (1924), 24
  Mussolini's Sicily visit (1937), 42–3, 44, 52
  Pact of Steel (1939), 45
  plebiscite (1929), 26–7
  porte aperte, 215
  Schirru plot (1931), 30, 127
  Second World War (1940–43), 46–9, 50–53
  Spanish War (1936–9), 43–4
Fascist Party, 8, 26, 52–3
  balilla, 20, 21, 28
Fava, Claudio, 228
Fellini, Federico, 184
Feltrinelli, 106
feminism, 145, 147
Fermi, Enrico, 143

INDEX

Ferro, Vito, 96
Feste religiose in Sicilia (Sciannia and Sciascia), 141
feudalism, 8, 10–12, 13, 15, 22–3, 59, 60, 67, 82–3, 103, 105, 106
film, 29–30, 32, 40, 41, 157–8
Finnegan's Wake (Joyce), 105
First World War (1914–18), 7–8, 15, 20, 34, 53
Florio, Ignazio, 31
Fodale, Salvatore, 140
Fogazzi, Giovanni, 241
food, 7, 10, 157
    Battle for Grain (1925), 27
    school lunches, 76–7
    Second World War (1940–45), 47–8, 51, 53, 57, 60–61
Foro Italico, Palermo, 43
Forster, Edward Morgan, 106
Forza Italia, 248
Foscari, Antonio, 212
France, 87, 158–9, 172, 212
    emigration to, 53, 84
    Enlightenment (c. 1685–1815), 38–9, 87, 98, 116
    Front Populaire (1936–8), 40
    May 1968 uprising, 136
Franchetti, Leopoldo, 13
Franchetti–Sonnino Inquiry (1875), 82
Franco, Francisco, 88
Franklin Bank, 188
Freemasonry, 122, 187, 190, 196, 203
friendship, 120, 157
Front Populaire (1936–8), 40
Fu Mattia Pascal, Il (Pirandello), 30
funerals, 20
furbi troppo furbi, 107
Furone, Giuliano, 189–90

gabellotti, 10–12, 15, 24, 60, 65, 82, 95, 105
Gabin, Jean, 40
Galasso, Roberto, 243
Galleria, 78
gambling, 54, 95, 221
Gandhi, Mohandas, 108
garantismo, 209

Garibaldi, Giuseppe, 9, 12, 20, 205, 241
de Gasperi, Alcide, 73, 81
Gela, Sicily, 97
Gelli, Licio, 189, 190
Genco Russo, Giuseppe, 58, 95, 111–12, 197
Genova, Liguria, 83, 137, 161
Genovese, Vito, 59, 60
Gentile, Benedetto, 155
Gentile, Giovanni, 36
Germany
    Federal Republic (1949–), 172, 246
    Nazi Germany (1933–45), 45, 48, 49, 50, 51, 55, 64, 144
Getty, John Paul III, 224
gialli, 39, 41, 99, 137, 174, 209, 234, 253
Giordano, Alfonso, 223
Giornale, Il, 243
Giorno, Il, 147
Giorno dei Morti, 4
Giorno della civetta, Il (Sciascia), see *Day of the Owl, The*
Giuliano, Boris, 125–6, 192–3, 198
Giuliano, Salvatore, 69–72, 69, 75, 107, 208
Giustolisi, Antonietta, 225, 239
Gli zii di Sicilia (Sciascia), 89, 101, 112, 210
goats, 10, 54
von Goethe, Johann Wolfgang, 4, 31, 122
Gogol, Nikolai, 240
Goths, 10
Goya, Francisco, 131, 233
Gran Sasso raid (1943), 64
Granata, Giuseppe, 36, 39–40, 44
Grand Tour, 11
grappa, 232
Grassi, Libero, 246
Greco, Emilio, 118
Greco, Michele, 197, 198, 223, 224, 225
Greece, 65, 135
Greek Sicily (c. 734–241 BCE), 10
Greene, Graham, 131, 244
Grey Wolves, 238

INDEX

Guardia della Finanza, 189, 202
Guccione, Piero, 155
Gulla, Antonio, 226
Gullo, Fausto, 67
Guttuso, Renato, 102, 117, *117*,
    122, 131, 138, 139–40, 153,
    154–5, 185, 251
    falling out with, 182, 186–7, 213
Guzzoni, Alfredo, 51

Hammett, Dashiell, 39
Heisenberg, Werner, 144
Hemingway, Ernest, 44
Henry VI (Shakespeare), 100
Hermann Goring Panzer
    Division, 55
heroin, 95, 153, 188, 193, 205,
    216, 219
Hiroshima bombing (1945), 143–4
Hitler, Adolf, 144
Hobsbawn, Eric, 103
Hollywood, 40, 44, 52
homosexuality, 145
hookworm, 54
Hotel dei Portoghesi, Rome, 92
Hotel delle Palme, Palermo, 95
Hotel Nazionale, Rome, 181–2
Hotel Pierre, New York, 188
Hotel Plaza, Rome, 191
Hotel Vernet, Paris, 158
Hugo, Victor, 18, 159
human rights, 209
humanism, 55, 76
Huxley, Aldous, 107

Ianni, Anna, 225, 239
Ignatius of Loyola, Saint, 141
illustrious corpses, xiv, 14, 192–5,
    216, 220, 237–8
illustrious widows, 226
'In Memoriam' (Sciascia), 74
inchieste, 129–31, 138, 142–5, 159,
    186, 209, 212–13, 242, 252
indentured labour, 5
industrialisation, 73, 82, 121, 137
Infantino, Luigi, 185
Inquisiciones (Borges), 129
Inquisition (1487–1782), 10, 16,
    130, 208, 215, 252

Institute of Physics, Rome, 143
insulin, 60
Interlandi, Telesio, 242
Inzerillo, Salvatore, 197, 198
Istanbul, Turkey, 220
Italian Civil War (1944–5), 53, 63,
    64, 65, 135
Italo-Ethiopian War (1935–7), 42–3
Italo-Turkish War (1911–12), 51
Italy
    Allied occupation (1943–4), 56–65
    Fascist Italy (1922–43), see
        Fascist Italy
    Republic of Italy (1946–), see
        Republic of Italy
    Risorgimento (1848–70), 9, 12,
        20, 76, 90
    Social Republic (1943–5), 64

J'accuse (Zola), 174
Japan, 143–5
Jesuits, 85
Jews, 4, 43, 130
John XXIII, Pope, 108
Johnson, Lyndon, 132
Joyce, James, 105, 124, 213
judiciary, 14, 126. 139, 141, 236
justice, 126–31, 159, 208–11, 215

Kalashnikovs, 96
Kalsa, Palermo, 216
Kazakhstan, 251
Keaton, Buster, 29
Khrushchev, Nikita, 89
kidnappings, 26, 65, 68, 70
    Moro (1978), xv, 165–79, 182–3,
        184, 186–7, 205–6, 209, 251
    Sossi (1974), 161–2
    d'Urso (1980), 183
Knight and Death, The
    (Sciascia), 232–4
Knight, Death and the Devil
    (Dürer), 232–3
Korean War (1950–53), 81
Kurds, 238

de L'Isle-Adam, Villiers, 245
La Cava, Mario, 78, 82, 89–90, 116,
    140, 191

INDEX

La Duca, Rosario, 120
La Matina, Diego, 130–31, 253
La Noce, Racalmuto, 6–7, 41–2, 93, 109–10, 133, 155–7, 174, 202, 211
La Torre, Pio, 198–9, 202, 205
Labour Day, 70
Lampedusa, Giuseppe, 105–6, 107, 154, 160, 170, 178, 194, 209
land reform, 66–7, 69, 70, 72
Laos, 193
Laterza, Vito, 84, 86, 101
latifondi, 82
Laughton, Charles, 32
Leggio, Luciano, xiv, 185, 197–8, 218, 223, 224
lemons, 10, 13, 31, 122
Leone, Giovanni, 169
Leone, Sergio, 157
Leoni, Giuseppe, 137
Leopard, The (Lampedusa), 105–6, 154, 160
Leopardi, Giacomo, 36
Leosini, Franca, 146
Lettere Luterane (Pasolini), vii
Levi, Carlo, 66, 95, 107
Levi, Primo, 132, 210
Li Causi, Girolamo, 66–8
Libera Stampa Prize, 89
Libertà d'Italia, La, 79
libri gialli, 39, 41
Liceo Ruggero Settimo, Caltanissetta, 34
Lichtenstein, 193
Lima, Salvatore, 121–2, 124, 153, 196, 200, 204, 226, 248
  Andreotti, relationship with, 196, 203
  assassination (1992), 246–7
  maxi-processo (1986–92), 231, 239
  Sciascia, petitioning of, 191–2
  Vitale's evidence (1973), 218
Linosa, 192
Lipari, 24, 138
literacy, 15, 18, 23, 55, 82, 107
Lloyd, Harold, 29
local elections (1925), 27
Lockheed, 168

London, England, 190, 220
  Blitz (1940–41), 47
  Calvi murder (1981), 190
Lopez de Cisneros, Juan, 130
Lorca, Federico Garcia, 44, 87
Lotta Continua, 136
lotte contadine, 67
lottery, 20, 95
Loy, Myrna, 40
Lucania, Salvatore, 58, 59–60, 95
Luce, Clare Boothe, 81
Lucky Luciano, 58, 59–60, 95
lupara, 96, 108

Macaluso, Antonio, 44
Macaluso, Emanuele, 44
Macaluso, Enrico, 27–8, 29
Macchiarini, Idalgo, 137
Machiavelli, Niccolò, 93, 235
Madrid, Spain, 212
Mafia, xiii, 11–17, 41, 94–104, 110, 123, 154, 185, 196–207, 216–26, 227–31
  Allied occupation (1943–4), 53, 58–60, 65, 94
  anti-Mafia commissions (1962–94), 110, 153, 185, 192, 194, 196, 238
  Banco Ambrosiano and, 187–91
  Borghese coup attempt (1970), 220
  cadaveri eccellenti, xiv, 14, 192–5, 216, 220, 237–8
  Catholic Church, relations with, 96–7, 108, 112, 113, 122, 123, 196
  Christian Democrats and, 73, 166, 191–2, 197, 199, 203–4, 246–7
  cigarette trade, 193, 197
  confino, 196
  Cupola, 196, 220, 224
  drug trade, *see* drug trade
  Fascism and, 21, 24, 67
  feudalism and, 11–13, 15, 22–3, 59, 60, 67–8, 95, 103, 105, 106
  de Mauro's disappearance (1970), 125–6

INDEX

maxi-processo (1986–92), xiv, 221–6, 222, 227–31, 237–40, 246, 248, 252
  meat trade, 95–6, 197
  Mori's suppression (1925–9), 23–6, 32, 33–4, 41, 94
  octopus metaphor, 14, 196
  omertà, 13, 24, 110, 181, 187, 208, 219
  L'Ora and, 96, 124–6
  pentiti, 210, 211, 217–20, 225, 239, 249, 250–51
  political influence, 14, 68, 73, 166, 196, 197, 199, 203–4, 238, 246–7
  Portella massacre (1947), 70, 71–2
  Sack of Palermo (1950s–80s), 95, 121–3, 124, 148, 153, 248
  separatism and, 66–8, 71–2, 73
  Via Carini massacre (1982), 201–5
  wars, 95–6, 110, 125, 196–205
  women and, 146, 219, 222, 223–4, 225
Mafia wars, 95–6, 110, 125, 196–205
  First (1953–8), 95–6
  Second (1981–3), 197–205
mafiologo, 103, 108, 193
mafiosità, 156
Mafiusi della Vicaria, I (Mosca and Rizzotto), 13
Magistrale 1X Maggio, Caltanissetta, 34
Maglie, Apulia, 175
mahia, 11
Majorana, Ettore, 142–5, 149, 159
malaria, 27, 30, 54
Malgrado Tutto, 244
Mancuso, Lenin, 193
Manhattan Project (1942–6), 144
Mani Pulite, 248
Mann, Thomas, 148
Mano Nero, 22
Manzoni, Alessandro, 18, 127, 130, 134, 176, 214, 240, 241
Maraini, Dacia, 123, 148
March on Rome (1922), 8
Marcinkus, Paul, 188
Mare colore di vino, Il (Sciascia), 145, 236
Marsala, Sicily, 9, 31, 216
Marshall Plan (1948), 73
Martelli, Claudio, 239
Martellucci, Nello, 200, 203
Martorelli, Genoveffa, 3, 32, 35, 41, 48, 74, 91, 132
Marx, Karl, 213
Marxism, 136, 162
  see also Communists
Matisse, Henri, 197
matriarchy, 146, 225–6
Matronas, 5–6
Mattarella, Piersanti, 194, 206
Mattei, Enrico, 125, 126, 150
Matteotti, Giacomo, 9, 28, 132
de Maupassant, Guy, 159
de Mauro, Mauro, 116, 124–5, 136, 150, 192
de Mauro, Tullio, 125
maxi-processo (1986–92), xiv, 221–6, 222, 227–31, 237–40, 246, 248, 252
May 1968 uprising, 136
Mazzarino, Sicily, 96–7, 122
McLuhan, Marshall, 169
meat markets, 95–6, 197
Meli, Antonino, 230–31, 239
Memoria, La, 155, 215
Messina, Rosa, 110
Messina, Sicily, 48, 59
methane gas, 83
mieloma micromolecolare, 241
Milan, Lombardy, 83, 92, 118, 137, 177, 196, 241
  Chiesa case (1992), 247–8
  Piazza Fontana bombing (1969), 135
  Sciascia debate (1987), 229
Milazzo, Silvio, 121, 123
Ministry of Public Education, 92
Mitgang, Herbert, 133
Moby Dick (Melville), 49
Monaco, Luigi, 44
Mondadori, 39, 106
Monde, Le, 132, 178
money laundering, 153, 188, 222

Monreale, Sicily, 56
de Montaigne, Michel, 38, 93, 105, 133, 134, 139, 157, 180, 215, 240
Montale, Eugenio, 36, 162
Montalto, Giangiacomo, 216
Montanelli, Indro, 176, 234
Montelepre, Sicily, 69, 70
Montgomery, Bernard, 55, 56
Morante, Elsa, 185
Moravia, Alberto, 84, 143, 163, 185
Moretti, Mario, 178
Mori, Cesare, 23–6, 25, 32, 33–4, 41, 94
Moro, Aldo, xv, 137, 165–79, 180, 182–3, 184, 205–6, 209, 251
Moro Commission (1979–2018), 182–3, 184, 186–7, 205–6
Morte dell'Inquisitore (Sciascia), 130–31
Morvillo, Francesca, 239
Mosca, Gaspare, 13
Mosjoukine, Ivan, 30
motor cars, 137
Motta, Antonio, 211
Movimento Sociale Italiano (MSI), 75, 81, 121, 135
mu a fa, 11
Murio La Verdad (Goya), 233
Muslim Sicily (827–1091), 2, 4, 10, 31, 60, 128
Mussolini, Arnaldo, 27
Mussolini, Benito, xiii, 8–9, 20–21, 23–4, 26, 28, 38, 40, 49, 52, 79
 anti-Mafia campaign (1925–9), 23–6, 32, 33–4, 41, 94
 Battle for Grain (1925), 27
 emigration restrictions (1931), 53
 Ethiopian War (1935–7), 42–3
 March on Rome (1922), 8
 Pact of Steel (1939), 45
 porte aperte, 215
 Schirru plot (1931), 30, 127
 Sicily visit (1924), 24
 Sicily visit (1937), 42–3, 44
 Spanish War (1936–9), 43–4
 World War II entry (1940), 46
Mussomeli, Sicily, 58, 111–12

Mystery of Majorana, The (Sciascia), 142–5, 149, 159
Myth of Sisyphus, The (Camus), 142

Nadeau, Maurice, 160–61
Naples, Campania, 210, 251
Napoleon I, Emperor of the French, 10, 20–21
Navarra, Michele, 72, 96, 198
Nazi Germany (1933–45), 45, 48, 49, 50, 51, 55, 64, 144
'Ndranghetta, 251
neo-Fascism, 79, 81, 121, 135–6, 190
Nero su nero (Sciascia), 185
New York, United States, 2, 54, 56, 58, 59, 188, 220
New York Times, 81, 102, 114
Nicolosi, Rino, 229
1912+1 (Sciascia), 214
Nisticò, Vittorio, 84, 86, 96, 123–4, 143–4, 152, 244
Nobel Prize, xiii, 38, 237
Noia del '937, La (Brancati), 41
Norman Sicily (1091–1194), 10, 31
nostalgia, 86
Notarbartolo, Emanuele, 14
nuclear weapons, 142–5
Nuova Cinema Paradiso (1988 film), 241
Nuovi Argomenti, 84

O'Connor, Flannery, 134
Observer, 250
Occhetto, Achille, 153
Occhio di capra (Sciascia), 212
Officina, 80
oil, 83
olives; olive oil, 60, 82
omertà, 13, 24, 110, 181, 187, 208, 219
Omnibus, 40–41, 46
One Way or Another (Sciascia), 141–2, 149, 163, 166, 180, 190, 236, 247, 251
Open Doors (Sciascia), 215
Operation Carlo Alberto (1982), 201

INDEX

Operation Gladio (1952–90), 135, 177, 252
Operation Husky (1943), 50–60
Operation Mincemeat (1943), 50
Operazione Milazzo (1958–9), 121
Opus Dei, 190
L'Ora, 84, 86, 96, 108, 114, 116, 123–6, 143–4, 152, 154, 244
oranges, 10, 13, 31, 47, 53, 122
orchards, 21
Order of Servi di Maria, 106
original sin, 20
Orlando, Leoluca, 219, 228, 239, 242, 248, 250
Orlando, Vittorio Emanuele, 14
Ortega y Gasset, José, 44
Orwell, George, 79, 152
L'Osservatore Romano, 44, 112
Other Voices, Other Rooms (Capote), 78
Ottoman Empire (1299–1922), 51
Oxford University, 53

P2 Masonic lodge, 189–91, 196, 203
Pact of Steel (1939), 45
Paese Sera, 176
Pais, El, 163
Palace of Justice, Palermo, 231, 249
Palazzo dei Normanni, Palermo, 23
Palazzo della Sapienza, Pisa, 136
Palazzo Steri, Palermo, 130
Palermo, Sicily, 10, 15, 114, 116, 152–5, 160
   Acquasanta, 110
   anti-Mafia campaign (1925–9), 23–6, 32
   belle époque (c. 1871–1914), 31, 116
   cadaveri eccellenti, 192–5, 216–17, 220
   car arson in, 96
   Cascio Ferro's extortion, 22
   Centro Giuseppe Impastato, 219
   Conca d'Oro, 31, 95
   Council, 152–5, 160, 181
   Foro Italico, 43
   Hotel delle Palme, 95
   Inquisition (1487–1782), 130
   Mafia war (1962–3), 110
   Mafia war (1981–3), 197–205
   maxi-processo (1986–92), xiv, 221–6, 222, 227–31, 237–40, 246, 248
   Mussolini's visit (1924), 24
   Mussolini's visit (1937), 43
   Orlando mayoralty (1985–90), 219, 228, 239, 242
   Palazzo Steri, 130
   plebiscite (1929), 26–7
   Sack of Palermo (1950s–80s), 95, 121–3, 124, 148, 153, 248
   Second World War (1940–45), 48, 49, 53, 56, 58–60
   Teatro Massimo, 31
   Ucciardone, xiv, 71–2, 223
   Via Carini massacre (1982), 201–5
   writers' congress (1953), 82
Palizzolo, Raffaele, 14
Palma di Montechiaro, Sicily, 82
Pannella, Marco, 181, 182
Panorama, 147, 232
Pansa, Giampaolo, 228, 229
Pantheon, Rome, 92
Pappalardo, Salvatore, 162, 201, 202, 219
Paris, France, 87, 158–9, 172, 212
Parishes of Regalpetra, The (Sciascia), 86, 90, 94, 126, 154, 212
parliamentary commissions
   on Mafia (1962–94), 110, 153, 185, 192, 194, 196, 238
   on Moro kidnapping (1979–2018), 182–3, 184, 186–7, 205–6
Parma, Emilia-Romagna, 46
Parri, Ferruccio, 73
Parrocchie di Regalpetra, Le (Sciascia), 86, 90, 94, 126, 154, 212
Parsifal (Wagner), 95
Pascal, Blaise, 87, 92, 113, 141, 176, 180, 244
Pasolini, Pier Paolo, vii, 79–81, 80, 82, 86, 124, 148–51, 163, 174, 180

INDEX

Patton, George, 55, 56, 57, 58–9
Paul II, Pope, 250
Paul VI, Pope, 167, 172
Pecorelli, Mino, 189, 247
Pedulla, Walter, 139
Pelosi, Pino, 150
pentiti, 210, 211, 217–20, 225, 239, 249, 250–51
Percoto, Friuli-Venezia Giulia, 232
Perreira, Michele, 124, 153, 154, 243
Pertini, Alessandro, 198–9, 210
pessimism, 16, 18, 38, 46, 103, 106, 133, 166, 175, 185, 207
Petri, Elio, 102, 158
Petruzzella, Francesco, 228
pezzi di novanta, 21, 73
phylloxera, 32
Piana dei Greci, Sicily, 24
Piazza Armerina, Sicily, 24, 88
Piazza di Spagna, Rome, 184
Piazza Fontana bombing (1969), 135
Piazza Magione, Palermo, 216
Picasso, Pablo, 131
Piedmontese Sicily (1860), 10, 12
Pietru, Maestro, 46
Pinelli, Giuseppe, 135
Pirandello, Luigi, xiii, 33, 36–8, 37, 49, 61, 63, 99, 109, 113, 134, 174, 214, 241
   Come tu mi vuoi (1934), 212
   death (1936), 173, 240
   death, views on, 206
   Fascism, views on, 37, 38, 44, 173
   Fu Mattia Pascal, Il (1904), 30
   Majorana's reading of, 143
   portrait, 240
   Rome, life in, 185
   Sciascia's writing on, 74, 82, 84
   unpublished work, 78
Pisa, Tuscany, 136
Pisciotta, Gaspare, 71
pistachios, 10, 19
Pitrè, Giuseppe, 13–14, 130
pity, 85
pizzicatu, 21
Pizzillo, Giovanni, 217
pizzo, 246

plague, 4, 18
Plague-Spreader's Tale, The (Bufalino), 120
plebiscite (1929), 26–7
Pluto, 4
podestà, 26, 27, 51, 52, 58
poetry, 23, 32, 47, 61, 74, 78, 80
poisonings, 72, 120, 140, 198, 201, 238
Poletti, Charles, 56, 59, 64
Ponte, Il, 78
Popolo d'Italia, 27
pork barrel politics, 248
pornography, 40, 41
Porte aperte (Sciascia), 215
Portella della Ginestra massacre (1947), 70–72
Porto Empedocle, Sicily, 4
Portrait of an Unknown Mariner (Antonello), 118
Porzio, Domenico, 234
potash, 83
poverty, 11, 26, 32, 43, 55, 57, 65, 75–7, 82, 83, 84, 85, 108, 181
Prata, Tuscany, 201
Premio Amici di Latino, 237
Primitive Rebels (Hobsbawn), 103
Pro Sicilia Committee, 14
Prohibition (1920–33), 22, 95
Promessi sposi, I (Manzoni), 18, 127, 240
proportional representation, 153
Prospettive Meridiane, 92
prostitution, 61, 221
Proust, Marcel, 106, 154, 159, 213
Provenzano, Bernardo, 197, 225
Puccini, Giacomo, 31
Puerto Rico, 238
Pugnalatori, I (Sciascia), 159

quaquaraqua, 228
quinine, 60

Racalmuto, Sicily, xiii, 1–9, 6, 12, 17, 27–30, 29, 32–3, 41–2, 82, 207, 212, 244
   anti-Fascists in, 28, 47, 49, 63–4
   Circolo Unione, 62–3, 86
   Don Calò's extortion, 22–3

INDEX

elementary school, 19–21, 75–8, 83–4, 108
emigration and, 54, 84, 85, 89
general election (1953), 81
Giuliano's banditry, 69
Inquisition (1487–1782), 130
La Noce, 6–7, 6, 41–2, 93, 109–10, 133, 155–7, 174, 202, 211
local elections (1925), 27
Mori's campaign (1925–9), 24
percorso, 253
Regina Margherita theatre, 29, 47, 241
Sciascia's writing on, 85, 86
Second World War (1940–45), 46, 47–9, 50–64, 78
sulphur mines, 2, 4–5, 5, 7, 16, 19, 27, 212
Rackham, Arthur, 131
Radical Party, 169, 181–3, 238
Radio London, 46
Ragusa, 83
Rahal Maut, 4
railways, 19
Ravaioli, Carla, 147
Red Brigades, xv, 136–7, 161–3, 165–79, 181
  Czechoslovakia, relations with, 186
  Moro murder (1978), xv, 165–79, 182–3, 184, 186, 205–6, 209, 251
  Sossi kidnapping (1974), 161–2
  d'Urso kidnapping (1980), 183
Reggio Emilia, 27, 84
Regia Scuola Mineraria, Caltanissetta, 73
Regina Coeli prison, Rome, 210
Regina Margherita, Racalmuto, 29, 47, 241
Reid, Ed, 98
religious festivals, 3–4, 76
remittances, 52, 54
Rennell, Francis Rodd, 2nd Baron, 59
Repubblica, La, 176, 182, 228, 231, 233
Republic of Italy (1946–)
  Andreotti government (1976–9), 166–70, 172, 175, 180, 189, 196–7

anti-Mafia commissions (1962–94), 110, 153, 185, 192, 194, 196, 238
Banco Ambrosiano, 187–91
Borghese coup attempt (1970), 135–6, 220
Craxi government (1983–7), 219
De Gasperi government (1946–53), 73, 81
divorce referendum (1974), 145, 148, 153
economic miracle (*c.* 1958–63), 137
Fanfani government (1960–63), 121
general election (1948), 71
general election (1953), 81
general election (1976), 166
general election (1979), 181
general election (1987), 238
general election (1992), 248
institutional referendum (1946), 73
local elections (1993), 248
maxi-processo (1986–92), xiv, 221–6, 222, 227–31, 237–40, 246, 248, 252
Moro Commission (1979–2018), 182–3, 184, 186–7, 205–6
Moro kidnapping and murder (1978), xv, 165–79, 182–3, 205–6, 209, 251
neo-Fascism in, 79, 81, 121, 127, 135–6, 190
Operation Gladio (1953–90), 135, 177, 252
P2 Masonic lodge, 189–91, 203
Piazza Fontana bombing (1969), 135
Red Brigades trial (1974), 162–3
regional elections (1975), 152–4
regional elections (1975), 152–4
student movement (1960s–70s), 136, 149
Years of Lead (*c.* 1968–88), xv, 135–7, 161–3, 182–3, 191
republic referendum (1946), 73
Rigoletto (Verdi), 29

Riina, Toto, 96, 197, 225, 247, 248, 251
Risorgimento (1848–70), 9, 12, 20, 76, 90
Rizzotto, Giuseppe, 13, 126
Rizzotto, Placido, 72, 96
Roatta, Mario, 49, 50–51
roba, 16, 36, 112, 146
de Roberto, Federico, xiii, 36, 106
Rognetta, Vita, 224
Roman Sicily (241 BCE–CE 476), 10, 155
Romania, 251
Rome, Lazio, 82, 92, 104, 181–5, 196
Roosevelt, Franklin, 50, 56, 66
Rosi, Francesco, 125, 158
Rosselli, Colette, 198
Rousseau, Jean-Jacques, 240
Ruffini, Ernesto, 108, 122
Russia, 251
Russo, Domenico, 201–2

Sack of Palermo (1950s–80s), 95, 121–3, 124, 148, 153, 248
Saetta, Antonino, 238
Salamanca, Spain, 212
Salò (1975 film), 150
Salò Republic (1943–5), 64
salt cod, 47
salt mines, 4, 62, 75, 85
Salvo, Ignazio, 126, 196, 205, 221–2, 226, 247
Salvo, Nino, 126, 196, 205, 221–2, 247
di Salvo, Rosario, 198
San Cipirello, Sicily, 70
San Giovanni in Laterano, Rome, 173
San Giuseppe Iato, Sicily, 70
San Sebastian, Basque Country, 87
sangue mio, il, 16
Santa Maria del Monte, Racalmuto, 3, 7
Saracens, 4
Saragat, Giuseppe, 136, 180
sarcophagi, 54
Sardinia, 221, 223
Sartre, Jean-Paul, 163

Savinio, Alberto, 45
Scalfari, Eugenio, 176, 228, 229
Scaraffia, Giuseppe, 240
Scarpinato, Roberto, 253
Schifani, Rosaria, 249
Schirru, Michele, 30, 127
Schleyer, Hanns-Martin, 172
Scianna, Ferdinando, 113, *114*, 122, 157
Sciascia, Angela, 1, 4, 93, 114, 132
Sciascia, Anna, 3, *35*, 41, 48, 61
Sciascia, Anna Maria, 74, 141, 181, 182, 210, 211, 228, 232
  Borsellino's assassination (1992), 249–50
  childhood, 91–3, 109
  father's death (1989), 243, 244
  marriage, 140
Sciascia, Giuseppe 'Peppino', 3, 19, 30, *30*, *35*, 41, 44, 45, 48
  suicide (1948), 73–4, 90, 109, 232
Sciascia, Giuseppina 'Nica', 1, 3, 7, 19, 27, 32, 41, 42, 61, 109, 132, *132*, 176
Sciascia, Laura, 62, 91, 92, 140, 141, 182, 210, 211, 242, 244
Sciascia, Leonardo, xv, 9, 30, *35*, 42, *245*
  A futura memoria (1989), 242, 243
  L'Affaire Moro (1978), 173–9, 209, 213
  Antimonio (1960), 44, 158
  artist friends, 117–21
  birth (1921), 1–2, 3
  Bologna conference (1974), 163
  Borsellino, relationship with, xv, 227–31, 238
  cancer diagnosis (1989), 241
  Candido (1977), 159–61, 174, 234
  Catholic Church, views on, 76, 85, 108, 112, 113, 140–42, 236
  childhood, 1–9, 16–17, 18–21, 29–30, 32–3, 34–46
  Christian Democrats, views on, 81, 123, 137, 140, 141, 142, 148, 166–79, 180

INDEX

Communists, views on, 81, 89, 90, 138–40, 152–3, 160–62, 166–7, 180, 182, 186
Council of Egypt, The (1963), 128–9, 236
Cronachette (1985), 215
Dalle parti degli infedeli (1979), 186
Day of the Owl, The (1961), see *Day of the Owl, The*
death (1989), 244–5
Death of an inquisitor (1964), 130–31
Death of Stalin, The (1958), 89, 229–30
divorce, views on, 145, 153, 181
Dolci, relationship with, 107–8
earthquake (1968), 114–15
education, 18–21, 32, 35–42, 46–7
Equal Danger (1971), 138–40, 158, 163, 166, 182, 236
European election (1979), 181
Fables from the Dictatorship (1950), 79–80, 126, 209
Fascism, views on, 20, 42–5, 66, 163, 230
father's death (1957), 90–91
film, love of, 29–30, 40, 41
general election (1979), 181
Giuseppe, relationship with, 30–31, 73–4
graphic art, love of, 87, 117–18, 131
Guttuso, relationship with, 102, 117, 139, 182, 213
inchieste, 129–30, 138, 142–5, 159, 186, 209, 212–13, 242, 252
Joyce, views on, 105, 124, 213
justice, views on, 126–9, 159, 208–11, 215
Knight and Death, The (1988), 232–4
literature, love of, 18, 21, 29–30, 35, 36–42, 48, 87, 109, 131, 155, 240
mafiologo status, 103, 108, 193
Maria, relationship with, 48, 61–2, 108–9

de Mauro's disappearance (1970), 125–6
maxi-processo (1986–92), xiv, 224–6, 227–31, 238
memory, views on, 155, 212–13
mentoring, 157
Moro Commission (1979–2018), 182–3, 184, 186–7, 205–6
Moro kidnapping crisis (1978), xv, 165–79, 251
Mystery of Majorana, The (1975), 142–5, 149, 159
Nero su nero (1979), 185
1912+1 (1986), 214
Occhio di capra (1984), 212
One Way or Another (1974), 141–2, 149, 163, 166, 180, 190, 236, 247, 251
Open Doors (1987), 215
L'Ora, writing for, 123–4
Palermo, city councillor in (1975–7), 152–5, 160, 181
Palermo, move to (1968), 114, 116
Palermo, trip to (1932), 31
Paris, trips to, 87, 158–9, 172, 212
Parishes of Regalpetra, The (1955), 86, 90, 94, 126, 154, 212
parliamentary membership (1979–84), 182–4, 191–2, 205–6
Pasolini, relationship with, 80–81, 86, 142, 148–51, 163
pentiti, views on, 218
Pertini, meeting with (1982), 198–9
pessimism, 103, 106, 133, 166, 185, 207
poetry, 23, 32, 47, 61, 74, 78, 80
Pugnalatori, I (1976), 159
Red Brigades trial (1974), 162–3
Rome, move to (1957), 92
Rome, move to (1979), 182–4
Scianna, relationship with, 114
science, views on, 142–5, 229
Second World War (1940–45), 46–9, 50–64

INDEX

Sciascia, Leonardo, (*Cont'd*)
  separatism, views on, 66–7
  Sicilia, La (1952), 78
  Sicilian Uncles, The (1958), 89, 101, 112, 210
  Sicily as Metaphor (1979), vii
  silence, 39, 183–4, 199
  Simple Story, A (1989), 241–2, 243
  Sindona's petition (1979), 188–9, 191, 205
  smoking habit, 40, 77, 119, 124, 150, 154, 156, 232
  Strega e il capitano, La (1985), 214
  teaching career (1949–57), 74, 75–8, 83–4, 108
  Theatre of Memory, The (1981), 212–13
  To Each his Own (1966), 112–13, 133, 145
  Tortora, relationship with, 210–11
  vertebra fracture (1979), 182, 211, 232
  Via Carini massacre (1982), 202–5
  wedding (1944), 61
  Wine Dark Sea, The (1973), 145, 236
  women, views on, 145–8, 181, 225–6
Sciascia, Leonardo Sr, 2, 2, 3, 4, 5, 6, 7, 8, 17, 19, 81
Sciascia, Maria Concetta, 1, 3, 8–9, 18, 21, 28, 36, 43, 48, 91, 132
Sciascia, Pasquale, 2–3, 5, 7, 8, 19, 31, 32, 45, 48, 61, 74, 90–91, 109
Sciascia, Salvatore, 1, 3, 28
Sciascia, Salvatore (publisher), 44–5, 78, 98
science, 142–5, 229
Scotten, William Everett, 59
sea, 18–19
Second World War (1939–45), 46–9, 50–65
  AMGOT (1943–4), 56–65
  Armistice of Cassibile (1943), 64
  Operation Husky (1943), 50–60
Segre, Emilio, 43, 143
Sellerio Editore, 118–20, 124, 154, 155, 176, 213, 215
Sellerio, Elvira, 110, 118–20, 155, 213, 241
Sellerio, Enzo, 118, 155, 213
separatism, 65–73
Shakespeare, William, 100
Sherlock Holmes books (Doyle), 39
Sicilia, La (Sciascia), 78
Sicilian dialect, 4, 212
Sicilian Uncles, The (Sciascia), 89, 101, 112, 210
Sicilianismo, 12, 66
Sicilianità, 118, 120, 157, 235
Sicilitudine, 87, 237
Sicily, 9–12, 66, 81–2, 86–7
  Allied occupation (1943–4), 56–65, 94, 188
  Aragonese period (1282–1479), 10, 16, 130, 208
  Bourbon period (1735–1860), 2, 9–12, 128–9, 131, 196
  British occupation (1806–15), 7, 11
  Byzantine period (535–902), 10, 31
  Fascist period (1922–43), *see* Fascist Italy
  Milazzo presidency (1958–9), 121, 123
  Muslim period (827–1091), 2, 4, 10, 31, 60, 128
  Norman period (1091–1194), 10, 31
  Piedmontese period (1860), 10, 12
  Roman period (241 BCE–CE 476), 10
  Second World War (1939–45), 46–9, 50–65
  separatist movement (1943–51), 65–73
  Spanish period (1479–1713), 10, 16, 130–31, 208, 252
Sicily as Metaphor (Sciascia), vii
Sicily Zone Handbook, 54
Siemens, 137

INDEX

Sign of the Cross, The (1932 film), 32
Signoret, Simone, 40
Simenon, Georges, 39, 98
Simple Story, A (Sciascia), 241–2, 243
Sindona, Michele, 188–91, 205, 238
Siracusa, Sicily, 54
Sirchio, 192
sirocco, 18, 55, 175
smoking, *see* tobacco
smuggling, 22
Socialist Party, 8, 9, 69, 81, 99, 103, 110, 121, 169, 219, 238
Sonnino, Sidney, 13
Sontag, Susan, 212
Sossi, Mario, 161–2
Soviet Union (1922–91), 46, 89, 136, 166, 177
Spain, 87–8, 116, 212, 251
   Civil War (1936–9), 43–4, 87, 90
Spanish Sicily (1282–1713), 10, 16, 130–31, 138, 208, 252
St Louis, Missouri, 22
Stalin, Joseph, 89, 229–30
Stampa, La, 144, 162, 194, 230
State, 13–15, 101, 102, 107, 111, 112, 168, 182, 187, 193, 194, 236
   in *Candido*, 161–4
   in *Day of the Owl, The*, 126–7
   in *Equal Danger*, 138, 139
   Falcone on, 220–21
   Moro murder and, 170, 172, 175, 187
   in *Nero su nero*, 185
   in *One Way or Another*, 142
   P2 network and, 189–91
Steiner, George, 253
Stendhal, 18, 39, 105, 109, 117, 133, 210, 240, 253
Stille, Ugo, 169
Storia della colonna infame, La (Manzoni), 127
Strega e il capitano, La (Sciascia), 214
Strega Prize, 106
strychnine, 72, 238

student movement (1960s–70s), 136, 149
suicide, 39, 73–4, 232
sulphur industry, 2, 4–5, 5, 7, 16, 19, 32, 37, 46, 62, 63, 73, 74, 75, 85, 129, 244
   decline, 27, 78, 82, 83, 212
   United States and, 4, 27
superstition, 1, 11, 13, 26, 34, 54, 76
sutrutu, 21
Switzerland, 188, 193
Syria, 95

Tandoy, Cataldo, 112
Tangentopoli, 248
tax collectors, 196–7, 221, 226
Teatro Massimo, Palermo, 31
Teatro Stabile, Catania, 102
Tempo Presente, 97–8
Termini Imerese, Sicily, 14
Terranova, Cesare, 185, 193–4, 198, 206
terribiltà, 127, 131, 252
terrorism, *see* Mafia wars; Red Brigades; Years of Lead
textiles, 137
Thailand, 193, 220
Theatre of Memory, The (Sciascia), 212–13
Times, The, 26
Times Literary Supplement, 133, 214
Tinebra, Baldassare, 63
To Each his Own (Sciascia), 112–13, 133, 145
To the Lighthouse (Woolf), 47, 48
tobacco, 40, 52, 77, 119, 124, 150, 154, 156, 232
   Mafia trade in, 193, 197
Tobagi, Walter, 194
Todo modo (Sciascia), 141–2, 149, 163, 166, 180, 190, 236, 247, 251
Todo modo (1976 film), 158
Togliatti, Palmiro, 66, 153, 186
Tolstoy, Leo, 148, 176, 215
Tornatore, Giuseppe, 241
Tortora, Enzo, 210–11

INDEX

torture, 25, 127–31, 208
Trabia, Sicily, 31
trade unions, 72, 167, 187
trains, *see* railways
Tranchino, Gaetano, 213
Trapani, Sicily, 71, 219, 237
Trappeto, Sicily, 106
Treaty of Versailles (1919), 8
Triads, 238
Truman, Harry S., 144
tuberculosis, 72
Tunisia, 53
Turin, Piedmont, 83, 118, 137, 162, 212
Turkey, 95, 220, 238
typhoid, 122

u pizzu, 22
Ucciardone, Palermo, xiv, 71–2, 223
Udine, Friuli-Venezia Giulia, 232
Ulysses (Joyce), 105, 124, 213
Umberto Eco, 90
Una vita venduta (1976 film), 158
unemployment, 82, 83, 107
Unification of Italy (1848–70), 9, 12, 20, 76
L'Unita, 28, 123, 139, 162, 200
unitari, 66
United Kingdom, 7, 11, 43, 158
  Calvi murder (1981), 190
  heroin trade, 193
  Second World War (1939–45), 46, 47, 50, 53, 55–7, 59, 64
United Nations, 172
United States, 2–3, 22, 158
  Black Hand, 22
  citrus industry, 31
  emigration to, 2–3, 52, 53, 84, 85, 89
  film industry, 40, 44, 52
  heroin trade, 193
  Mafia, 25, 58, 59, 95, 98
  Manhattan Project (1942–6), 144
  Marshall Plan (1948), 73
  Moro kidnapping crisis (1978), xv, 168
  Operation Gladio (1952–90), 135, 177, 252
  Prohibition (1920–33), 22, 95

Second World War (1941–5), 50–65, 78
sulphur industry, 4, 27
Vietnam War (1955–75), 132, 136
University of Trento, 136
d'Urso, Giovanni, 183
Uruguay, 189
Ustica, 24
Utrillo, Maurice, 87

Van Gogh, Vincent, 197
Vandals, 10
Vatican, 44, 68, 73, 112
  Banco Ambrosiano and, 187–91
Vatican Bank, 188
Veleni di Palermo, I (La Duca), 120
Veneto, 51
vento del nord, 66
di Verdura, Fulco, 31
Verga, Giovanni, xiii, 36
Versailles Treaty (1919), 8
Via Carini massacre (1982), 201–5
Viceroys, The (De Roberto), 36, 106
Victor Emanuel III, King, 8, 48, 53
Vidal, Gore, 133
Vietnam War (1955–75), 132, 136
Vilardo, Stefano, 35–6, 42, 44–5, 46, 61, 62, 78, 92, 93
Villa Palagonia, Bagheria, 122–3
Villa Sperlinga, Palermo, 154
Villalba, Sicily, 22–3, 25, 58, 59, 67, 95, 197
Vitale, Leonardo, 218, 219
Viterbo, Lazio, 71
viticulture, 32, 82
Vittorini, Elio, 45, 78, 82, 84, 90, 92, 106
Vizzini, Calogero, 22–3, 22, 25, 58–9, 60, 63, 66, 67–8, 94–5, 197
Voghera, Pavia, 238
Voltaire, 38, 87, 109, 117, 134, 141, 142, 152, 157, 159, 185, 236
Vuillard, Édouard, 131

Wagner, Richard, 95
Waldheim, Kurt, 172
waterboarding, 25

294

Weil, Simone, 152, 252
wheat, 4, 7, 10, 12, 27, 34, 47–8, 60–61
whisper of books, 90
Wilder, Thornton, 47
Wine Dark Sea, The (Sciascia), 145, 236
witchcraft, 1, 11, 26, 214
women, 145–8, 181
  Mafia and, 146, 219, 222, 223–4, 225
Woolf, Virginia, 47, 48
writers' congress (1953), 82

Years of Lead (*c.* 1968–88), xv, 135–7, 161–3, 191
  Bologna bombing (1980), 191
  Moro murder (1978), xv, 165–79, 182–3, 186–7, 205–6, 209, 251
  Piazza Fontana bombing (1969), 135
Yeats, William Butler, 124

Zaccagnini, Benigno, 171
Zafferana Etnea, Sicily, 141
Zagarella, Sicily, 247
Zola, Émile, 174, 240

About the Author

Caroline Moorehead is a bestselling and prize-winning author, and the biographer of Bertrand Russell, Freya Stark, Iris Origo, Madame de la Tour du Pin and Martha Gellhorn. Her recent books – a quartet focussed on resistance to dictatorship, particularly in Italy – were shortlisted for the Samuel Johnson Prize, the Orwell Prize and the Costa Biography Award. She lives in London.